PUBLISH YOUR SPECIALTY

Other books by the author:

Publish Your Genealogy: A Step-by-Step Guide for Preserving Your Research for the Next Generation

Publish Your Family History: A Step-by-Step Guide to Writing the Stories of Your Ancestors

Publish a Local History: A Step-by-Step Guide from Finding the Right Project to Finished Book

Publish a Memoir: A Step-by-Step Guide to Saving Your Memories for Future Generations

Publish a Biography: A Step-by-Step Guide to Capturing the Life and Times of an Ancestor or a Generation

Publish a Photo Book: A Step-by-Step Guide for Transforming Your Genealogical Research into a Stunning Family Heirloom

Publish a Source Index: A Step-by-Step Guide to Creating a Genealogically Useful Index, Abstract or Transcription

Publish Your Specialty: A Step-by-Step Guide for Imparting Your Research Expertise to Others

Set Yourself Up to Self-Publish: A Genealogist's Guide

PUBLISH YOUR SPECIALTY

A Step-by-Step Guide for Imparting Your Research Expertise to Others

by Dina C. Carson

IRON GATE PUBLISHING
Niwot, CO

Publish Your Specialty:
A Step-by-Step Guide for Imparting Your
Research Expertise to Others

by Dina C. Carson

Published by:

Iron Gate Publishing
P.O. Box 999
Niwot, CO 80544

Copyright © 2015 by Dina C. Carson, Iron Gate Publishing
Printed in the United States of America
       ISBN   1-879579-76-6   ISBN 13 978-1-879579-76-7
       LCCN   2014914859

Publisher's Cataloging-in-Publication Data

Carson, Dina C, 1961 -

    Publish Your Specialty: A Step-by-Step Guide for Imparting Your Research Expertise to Others
by Dina C Carson.

          p.   cm.
    Includes index.
    ISBN 978-1-879579-76-7 (softbound) $24.95

     1. Reference—Writing.
2. Language Arts & Disciplines—Publishing.
3. Self-Publishing—United States   I. Title.

CT5. C239 2014   [Z285.5 C239 2014—Self-Publishing]
070.593

To Mom,

With a smile, she endured endless readings of my favorite childhood stories.

She encouraged me to read and to imagine.

She made me a better scholar.

She and Dad sacrificed a great deal to give me my most coveted possession—my education.

Acknowledgments

My kindest, most deeply held thanks to:

Dad—who supported my efforts in genealogy and who loved hearing about every delicious find I have made.

Mom—who had enough patience to read every word in this series of books and made each book better.

Charly Miller—whose Harry Potter Places travel guides have charmed me through and through, and who has supported every last thing I have done to make these books possible.

Buzzy Jackson—who wrote the stories of her ancestors in an enviable way, and was kind enough to lend her expertise to launch this project.

Silvia Pettem—whose remarkable local histories encourage me and so many others to poke about Boulder and write about our discoveries.

Dr. Thomas W. Jones—whose kind words and brilliant edits inspired me to share what I know about publishing.

Pat Roberts and Mona Lambrecht—who inspired an entire workshop on writing, research and publishing that lead directly to this series of books.

Sandi Pearce—my grammar goddess, who keeps me from tumbling headlong over my own words.

Gena Philibert-Ortega—for the most amazing week of social history studies. I have never had so much fun in a class.

Dr. John Philip Colletta—for providing the inspiration to take the next step to finish these books.

My friends at the Boulder Genealogical Society, the Jewish Genealogical Society of Colorado, the Boulder Heritage Roundtable, and the Colorado Council of Genealogical Societies—who have encouraged me to write, to lecture, and through steadfast community spirit have kept me going.

An expert is someone who knows some
of the worst mistakes that can be made in his subject,
and how to avoid them.

—Werner Heisenberg

I am learning all the time.
The tombstone will be my diploma.

—Eartha Kitt

Updates

Websites come and go or change their structures. If you find a broken link or a website that has moved or changed its name, please help me update the book for the next generation of readers. Send an email to: alert@irongate.com.

Contents

Section 5: Marketing

Preface

Because publishing is my specialty and how-to or instructional guides have been primarily what I have written in the past, this series of books has been my way of passing along my expertise to genealogists, and family or local historians.

The question I get most often when I lecture on the topic of writing and publishing, is "How did you go about it when you wrote your first book?" For me, writing about non-fiction topics came quite easily, writing the stories of family history, however, did not.

In the preparation for writing my own family history, one thing I found frustrating was that there were so many authors or instructors who told me *what* should be done, but very few who told me *how* it should be done, and done well. A lot of that, I had to figure out on my own.

I had to determine whether I could borrow from fiction, memoir writing or creative non-fiction. If so, just how much? Or, must I stay within the rules of non-fiction and write like an historian, although historical fiction could hold some lessons? If there is a line we cannot cross as genealogists and family historians, where is it? And how close can we come to it? To write about my expertise, are the lessons best taken from technical writing, or classic, how-to, non-fiction?

To answer my own questions, I started with a well-researched register-style genealogy. I am confident *that* book will be of use to the next generation of researchers, but I also wanted to leave behind a family history my non-genealogical relatives would read. So, I wrote a narrative family history. Then I re-wrote it. And I re-wrote it again. Each time experimenting with how to entice the best stories to come out. I also wrote about my expertise which is publishing and book production, so much of this book comes from my experience.

I sought out professional writing assistance, and I have had the pleasure of learning from the best. I studied genealogical writing with Tom Jones during his "Writing and Publishing for Genealogists" course at the Institute for Genealogical and Historical Research (IGHR) held at Samford University, and John Colletta's "Producing a Quality Family Narrative" course at the Salt Lake Institute of Genealogy (SLIG). I am not going to give away their secrets here. It is well worth attending these Institutes yourself.

I am willing to try anything and everything that promises to make my work better, and I am not afraid to make mistakes. If, like me, you have ever been called out for using a malapropism, grouched at for run-on sentences (or other grammatical horrors), or even for missing the point of the writing assignment entirely—at those tender moments in a class full of fellow writers, you know *exactly* what you do not know, and then some. I have spent enough time in writers workshops, genealogical institutes, local history seminars, and national conventions featuring the best writers and speakers, to put the pieces together.

At the point at which years of ruminating over classes and seminars and books about writing became "A-ha!," that I wrote this book and the others in this series.

It turns out that explaining one's research expertise is not that unlike writing a genealogy. You will be turning over your hard-earned research lessons to the next generations of researchers so that their path of discovery begins on solid, well-documented ground.

Passing on your expertise is a generous gift.

Take heart.

You do not have to be the world's foremost expert to publish a guide to what you know. Frankly, every how-to or instructional guide is a step up for the next expert in the field who may, some time in the future, write a more comprehensive guide than what you are planning. No worries. Write your guide anyway. The methods and available resources for research are changing all the time. Expect it, and publish anyway.

And, you do not have to have any experience with publishing to take your knowledge and mold it into a useful book.

Just keep reading.

Introduction

This book is a guide for anyone interested in sharing your expertise with others—to create an easy-to-use, easy-to-understand how-to or instructional guide.

This book is a conversation between you and me—one expert to another. I have been where you are. My expertise is in publishing as well as local and family histories. I have slogged through far-away repositories and courthouses. I have accumulated a pile of research and scratched my head over how to put it together in a way the novice would enjoy. I have made sense of it, and so can you.

So, what if:

You have an abundance of knowledge but no research to document it?

You have research not quite enough to make you the go-to expert?

You have facts but no images to help novices understand the subject?

For the beginner, this book contains the elements needed to start with an idea and end with a finished book. For the intermediate, there are ideas for organizing your research, adding social or historical context, and writing in a concise, believable way. For the advanced, it is a polishing cloth for your writing and your research, to make your book the best it can be.

This book has technical explanations. If you are technologically challenged, there are suggestions for hiring help in critical areas that you may not wish to tackle yourself.

This book contains some drudgery. Writing is hard work and some of the rules for publishing are no fun to implement, but are endured by publishers everywhere for the sake of the reader.

This book is not death by grammar. There are suggestions for catching and correcting the little bugaboos we all use because our first inclination is to write as we speak. Even the most prolific professionals do not write perfect books on the first try. They, however, have the benefit of professional editing. Most of us do not. Trust me when I say that I can turn my editor, my grammar goddess, into a grammar grouch in one short phrase. The painful process of editing is not a punishment, it is performed so that the words on the page for posterity convey your meaning.

This book is lengthy. If you would rather jump right in and start with what interests you most, go right ahead. For the rest of you, I have organized the book in the steps that publishing projects follow.

PUBLISH YOUR SPECIALTY

Section One is full of ideas for additional publishing projects, describes how to pick a doable project, explains how traditional and self-publishing works, and examines the tools to facilitate the jobs of organizing, researching, writing, type-setting and layout.

Section Two describes the preparation for writing—identifying who you are writing for, conducting a research review of what you already have, adding research and images to make your explanations clear and believable, what happens when you stare at a blank page one and have no idea what to do next, and how to create an outline to jump start the first draft.

Section Three is all about the writing—conveying your expertise, saving time by creating a style sheet, writing the first draft, and editing.

Section Four tackles the ins and outs of print publishing. The books that look the best are also the easiest on the eyes to read. This section will give you the instructions you need to make your book look its best.

Section Five will show you how to spread the word far and wide that your book is finished and available.

By the end of this book, you can expect to choose a doable project, to perform the kind of research that will give you a sound footing on which to explain your expertise for the benefit of the novice and more advanced alike, to write in a way that is compelling to readers, to successfully publish a book, and to let the world know it is available.

Throughout the book you will find references to:

Baby Steps. Baby Steps are essential. My objective, always, is to encourage you to do what you feel comfortable doing and to enjoy the process. It is not to make your book project a burden. If the only steps you take are the Baby Steps, no problem. Baby Steps also may identify more complicated tasks that you can skip if you are feeling overwhelmed, and still create a useful guide.

Next Steps. Next Steps build upon the Baby Steps and require more effort but will make the book look and read better. Many of these steps are about time—time to make another trip to the archives, time to learn the advanced features of your software, or time to re-write a section or two.

Giant Leaps. Giant Leaps build upon Baby Steps and Next Steps and require significantly more effort, but are steps that professional writers, editors or publishers would take to make the book the best it can be. My original contention bears repeating. If you can do the research, you can write and publish. In fact, you can take the Giant Leaps. You can write a compelling how-to book and package it in a way that even the snootiest, uptown publishing house cannot tell is self-published.

Enough with the soliloquy—on with the show.

2

SECTION 1

The goal in this section is to give you enough of an understanding about how publishing works to make you comfortable with the decision to self-publish.

Baby Steps

Take a look at the stages of all publishing projects—planning, writing, production and marketing. Consider a myriad of ideas before honing in on your own publishing project.

Next Steps

Learn how traditional book publishing works, and discover how everything a traditional publisher could do for you, you can do quite easily for yourself.

Giant Leaps

Examine the tools you will need to make your way from bright idea to a book in your hands.

Chapter 1

Who Needs This Book?

You need this book if:

- You want to pass on your expertise to another generation of people interested in the subject, and you do not know where to begin.
- You are someone with broad expertise, but you want to focus your efforts on what to include in your first book.
- You want to issue a private publication that only you or your colleagues will have access, without worrying about privacy or proprietary information issues.
- You want to share what only you have access to, such as one-of-a-kind research, photographs, illustrations, diaries or letters.
- You are an experienced researcher, and you want to cut your publishing teeth on a subject that is already well researched.
- You want to become a better instructional storyteller who uses clear, convincing steps to bring those with less knowledge in the field up to a higher level of expertise.

Rest assured. The skills you have developed (or will develop) as a researcher will help you as a writer, and the questions you raise as a writer will help you conduct better research. Together those skills will enable you to write a how-to or instructional guide, that is also a pleasure to read.

Keep reading. If you have a subject interesting enough to research, there are others who will benefit from your work.

Why Publish a How-to, Guide or Instructional Book?

With a little bit of knowledge, you can take your expertise or research, tell those who are interested how you gained your expertise and how they can benefit, and then make it available to family, friends or other researchers. Modern publishing technology makes it possible. In fact, publishing is one way to assure the legacy of your research.

Not only will other interested people appreciate knowing more about the subject, the hours you spent (or will spend) researching, investigating or experimenting deserves to become an everlasting record.

Where Do You Start?

Have you ever said to yourself, "I'll write a book when I finish the research?"

Many of us—yes, myself included—could pitch a tent at the National Archives and still not obtain every source we desire. There is always another graveyard to find or courthouse to search. At some point, you need to put aside the quest for every bit of information, and focus on the most important parts to pass along— just long enough to write the results of your research down so the reason you performed the research in the first place is not lost.

Kirk Polking in his book *Writing Family Histories and Memoirs* describes a woman who entered a "Why am I a Writer?" contest. Her answer to that question was that she had read about a man who had always wanted to be an artist. After he had died, family found his house full of unopened pots of paint and empty canvases. On the day the woman read that story, she put pen to paper with the thoughts she had been saving up for that someday when she would be a writer.

For you, that day has come.

Chapter 2

Publishing Projects

Every publishing project, whether it is a how-to, instructional guide, or the next blockbuster novel, goes through four stages—planning, writing, production, and marketing.

Planning

The first step in any publishing project is the planning stage, where you decide what type of book to write—how much to include or how little. If you think you must include everything you know about your subject in a single volume, you do not. In fact, I want discourage the data dump—purging your research notes of every available tidbit and source into one enormous manuscript. It may feel good to see how much research you already have. But once you start adding the images and the historical or social context, the project may become overwhelming.

In the next few chapters, I am going to help you pick a doable project and suggest material to make the book more interesting. Then, you will finish gathering the materials you will need to begin writing.

Writing

The writing stage is perhaps the most feared part of the publishing process. All writers face that first blank page. All writers have doubts. "What if I can't think of anything to say? What if I don't like what I've written? What if no one else likes what I've written?"

Anxiety about writing is normal. Thankfully, the writing stage is not all writing. For most authors, it is a writing and research stage. Research, for many of us, is a much more comfortable, more familiar place. Feel free to retreat into the comfort zone every now and again to gather material to strengthen your instructions or explanations. Be wary, however, of letting a small detour back into the research become an excuse to avoid writing. Eventually, you will want to finish the book.

Once the manuscript is complete, you must edit. Not even the most accomplished writer can produce a perfect manuscript in the first draft. Editing always means fixing typos and catching errors. Editing often means rewriting. Editing will make your manuscript better, more enjoyable for the reader.

Production

During the production stage, you will design the look and style of the book, and follow a set of rules to make the book easy on the eyes.

Production decisions include page layout, image placement, typesetting, cover design and final files. Fear not. There are ample tools to help you lay out the pages and make the images look their best.

During the production phase, you will decide whether to produce the book solely in print, whether an electronic or an online format may be better, or perhaps some combination of all three.

Marketing

Marketing is not necessarily about generating sales. It is a means of letting people who have an interest in your subject know that the book is available.

You may choose to give the book away as gifts or conduct a private sale, so only members of a class you teach can obtain a copy. You may want to sell the book to avoid financing the entire production yourself. Or, you may have a book with broader appeal that would warrant a sales campaign.

Marketing a how-to or instructional guide is a long-term process because most do not go out of style and should not go out of print. If you find new information, you can issue a second edition or publish a new book. The most important part of marketing is letting interested hobbyists and other researchers know that your book is available.

❧❦

None of these stages has nice, neat beginnings and endings. Occasionally, you may need to return to the planning to gather more information to make the writing easier. You may discover errors or missing elements while you are typesetting that require research or may initiate a re-write. Later, you may discover some piece of blockbuster information that will inspire a second edition.

No instructional book will roll off the press complete or perfect. Times ticks on. New information comes to light. Expect it and publish anyway.

Chapter 3

Pick a Project to Publish

The most important consideration for your publishing project is that you can complete it. The challenge for you, right now, is to pick a part of your research that you are willing to focus on—to the exclusion of other interesting finds—and narrow the scope enough so that the project does not become overwhelming.

In Chapter 7: Conducting a Research Review, you are going to take a critical look at the research you have already done, and decide whether what you have fits the project you have in mind, whether it will with a little more research, or whether an entirely different project may be best, for now. In the meantime, let us explore a few ideas in more detail.

Each of the books in this series was written with the genealogist, family or local historian in mind. You, however, may have a project idea or expertise unrelated to any type of genealogical research. That is fine. This book will help you take your expertise from idea to finished book. Each of the book projects below has a corresponding guide book with information specific to each book type.

A How-To or Instructional Guide

No matter your expertise share it—especially if you have conducted extensive research in any one aspect of genealogy or local history. Everyone can benefit when you help others become more knowledgeable about your area of expertise or how to avoid the pitfalls of conducting family or local history research.

The following are ideas for how-to books:

Tips and Tricks. Give snippets of advice for people who are new to an area of research. This is especially useful for new members of groups such as re-enactors, so they can catch up with the more experienced members quickly.

Process. Describe how to do something from start to finish. This is where your knowledge of an earlier time may help readers understand what their ancestors did and how they did it. How were houses constructed in the 17th Century? How did hunters keep enough food on the table at a western fort? How did Paul Revere make copper-bottomed pans? The ideas for books about processes are endless.

Lessons Learned. Reveal the techniques that *did not* work in your research so others can avoid making the same mistakes.

Record Type. You may have experience in land records or military records, for example, and can help others use those records effectively.

Research Facility. Do you have shortcuts to help make the best use of your time at a major repository? Or, perhaps you can shine a light on a repository that few researchers know about.

Recording or Preserving Records. Do you have photography tips for taking the best travel or cemetery pictures to use in a family history book, or advice for best practices to preserve the family bible?

Location. You may have conducted extensive research in a particular location (city, county, state or country) and could create a guide to what is available there.

A Family History

What is the difference between a genealogy and a family history?

In technical terms, a *genealogy* begins with an ancestor and moves forward in time through his or her descendants. A *pedigree*, on the other hand, starts with a descendant and moves backward in time through the ancestors.

For our purposes, consider a genealogy a way to pass on your well-documented *research* (with or without a lot of narrative). A family history, on the other hand, is less a numbered lineage, but rather the *stories* of your family.

The challenge with any family history project is limiting the scope enough that you can tell the stories well. One consideration is the time period in which the chosen family lived. For your generation, you have personal knowledge of the people and can tell their stories from your experience. And, most probably, there are hundreds if not thousands of photographs for you to choose from to help you remember events in order to write about them and help illustrate the stories once they are written.

To write about the generation before you, you may know each family member, or you may need to consult other family members for their stories. For your grandparents' generation (and further back), you may not have as many people to consult or as many photographs to view. Once you get back beyond the Civil

War era, you may not have any photographs at all. At some point in the past, you will be relying entirely upon research.

The following are ideas for planning a family history:

Start to Finish. Pick the ancestor you wish to use as the first generation. Describe the circumstances of that ancestor's entry into the family—not necessarily his or her birth, rather setting the scene for his or her early years. Follow the family through the number of generations you have chosen to include describing the events that affect most families—the births, schooling, marriages, professions, and deaths. Add the migrations, moves or turns of events that involved your family. Enrich the stories with enough social history so that the reader understands what it was like to live in the time and place your ancestors lived.

Photographs or Memorabilia. If you have inherited a box of photographs or memorabilia, plan your project around the people and events you find in that collection.

Letters or a Diary. Write about the people or person who wrote the letters or diary, weaving the actual text into the stories, or using the events described as the timeline for the book.

A Tragedy. Write about a defining event that affected the family, such as a natural disaster, becoming a prisoner of war, losing a fortune, or surviving the Great Depression or the Holocaust.

A Triumph. Triumphs are also defining events, such as suddenly becoming wealthy or famous, being elected to an important public office, and so on.

An Ancestor and the People Known to Him or Her. A book of this type could include parents, siblings, grandparents, children and grandchildren, cousins, aunts and uncles—essentially five generations—the two before and the two following your main character.

A Single Generation. If you would rather focus on an individual or a couple (e.g. your parents or grandparents) than a multi-generational family line, consult, *Publish a Biography: A Step-by-Step Guide to Capturing the Life and Times of an Ancestor or a Generation*. The difference is mostly in the level of detail required.

If you have done the research and are ready to write the stories of your family, you will find a detailed chapter on storytelling in *Publish Your Family History: A Step-by-Step Guide to Writing the Stories of Your Ancestors*.

A Genealogy

By my definition (above), a genealogy is a little less about writing and a little more about passing along your research to other researchers. Publishing your research is a valuable effort, in an of itself. If you have plenty of research to choose from, but are not quite ready to write the stories, publishing a genealogy will give you experience with the publishing process.

The following are ideas for planning a genealogy:

Every Descendant of a Single Ancestor. That may be your grandparents or the first immigrant. The more generations you go back, the more challenging it will be to ensure that the lines are complete.

Direct Descendants of a Single Ancestor. Include the siblings in each generation, but the detailed information only for your direct line.

Female Lines. Your mother and her mother, and her mother, and so on, as far back as you have researched.

A Surname Line. Beginning with the first ancestor of a given surname (a female), following her surname (male) line backward. Another section could include the wives of the male ancestors as collateral lines.

A Direct Line to a Specific Ancestor. Beginning with yourself, you could trace back across different surnames to a specific ancestor, such as an American President or a Salem witch (the kind of research to join a lineage society).

A Surname Study. Focus on a surname in a particular region (e.g. The Bakers of Campbell County, KY), within a national database (e.g. Revolutionary War soldiers or patriots), or across a complete record set (e.g. federal census records).

If you have done the research, but are not quite ready to write the narrative, you will find additional details about numbering systems and formal genealogical writing in *Publish Your Genealogy: A Step-by-Step Guide for Preserving Your Research for the Next Generation*.

A Local History

There are endless possibilities for writing local histories. All families have elements of local history in their stories, right? They attended local schools, worked in local businesses, joined community organizations, participated in local government, and lived in neighborhoods or rural communities.

The following are ideas for elements of local history to enhance your family history. Any of these ideas could become a local history unto itself:

Professions. Farming, mining, ranching, medicine, crafts, craftsmanship, banking, manufacturing, logging, science, technology, information, inventions, merchants, wholesalers, working conditions, etc.

Institutions. Schools, courts, military units, libraries, government agencies, fire departments, law and order, etc.

Associations. Sports teams, Masons, Odd Fellows, Boy Scouts, Girl Scouts, 4H, philanthropic, social, fraternal, activist, etc.

Religious Groups. Churches, synagogues, mosques, religious movements, religious colonies, etc.

Transportation. Freighters, wagon roads, railroads, stage companies, stations or airports, riverboats, barges, trails or roads, aerospace, aeronautics, etc.

People. Famous or notorious, leaders, office holders, women, children, what became of (e.g. a school class), the poor, ethnic groups, religious groups, etc.

Events. Natural disasters, on this day, during this year, anniversaries, economic depression, loss or gain of a major employer, politics, etc.

Architecture. Neighborhoods, downtown, building styles, building techniques, public buildings, historic homes, etc.

Transitions. Town into city, fort into town, farm into metropolis, etc.

Customs. Marriages, burials, holidays, celebrations, 4th of July, parades, rallies, expectations, manners, roles for men and women, expectations of children, economic class, etc.

Entertainment. Music, art, dance, theater, movies, plays, books, museums, carnivals, festivals, leisure, etc.

If you are considering writing a local history, consult, *Publish a Local History: A Step-by-Step Guide from Finding the Right Project to Finished Book.*

A Photo Book

There are some family stories best told by focusing on the photographs or illustrations with snippets of text to accompany the images.

The following are ideas for family photo books or pictorial histories:

Heirloom Catalog. Share family heirlooms in pictures by showcasing them in a book. This is one way to preserve the many historical items that belong to your family, even if they have been scattered across the globe.

13

Holiday Traditions. Maybe you have Christmas or other holiday cards or letters saved over the years that could accompany yearly pictures. Or, perhaps you have photos of other holidays celebrations that would make a good transition-through-time photo journal.

School Pictures. Starting in the 1950s, most school children had individual photographs taken each year as well as a class picture. Collecting the school pictures is one way to show what the family was doing every year across a decade or a generation.

Themes. Does your family have something in common? Eye or hair color? Freckles or jawline? Hobbies? Can you find a picture of different members of the family with their bikes, while skiing or fishing? Perhaps you have a collection of wedding photographs across many generations.

Travel Diary. If you have made the trip of a lifetime, or a trip to research your family's origins, show your family what the old country looked like through your modern-day experiences and photographs. You could also provide tips for other family members who wish to make the trip themselves.

Preservation. If you have a photo album or scrapbook made by one of your family members, preserve it by creating a more modern edition while adding stories gleaned from interviews or research.

Letters Home. Perhaps you have letters from a soldier written to those at home during a war, or from a student who traveled abroad.

Talents. Was your grandmother a knitter, or did she embroider or tat? Do you have examples of her work to show in a pictorial history? Perhaps your family's talent was acting or painting, scroll work or whittling, jewelry or quilting?

If you are considering a picture history consult, *Publish a Photo Book: A Step-by-Step Guide for Transforming Your Genealogical Research into a Stunning Family Heirloom*, for more details on image preparation in full color.

A Biography

A biography is different from a family history in that it focuses on an individual or a couple rather than trying to follow a family across generations. A biography requires a greater level of detail about individuals including where they lived, the era they lived in, what kind of schooling they had, associations they joined, and how they worked.

The following are ideas for general biographies:

Accomplishment. There are people who warrant our attention because of their accomplishments. If you have discovered someone like a Steve Jobs of Apple who had extraordinary vision for innovative products, a book highlighting your subject's accomplishments would make a good biography.

The Tragic Historical Figure. You may have discovered someone with an interesting story whose life met a tragic end. One example is: *Silas Soule: A Short Eventful Life of Moral Courage* by Tom Bensing.

A Shadowy Figure. Perhaps you are interested in someone who lived a hidden life. The life of Hugette Clark for example: *Empty Mansions: The Mysterious Life of Hugette Clark and the Spending of a Great American Fortune* by Bill Dedman and Paul Clark Newell, Jr.

Someone Famous. You may wish to write about a famous historical figure. Often the famous have been written about numerous times, but each author can give a famous historical figure a different look, such as that in: *Blood and Thunder: The Epic Story of Kit Carson and the Conquest of the American West* by Hampton Sides.

Someone Quite Ordinary. Throughout history, ordinary people have made contributions that are representative of the experience of so many others. *The Civil War Diary of a Common Soldier: William Wiley of the 77th Illinois Infantry* by Terrence J. Winschell reveals what it was like to experience battle firsthand by an ordinary soldier.

Some of the top selling biographies in the last two decades are autobiographies such as, Dave Peltzer's, *A Boy Called It*, Peter Kay's, *The Sound of Laughter*, and Barack Obama's, *Dreams from My Father: A Story of Race and Inheritance*. In the top ten best-selling biographies in recent years, all are about historical figures, and only one, *Steve Jobs* by Walter Isaacson, is about a modern figure. The numbers one and two based upon sales volume are: *The Bully Pulpit: Theodore Roosevelt, William Howard Taft and the Golden Age of Journalism* by Doris Kearns Goodwin, and *Bach: Music in the Castle of Heaven* by John Gardiner. The two highest selling biographies in 2014 according to the number of weeks atop the New York Times Bestsellers list are: *Unbroken* by Laura Hillenbrand, and *Killing Patton* by Bill O'Reilly and Martin Dugard.

Any person who is interesting enough to research and write about could make a good biography.

The following are ideas for family biographies:

Parent(s) or Grandparent(s). This book could be a tribute to a couple or an individual. These are people you may have the most information about, because they are people you know or knew well which means you can draw from memories as well as research.

Famous Ancestor. Whether famous or notorious, did your ancestor participate in a well-known historical event? Was he or she a professional athlete, or famous entertainer? Did he or she establish a town, or start a business?

Interesting Profession. Perhaps you had an ancestor who was a hatter, a furniture maker, or a smelter. Maybe your ancestor was an inventor who changed the lives of many people? Researching how an ancestor worked may be interesting to other people whose ancestors held similar jobs.

If you are interested in writing a biography, consult: *Publish a Biography: A Step-by-Step Guide to Capturing the Life and Times of an Ancestor or a Generation.*

A Memoir

While it may seem a strange exercise for family historians to do research on yourself or your generation, telling your story should not be. A generation from now, your children or grandchildren will be interested in how you lived.

The following are ideas for writing a memoir:

An Aspect of Your Life. Pick a part of your lifespan to write about—childhood, teenage years, college experiences, married life.

Professional Life. Perhaps it is your education, preparing for a profession, or your work life that you would most like to write about.

Military Life. Even if you did not choose the military as a profession, tell the stories of your experience in the service—during peacetime or at war.

Remembrances. If you have greeting cards or letters that help tell your story, consider weaving those into a memoir.

Journal or Diary. If you have kept a journal or diary, expand upon what you were thinking at the time you wrote the original entries.

Travel. If you have traveled extensively, create a lasting journal of the places you have gone, the experiences you had, the people you met along the way, and the things you saw.

If you are interested in writing a memoir, consult: *Publish a Memoir: A Step-by-Step Guide to Saving Your Memories for Future Generations.*

A Source Index

Recently, I heard a speaker state that only two percent of all the material that could be digitized has been digitized. So, good records extractions will be necessary for a long time to come. If nothing else, creating an index that makes a record set easier to use is a valuable gift to other genealogists or researchers.

There is no limit to the places where records are kept. To name a few: government (e.g. schools, agencies, cities, counties, etc.); company (e.g. mortuary, ditch companies, banks, merchants, etc.); associations (e.g. religious groups, Masons, Odd Fellows, service clubs, philanthropic clubs, community groups, sports teams, etc.); publications (e.g. journals, newspapers, etc.), transportation (e.g. trains, freighters, ships, planes, etc.), or cemeteries (e.g. headstone transcriptions, lot purchasers, burial certificates, etc.).

The following are ideas for records extractions:

An Index. If you are in the records, you may as well do a thorough job and collect every name, every subject, and every location. In addition to record sets, many 19th century local histories could use an index.

An Annotated Index. If you want to take an index one step further, you could add useful information such as the role each individual played (e.g. juror, judge or witness) and the date each event occurred.

An Abstract. Without going as far as a full transcription, you could abstract the basic points of court cases, probate files, or meeting minutes.

A Transcription. While your first duty is to do no harm to the archive that holds the records, you can write a transcription in a way that encourages readers to visit the archive to obtain copies of the original records, so that the collection does not become less valuable as a result of your transcription.

An Annotated Transcription. You may be familiar enough with the records, or the people whose names appear in the records, that you could add information (an annotation) to make the transcription more useful.

Preservation Plus Extraction. Some records are so fragile that they are difficult to use without damaging them. In this case, photograph the records to display them in the book in their original form, along with an index, an abstraction, or a complete transcription.

A Comprehensive Index. Consider indexing each source within a single collection (e.g. California gold rush participants in the Bancroft Collection), or across many collections to create a comprehensive index (e.g. Boulder Pioneers in the Colorado State Archives).

If you are interested in publishing a source index, consult: *Publish a Source Index: A Step-by-Step Guide to Creating a Genealogically Useful Index, Abstract or Transcription.*

Hybrid Projects

You may have a project in mind that does not fit neatly into any one category. Your book does not have to fit a mold. Be creative with some hybrid ideas.

The following are a few of the many possibilities for a hybrid family history:

Biography/Cookbook. While you write a biography, include a few recipes or family traditions sprinkled through the text.

Cookbook/Biography. Organize this one as a cookbook, but include some biographical information about the people who contributed the recipes, or how your family used the recipes according to tradition.

Biography/Professional Manual. You may have enough information about an ancestor's work or business to write a professional guide along with biographical information.

Photographic Timeline. Show how each family member fits into the photographic tree, or how they fit into the timeline of history.

Memoir/History. Use recollections from a memoir, letters or a diary, alongside the real-world history taking place.

Travel Guide/Family History. Let your family members follow your footsteps as you traveled to the homeland, along with information about the people who lived in the places you describe. Include travel guide information to help the reader make the trip, as well.

Perpetual Calendar. Include birth and death dates, anniversaries, graduations, immigration, travel—anything that puts family members on the calendar.

On This Day. Place historical events from your family history research or local history into a day-by-day collection.

Genealogical Gifts

While books are the most appreciated gifts according to reunion-goers, there are many other ways to give away your genealogical research as gifts.

The following are a few of the many possibilities for genealogical gifts:

Charts. You can create phenomenal family tree charts using software that makes it easy to upload your tree—fan charts, half-circles, full circles, or bow-tie charts. You can add photographs or background images, and information in as much detail as you desire.

Scrapbooks. There are books, clubs and stores devoted to creating amazing scrapbooks. If you can picture it as a pedigree, you can scrapbook it in a way that shows family relationships.

Photographs on Products. You can put a photograph on nearly anything—cakes, wall hangings, button covers, place mats, cups, mugs, and much more.

Cookbooks. Many companies specialize in producing cookbooks since so many groups use them as fundraisers. Use your next holiday or reunion to gather up the family's favorite recipes.

Card Decks. There are companies that specialize in playing card decks that you can create using photographs of your family. Sports cards are another idea along the same line.

Quilts. Quilting was one way to re-use scrap material and create a warm blanket before there was central heating. Quilting patterns can reveal something about your ancestors' ethnic heritage or the area where they lived. Other textiles such as tartans have similar meanings to family groups.

Replica Items. You may find a replica item of something your ancestors owned or could have owned that may be a meaningful gift. Look in historical museum catalogs for these items.

Slide Show. There is software to help you gather photographs and add captions for a slide show that you can distribute or place online for your family to see.

❧❧

Now that you have a great many ideas for turning your expertise or research into a book, read about the publishing process to determine the easiest way to finish your book and make it available to interested readers.

Chapter 4

How Publishing Works

Publishing has two essential parts—production and distribution. Before you determine whether to publish your book in print, electronically, or online, think about how your audience will want to read the book, and how you are going to deliver it to them.

It is hard to go wrong choosing print. The upside is that nearly everyone can read a printed book. The downside is that printed books must be produced and distributed (shipped) which cost money. Thankfully, print-on-demand technology has made it possible to print and ship books one at a time. Gone are the days when you had to order hundreds of books to keep the cost of each book down.

Publishing in an electronic format is tempting because there is almost no cost of production or distribution. Books can be sent to the reader electronically. The downside to electronic formats is that not everyone wants to read a book on a computer screen, dedicated eReader or tablet.

Publishing online is also tempting because most people have access to the Internet. Anyone with a web browser can read the book. The downside is that Internet companies come and go, so if your book is sitting on the server of a company that folds, the book disappears with it.

What is the best option? You do not have to make a decision about this yet. You may choose to publish in more than one format.

Before we move on to production, let us look at each publishing option in a little more detail.

Print Publishing

Before print-on-demand made publishing easy for anyone, there were four ways to publish a book in print. There still are. You can write a query letter to interest a traditional publishing company, pay a vanity publisher, hire a book packager, or self-publish. Before you decide to self-publish, what follows are the more traditional routes to book publishing and how they work.

Traditional Book Publishers

There are more than a few types of traditional publishers. There are the big publishers, such as Random House. Random House is one of the remaining Big Five, and companies such as this one are looking for the next blockbuster. They are not likely to be interested in a how-to or instructional guide unless the topic is of interest to the general public. There are also smaller publishers, mostly niche publishers, such as Arcadia Publishing that specializes in local history books.

In order to get the attention of one of the big publishers, you may need a literary agent to make a pitch to the company for you. Writing a good query letter introducing yourself and your book may work with a smaller publisher. Most how-to books, will not interest a traditional publisher enough to offer you a contract.

Even so, if you have an interesting specialty to write about and can interest a publishing company, they will buy the rights to publish a version of your work (e.g. print, electronic, audio, foreign language, or all rights) in exchange for a royalty—a percentage of the sales price. Most publishing contracts are based upon the sales price rather than the retail price because so many books are sold at a steep discount to bookstores or book clubs.

When the book sells, the publisher is paid, and they will handle any returns. You will be paid approximately ninety (90) days after the publisher, to allow time for returns.

A well-known author can expect a royalty of about fifteen percent, a lesser known author about ten percent, and an unknown author something less than ten percent. For most authors, a small percentage of the sales price (your royalty) means you have to sell a great number of books to make any money. For most how-to or instructional guides, this is not likely.

A traditional publisher will have total control over the physical production, distribution, and sales. The publisher will choose the cover design. Oftentimes, they will choose the title. Most importantly, they will control the content through the editing process. As the author, you will start the process, but once you sign a contract, and the manuscript is turned over, the publisher is in control.

If your book needs revisions or corrections, that will take place only after the initial print run sells out. For many books, the first print run never sells out. (One advantage to self-publishing using a print-on-demand printer is that you can make revisions at any time.)

A traditional publisher will decide how long the book will stay in print, and how long marketing will continue. For many books, once the sales slow, the marketing ends. (If you self-publish, the book will stay in print as long as you want it to.)

Vanity Publishers

Please do not enlist a vanity publisher to "publish" your book and "market" it to potential readers. In reality, these companies are offering to take as much of your money as you are willing to give them, and do nothing for you that you could not do cheaper. It is best to avoid these companies altogether. That goes for some author services companies, as well.

Book Packagers

Book packagers offer the different parts of the publishing process as services a-la-carte. If you do not want to handle the book cover design, for example, you could hire one of these companies to do so for you. You sign a contract for a specific service at a specific price. Book packagers can be helpful if you do not want to learn everything there is to know about book production, but still want a professional looking book.

Author Services

Author services companies offer many of the same services that book packagers do, as well as editing and marketing. Some of the biggest print-on-demand printers also offer author services. CreateSpace (www.createspace.com and its author services company BookSurge, www.booksurge.com), Lulu (www.lulu.com), and Blurb (www.blurb.com), offer packages of author services, such as copy editing, eBook conversion, layout, and cover design.

Most of the time, you will be able to do for yourself most of what they are offering to do for a fee. A better solution may be to find a local person—a book packager—who can design a cover or typeset the book for you at a fee you can negotiate, rather than accepting a package price for more services than you want or need from an author services company.

Caution: Author Solutions (www.authorsolutions.com—the author services provider of Penguin Random House via its imprints AuthorHouse, Trafford, Booktango, WordClay, FuseFrame, PitchFest, Author Learning Center, Author Hive, Xlibris, Palibro, Inkubook, Partridge and iUniverse) had a federal class-action lawsuit filed against them in 2013 alleging that they have been cheating writers out of their royalties and charging outrageous prices for services—for years. What follows are the names of companies that have aligned themselves with Author Solutions. Please avoid these vanity presses: Archway (Simon & Schuster), Partridge (Penguin), Westbow (Thomas Nelson/Harper Collins), Balboa Press (Hay House), Abbott Press (Writers' Digest), Dellarte Press (Harlequin). Many thanks to David Gaughran, author of *Let's Get Visible: How to Get Visible and Sell More Books* for helping fellow writers avoid trouble.

Self-Publishing

The best option for most specialists is self-publishing. You are the publisher. You are in control of the whole process. You decide what goes into the book and how it looks. You control who can buy the book, if you want to use your book as an exclusive benefit for a class you teach, for example. You control the contents and the process. You also do most of the work. Fortunately, printing technology and software to create book layouts and electronic files has made self-publishing not only possible, but relatively easy.

Now that you have a better understanding of the role of the publisher let us take a look at some of the nuts and bolts decisions about print production.

Book Printers

Please use a book printer, not the local copy shop. Producing books one at a time at the local copy shop is not only expensive, but most copy shops do not have the kind of equipment to create books with permanent covers—either softbound (perfect bound) or hard-bound. The local copy shop may be good if your manuscript will only fill a booklet (under 48 pages) rather than a book, and if you only plan to print a limited number.

To create quality softbound or hardbound books, there are two options—print-on-demand or offset presses.

Offset Book Printers

Using an offset book printer has its advantages, especially if you can sell or give away a large print run. Ordering books in quantity will keep the price per book down. The downside is that you have to print and pay for a minimum number of books up front—often 250 or more.

Offset printing is best for books with custom sizes or books that require high-quality reproduction such as photography or coffee table books. High-quality, full-color books are often printed in Asia because the cost is lower, even with international shipping.

Print-on-Demand Book Printers

Print-on-demand (POD) book printers are exactly as their name suggests—you can print a single book when you need it. There is a wide variety of print-on-demand printers. The following is a representative example of what you will find.

Lulu

Lulu (www.lulu.com) is a POD book printer that also offers author and marketing services. Their business model assumes that you, the publisher, have no experience, so their website will guide you through the process step by step. Anyone can create a printed copy of a book through Lulu. The only downside is that there is no quality control during the process, and some people—mostly those in the book industry—may assume that your book is amateurish if you publish through Lulu. If you are not worried about selling the book except to friends, family or close associates, then there is no need to worry about where you have your book printed. The ease of using Lulu's website is an attractive plus.

Lulu is one of the few POD book printers with privacy options. At Lulu, you can make the book available only to you or by private web link to only those people you allow to buy the book. Publishing privately is an attractive option for proofing books and for keeping books out of the hands of the general public if they contain information about living people, for example.

Lulu also has an online bookstore if you want to make your book available for sale. Lulu's catalog also appears in other major online bookstores' catalogs. Both Lulu and the other bookstores will take a cut before you earn a royalty, if you print your book through Lulu but sell it through Amazon, for example.

At Lulu, your wholesale prices may be higher than at other POD printers. If you are selling the book to make a little money, investigate additional options.

CreateSpace

CreateSpace (www.createspace.com) is Amazon's POD printer. They expect you to know a little bit more about the process, so the website is not as easy to use as Lulu. CreateSpace will have a staff person review your book before approving it. Your book will not become available in the Amazon catalog without approval. Gaining approval can be a hurdle if you have unusual page numbering or something that makes the staff unsure of the quality of the work.

The upside is that your book will be available at the largest online bookstore on the Internet, and your wholesale prices will be lower at CreateSpace than at Lulu. Amazon's reach is enormous, meaning your book will be available literally around the world if you print through CreateSpace.

Lightning Source

At the far end of the scale is Lightning Source (www.lightningsource.com). Lightning Source is an Ingram Company. Ingram is the largest book wholesaler in the United States, and selling through their catalog means access to 30,000 wholesalers, retailers and booksellers in more than one hundred countries.

Lightning Source *only* works with publishers. They expect you have experience with the process.

At Lightning Source, you must have your own International Standard Book Numbers (ISBNs), unlike CreateSpace and Lulu—both offer free ISBNs. All books, including different versions of the same book (an eBook or a 2nd Edition) must have an ISBN. ISBNs are like the Social Security number for a book. ISBNs distinguish one book from another or a newer version from an older version. The benefit of a free ISBN is cost savings since a single ISBN costs $125.00. A package of 10 ISBNs costs $295.00; 100 ISBNs cost $575, and so on. The more you buy, the less they cost per ISBN. You can purchase ISBNs through the Bowker Company's Identifier Services (www.myidentifiers.com).

Note: If you use a free ISBN from your printer, that company will become the publisher of record, not you.

Lightning Source charges fees to establish and maintain each book in their catalog. There are also fees for every update or revision. In other words, you need a next-to-perfect manuscript and a properly-sized and prepared cover to use this service, unless you are willing to spend a lot of money in fees and proofs until you get it right. There is no hand holding through the process.

The upside to printing through Lightning Source is that your wholesale costs will be lower than other POD printers, and your book will be available to a vast distribution network of wholesalers, retailers and booksellers—including Amazon and Barnes&Noble.

Espresso Book Machine

The Espresso Book Machine (EBM) (www.ondemandbooks.com) takes print-on-demand a whole step further. They provide equipment to select locations allowing readers to choose a book and have it printed in about fifteen minutes while they wait. You will not find EBMs in every city, at least not yet, and in some states, there are few locations. EBMs offer some exciting possibilities, however. Think about creating a book with recipes or stories gathered during a family reunion and being able to deliver the book to family members a few hours later.

Print Production Basics

One of your first major decisions is whether to print the book in color or in black-and-white. The cover, of course, will be in full color since that will not cost you more, and color covers are standard across the industry. Color *interiors*, however, add significantly to the cost. At print-on-demand printers, if you choose a color interior, every page will be considered a color page, even if it only has black-and-white text on it. If the book is in color, it is color throughout. An offset printer may be able to insert color pages either as a section in the middle or select places throughout the book. Either way, the cost of full-color books is much higher than books with black-and-white interiors.

Consider that you may be able to create a 200 page, 8.5"x 11" book in black-and-white for around $7 wholesale. Whereas, a color version of that same book could run $80 or more. **Tip**: One way to provide a complete set of instructions in black-and-white and the photographs in full color is to print the instructional book with the images in black-and-white along with a companion photo book for the best images. That way, you print the black-and-white book for $7 wholesale, along with a 20-page color photo book for $10 to $15—together, still cheaper than a full-color interior.

Interior Files

All books have interior files and cover files. The interior file will contain everything from the title page to the index, including the images. You will set up your manuscript in the physical size of the final book, called the trim size. The paper will be slightly larger than the final size so it can be trimmed off neatly to give the book a finished look.

The most common trim sizes are 6" x 9," 7" x 10" and 8.5" x 11." You can create a book of nearly any size, but if you will use one of these common sizes, the production cost will be lower and your options for printers will be greater.

Choose a trim size based upon how many pages there are in the manuscript, and how large you wish to display the images. When you are ready to create the layout, you should have an idea of whether your book will run 50 pages or 500.

The 6" x 9" or 7" x 10" size is nice if you think the reader will sit down and read the book cover to cover because these books are easy to hold. If the book becomes too thick at one of the above sizes, you can increase the page size to 8.5" x 11"—the size of a traditional piece of paper in the United States. This size is a little less comfortable to hold while reading, but ideal for a book meant for research, and has more room on each page to display images.

Cover Files

You will not create your cover file until you have chosen the trim size, the binding, and have the manuscript ready because the number of pages will determine the spine width.

Most printers offer the following binding options:

Hardbound also Called Case Bound. Hardbound covers consist of thick cardboard pieces covered in material, glued or sewn to the interior at the spine. You will have the option of a plain cloth cover, wrapping the cloth cover with a dust jacket, or a full-color, glossy paper cover—such as a textbook.

Softbound also Called Paperback or Perfect Bound. Softbound covers consist of thick, paper cover glued to the interior pages at the spine.

Lay-flat. Lay-flat is a more expensive option than softbound, but best for workbooks or cookbooks that need to lay flat for easy use.

Each of the following binding styles is disliked by librarians and bookstore owners because they do not have spines, so the book must be removed from the shelf in order to read the title.

Saddle Stitch. Saddle stitch books are laid out in two-page spreads, folded in half, then stapled at the spine. Standard 8.5" x 11" paper becomes a 5.5" x 8.5" book, or an 11" x 17" paper becomes an 8.5" x 11" book. The covers are created from thicker card stock placed on the outside of the collated pages before folding and stapling. Saddle stitch is best for books under 48 pages.

Side Stitch. In a side-stitched book, pages are collated; loose card stock covers are placed on the front and back, then stapled on the left-hand side near the edge.

Spiral or Wire-O. These books look like a spiral notebook. One problem with spiral or wire-o is that every time the pages are turned, they rub against the binding. Eventually, the pages will tear from the book easily.

For a how-to or instructional guide, softbound or hardbound is best. Either looks professional, has a nice spine so you can read the title when the book is on the shelf, and lasts longer than spiral, wire-o, or old-fashioned comb binding which is expensive and does not hold up well over time.

Final Files

Most printers will accept Portable Document Format (PDF) files. Once you have your manuscript looking the way you want it to, save it as a PDF and send it to the printer. (More about the mechanics of saving PDF files in Section 4.)

Print Distribution Basics

To deliver a printed book to an interested reader, the book could be sold through a bookstore—a brick and mortar store or online. You could distribute them yourself by selling them on your own website; print a bunch and take them to a gathering to sell to readers directly; ask interested readers to send orders to you; or, use an online print-on-demand service where buyers could purchase a copy for themselves. These are all easy options for distributing printed books to readers.

Selling books through a brick and mortar store is a little more complicated. Most bookstores order directly through one of the major wholesalers—Ingram (Lightning Source) or Baker&Taylor. To sell books to a chain bookstore, you must have an account with one or both of the major wholesalers. For a how-to book, however, chances are that the trouble you will go through to obtain an account will not be worth it.

There are exceptions. If you have information with widespread public interest, then traditional bookstore distribution channels may be an option for you.

Another exception is selling through a local independent bookstore. A local store owner may be willing to stock a few books bought directly from you, but expect this to be the exception rather than the rule. You may have more luck with a local museum shop where making small purchases from local authors is more common. Museum stores will purchase a few copies at a time, so give them an easy way to re-order.

Be aware of the expectations of booksellers. Wholesalers will expect up to a 50 percent discount, so they can make money and allow the end seller (the bookstore) to make a few dollars on the sale as well. You can probably offer a smaller discount to a local bookstore or museum shop, more like 20 to 30 percent if you are not using a wholesaler.

Then there is the matter of returns. Bookstores and wholesalers expect to be able to return books if they go unsold. Returns are an accounting hassle for you, not to mention that the wholesaler or retailer may send the book back years later, in no condition to re-sell, but expect credit for the return anyway. For small publishers, the only way around this is to sell books on a *non-returnable* basis. You may have to offer a bigger discount to induce the bookstore or museum shop to a non-returnable sale, but the greater discount is almost always worth not dealing with returns.

Electronic Publishing

Except for adult fiction, printed books still hold about ninety percent of the book market. However, people are reading more and more via dedicated eReaders and on other electronic devices such as tablets. On tablets, readers use an application (app) to display the book as the dedicated eReaders do. As smartphones, tablets, and other mobile devices become more widely used in schools and offices, electronic books will become even more popular. Electronic books are cheaper, mobile and easier to store.

Currently, there are three primary formats for electronic publishing—PDF, MOBI, and EPUB.

Portable Document Format (PDF)

Creating a PDF does not require a publisher or a distributor. PDF is a file type developed by the Adobe Corporation that solved cross-platform problems between computers. Before the PDF, sending a file to a person using a different operating system (PC or Mac) or software (Word or Word Perfect) meant that the recipient could not open or read the document.

You can convert almost any file to a PDF, and almost every computer comes with the free Adobe Acrobat Reader pre-installed. If your computer does not have Acrobat Reader, download it free from Adobe (www.adobe.com). PDFs can be opened and read on most electronic devices including tablets.

One upside to PDFs is the ease of creation. Most word processing and page layout software will save their files to PDFs. Saving to PDF keeps the page formatting exactly as you designed it. Everything will stay in place—the text, the pictures, and the captions.

A downside is that documents designed using 8.5" x 11" pages are easy to read on a computer screen or iPad, but may be almost impossible to read on a smaller device such as a mini-tablet or a phone. The pages are a fixed size, more like viewing a photograph than reading a text document. A better option for smaller devices is to use a format that allows the text to reflow, such as MOBI or EPUB.

MOBI and EPUB

Where electronic publishing gets a little more complicated is in the creation and distribution of different formats for different devices. There are two primary formats for eReaders or apps that imitate eReaders—Kindle's proprietary format MOBI and the EPUB format used by many other devices. Acting as your own publisher for these formats is not impossible, but not simple either.

Publishing for Kindle

The Kindle is Amazon's dedicated eReader. To publish for Kindle, use the Kindle Direct Publishing (KDP) service (kdp.amazon.com). You will be able to upload a Word document or a PDF, and Amazon will convert it to their proprietary MOBI format. Amazon will handle all sales and distribution. Readers will make their purchase through Amazon and download the book to their Kindle or a device with a Kindle app.

Amazon pays you a royalty based upon the book's retail price. In 2015, any book with a retail price under $9.99 will generate a 70 percent royalty, whereas books priced at $10.00 or higher receive a 30 percent royalty.

One nice feature of Kindle books is their ability to sync across devices, meaning that readers can switch from their Kindle to their tablet or smartphone and sync the files to maintain their place in the book.

Publishing for Other eReaders

While most word processing software will create a PDF, you may need special software to create an EPUB file. Since so many devices are using this format, it may become easier to create an EPUB in the future. If you have a Mac, Pages software will create EPUB files. Adobe InDesign will create an EPUB file on a PC, but the software is expensive. Microsoft Word will allow you to save your manuscript as an HTML file, and then you can use the free Calibre software (calibre-ebook.com) to convert an HTML file into an EPUB.

If you create your own EPUB files, download Adobe's free Digital Editions software (www.adobe.com). Use Digital Editions to preview how the book looks before sending it to readers or elsewhere for distribution.

Electronic Production Basics

Electronic books, like printed books, need an interior file and a cover file, but there are differences in how the files must be prepared—sometimes big differences.

Interior Files as PDFs

Setting up your manuscript for a PDF is almost the same as setting it up for print production. You can set the interior up as two-page spreads, so that the reader experiences the book the same way they would if they were reading a printed version, or you can set it up as a single page document without right-hand or left-hand pages. Single pages allow the reader to keep a single page on the screen that will make it easier to read on a device such as an iPad.

You can use a word processor or page layout program to create your PDF file, or you can use a presentation program such as PowerPoint or Keynote for the Mac. Word processors have the best spell and grammar checkers, but presentation programs may give you greater control over combining text and images. The slide sorter view, for example, lets you move information around much easier than cutting and pasting in your word processor. Page layout programs (albeit the most expensive software option) will give you the greatest control over both text and images.

Interior Files as MOBIs or EPUBs

Preparing a manuscript for conversion to MOBI or EPUB is, in some respects, easier than laying out and formatting a PDF for electronic or print production. Electronic books must be simple, and without a lot of complicated formatting because the look of an electronic book is controlled largely by the reader. The reader can adjust the type size to suit their needs so the text must re-flow within the eReader's window.

While it is possible for you to create a MOBI or EPUB file yourself, it may be easier to let an eBook aggregator or distributor create the file so that there are no glitches when the file is read by electronic devices.

Cover Files

While it is not necessary to include a cover file with your electronic book, many eReaders will show the cover in the device's catalog, and most eBook outlets will show a thumbnail. Make sure your title is readable in a small thumbnail.

Electronic Distribution Basics

How electronic books are distributed depends upon the format.

Distributing PDFs

Distributing a PDF is simple. You can send it directly to the reader in an email. Fortunately, PDF files can be optimized which makes the file small enough to send even long manuscripts with photographs and illustrations by email.

Another option is to post your PDF online for readers to download for themselves. You could send interested readers a link, or they could use a search engine to discover it. You could also create a website and post your PDF behind a password so that only paying customers can access it.

One downside to *selling* your book as a PDF, however, is limiting distribution to paying customers. There are tools that allow you to mark copies with the name of the original buyer so if the book is widely shared, you will know who made it available. Other tools allow you to lock the PDF from printing or to password protect the file. Practically, however, once you distribute your book in a PDF format, it may be re-distributed without your knowledge.

Distribution for the Kindle

Amazon distributes Kindle books. You can publish your eBook directly through their distributor CreateSpace (which also handles printed books) (www.createspace.com), or Kindle Direct Publishing (kdp.amazon.com), if you plan to publish only in the Kindle format. Right now, Kindle holds a majority of the eBook market through either its dedicated reader or through the Kindle app available for tablets or smartphones.

Distribution for Devices Using the EPUB Format

Hundreds of different devices use the EPUB format. If you can create an EPUB file, you can distribute the book yourself, much the same way as you would a PDF file (above). There are also hundreds of distribution outlets for EPUB books including:

- iTunes (www.itunes.com)
- The Android App Store also called Google Play (play.google.com)
- Google Books (books.google.com)
- Kobo (www.kobobooks.com)
- Smashwords (www.smashwords.com)
- Gumroad (gumroad.com)

These online bookstores sell electronic books, acting as a wholesaler between you and the end user.

Rather than dealing with hundreds of online bookstores, consider using an aggregator. Aggregators charge a fee, but they will prepare your manuscript for distribution across multiple platforms making sure the file passes the standards tests for different devices. They will also prepare the file for the many apps that mimic eReaders such as the Nook app or the Kindle app.

Aggregators will handle sales through the different electronic book outlets, take a percentage as their sales commission and pay the rest to you as a royalty. The following are all eBook aggregators:

- Bookwire (www.bookwire.com)
- Ingram (www.ingramcontent.com)
- INscribe (inscribedigital.com)
- Smashwords (www.smashwords.com)
- BookBaby (www.bookbaby.com)

Distribution of Other Electronic Files

Services such as Gumroad (gumroad.com), allow you to upload your electronic file(s) to their servers. Gumroad accepts audio, video or zipped bundles, if you have more than one book available or want to include an audio file along with your book file. To sell your book, place a link on your website taking viewers to Gumroad to buy it. You price your book; Gumroad keeps a percentage as a hosting and processing fee; they pay you the rest. In essence, Gumroad is taking care of the credit card processing and electronic delivery. Once the item is paid for, the buyer will receive a download link.

Distribution to Groups

If you want to sell books to an organization in quantity, for example, you can use Amazon's Whispercast service (whispercast.amazon.com). The organization will create an account and send an invitation URL to its members. If the member accepts the invitation, the organization buys a copy for that person. After the member receives the book, Amazon charges the organization's credit card for the sale. This would work for an association. By pre-selling books during an association gathering, setting up a bank account with a debit card on behalf of the group and using the funds collected to pay for books through Whispercast.

Global Distribution

One of the biggest advantages to publishing electronically through one of the major distributors such as Amazon's Kindle Direct Publishing (kdp.amazon.com), or Barnes & Noble's Nook Press (nookpress.com), is that they will make your eBook available to people across the globe. There is no negotiating of foreign rights or dealing with a foreign publisher to distribute the book on another continent. If you have interested readers across the world, publishing electronically may be a good option for you.

Distribution by Gift Card

Enthrill Books (enthrillbooks.com) enables you to use a pre-activated gift card allowing the recipient to download your book either in the EPUB or MOBI format. You could take the pre-activated cards to a book signing or conference, for example, to sell or give away to interested associates.

Distribution to Libraries

One final consideration is placing your book with the major genealogical collections across the country and into local libraries if your specialty is locality specific. While most libraries still focus on print books, they are coming around to the idea of purchasing licensing rights for eBooks. The electronic format would allow the library to lend the book to patrons with eReaders. OverDrive (www.

overdrive.com), is one of the leading digital distributors of electronic books to libraries, schools, and some retail outlets. If you are interested in selling your eBook to libraries, check out the publisher services on their website.

Online Publishing

For those of you who may want to make your book widely available and are not interested in selling it, publishing online may be a good option. There are a couple of ways to do so. You can use an online book publisher (Google Books), or you can act as your own publisher by using online publishing tools such as blogging software, website builders, or social media.

The difference between an online book and an electronic book is how it is delivered. Online books and electronic books are both in an electronic format. An online book stays on a server somewhere where readers can use a web browser to access the book via the Internet. An electronic book is more likely to be distributed to a reading device such as a Kindle, Nook or smartphone.

The upside to publishing online is that anyone with Internet access can find and read your book. Many of the options below cost nothing to set up and use, although, you are completely at the mercy of the host as to whether your site stays up and running. If the company folds, your free site folds with it. Another option is to pay for your own website which will give you more options for the look and feel of the material or whether you want to sell the book rather than give it away. But, you must continue paying the hosting fee or the site will come down and your book with it.

The following are options for publishing a book online:

Online Book Publishers

Google Books is one of the only online book publishers I have found to date, meaning that they sell books meant to be read via the Internet using a web browser. Google Books allows readers to choose between PDFs formatted exactly as the publisher formatted the book, or read through a proprietary browser platform that presents the book in side-by-side pages as if reading a printed book. Google's browser-based software also gives readers the option of reading the book like other dedicated eReaders. The reader can change the type size or the font, and the book text will reflow. If you want to publish a book through Google Books, sign up through their Google Play Books Partner Center (play.google.com/books/publish/).

Amazon offers something similar allowing readers to purchase a book for their Kindle, also allowing them to access the book from a web browser through the Kindle Cloudreader software (read.kindle.com). The experience of reading a Kindle book online is similar to reading from the Kindle device itself.

Publishing a Book by Blog

Blog is short for web log. Blogging software allows publishers to post new content easily and quickly. If you can use email, you can blog. The process is similar. You will use a headline to alert the reader, and the body text to tell the story and display images.

The difficulty of publishing a book on a blog is organizing in a way that the reader understands what to read in what order, and keeping the segments short enough to avoid scrolling (and scrolling and scrolling).

Publishing a Book Using Social Media

Facebook (www.facebook.com) is the most popular social media site right now, although it has not always been, and may not be in the future. The appeal of Facebook is that it is so easy to connect with other people interested in reading your material. The downside of using something such as Facebook to deliver your book's content is that each post can be only so long, shorter, even than blog posts. You will be delivering your book in little dribs and drabs. Facebook may be a better place to obtain additional information or tips from colleagues while you are writing, more so than playing host to your finished book. (You will find more detailed information regarding publishing by blog or social media in *Set Yourself Up to Self-Publish: A Genealogist's Guide*.)

Publishing a Book on Your Own Website

If you create a website to publish your book, you can install blogging software such as WordPress, or more traditional HTML coding using any number of HTML editors (website building software) such as Adobe Dreamweaver (www.adobe.com).

If you create your own website and use an HTML editor to build it, you will have complete control over how the site looks, and how you will organize your book as web pages.

Publishing a Book Using a Wiki Platform

Wikis are user-generated content that can be edited directly using an ordinary web browser. A wiki is a great opportunity for collaboration, but it is also an opportunity for malicious users to spread misinformation or to delete a lot of hard work. The power and the bane of wikis is the ability of anyone to contribute.

Online Production Basics

If you publish online, preparing your manuscript is relatively easy. Although, how you prepare it depends upon where you are going to place it on the Internet. Let us start with Google Books since they are the exception to the rule, and then we will look into making your book into blog posts or web pages.

PUBLISH YOUR SPECIALTY

Files for Google Books

If you publish online through Google Books, you can upload both a PDF version and an EPUB version, so the reader can choose whether to view the book exactly as you have it laid out, or as flowing text they can control through Google's browser-based platform. PDF and EPUB are the only two file formats Google Books accepts for upload. They will also accept a printed book and scan it for you, making it possible to create a new eBook out of an older, out-of-print title.

Google Books uses thumbnail-sized cover files in their online catalog.

Files for Blog Posts

While you can organize your material as a complete book on a blog, you must organize in a way that lets readers know how to follow the stories one after the other, and split the manuscript into short segments (posts) to keep scrolling to a minimum.

Each post requires a headline and body text, similar to composing an email. Blog posts can include images and captions. You can also add keywords to categorize each post so that readers can find the blog using a search engine.

Readers familiar with feed reader programs can subscribe to your blog so that they are notified every time you create a new post.

You can use your book cover image as a part of the blog's header so that it is always visible no matter which post the reader is viewing.

Files for Social Media

Publishing to a social media site is similar to publishing to a blog. Posting to a blog or social media keeps your short snippets in one place with the latest post at the top. The older posts will move down as the new posts appear.

On social media, if you create a page (sometimes called fan page) dedicated to your book, readers can come to that page to see everything you have posted, similar to visiting a blog, but if readers are "following" your page (i.e. they have "liked" it), then the snippets will be delivered to the reader through the newsfeed on their own pages.

For each post, use a headline to catch the viewer's attention as they skim their newsfeed (the posts coming in). Place the text in the body, and add images. Some social media platforms allow you to caption each image, and "tag" the people in the image. Tagging is similar to adding a keyword to the image. It helps people find the image using the site's search feature or by using a search engine.

Use your book cover image in the header area or as the profile image so that every time you post, the book's cover is shown in the little icon next to the post. Facebook uses square profile images, and book covers are longer than they are wide, so you may have to add white space on either side of your image to make it square. Otherwise, it could be cut off at the top and bottom when displayed.

36

Files for a Website

Creating your own website gives you a lot of flexibility for how and what you make available to readers.

Web pages can hold text, images, video or audio files and contain links to other resources on the Internet. To publish your book as a website, use an HTML editor to create a page for each story or chapter and navigation links to help the reader move from story to story logically.

Keywords are used on web pages the same way they are used on blog posts to help the search engines find the web page. HTML editing software and most website building tools online offer a way to include keywords in the metadata for each page.

Use your book cover image in the website's header, or alongside the text on the home page.

Copy and Paste Text Cleanly

The easiest way to prepare text for any online option is to copy and paste from your word processor. However, many word processors add code for formatting features such as margins, fonts, font size, bold or italics. These codes do not always translate cleanly to email, blog posts or websites. Word processors use an 8-bit environment for formatting, while many of the tools of the Internet use a 7-bit environment which can cause conflicts. What you can end up with is unexpected characters in your text, mostly where you expect punctuation to be.

For example, this is what happens when a quote is copied from a Word document into an email:

From Word: "Jacob's intended return ..."
Copied into email: "Jacob@s intended return ..."

One way to avoid these unexpected ASCII characters is to copy the text into a plain text editing program such as Notepad first. Notepad will remove all formatting, leaving a plain text (.txt) version of whatever you are copying and pasting. The plain text version can then be used in an email, a blog post or a website without any unexpected characters surfacing.

Create Web-Friendly File Names

Tools of the Internet also prefer standard filenames. So, file names that are acceptable on your local computer may contain unexpected characters when posted online. For example:

Local file: Jacob Wilson's will.pdf
Online becomes: Jacob%20Wilson%20s%20Will.pdf (depending upon the server settings)

For clean file names, avoid punctuation except for periods and use underscores for spaces. Either of these file names would be fine, for example:

Jacob.Wilson.Will.pdf
Jacob_Wilson_Will.pdf

Online Distribution Basics

If you publish online, you have largely determined how the book will be distributed to the reader—on a blog, a website or within a social media platform. You do not have to distribute it; the readers will come to the book. You need only take the steps necessary to help readers find the book online—good, descriptive keywords, great content, and a willingness to get the word out.

❧❧

What is the easiest way to prepare a book and distribute it at the least cost? That would be a PDF. As long as the PDF is designed for easy reading on the screen, the book can be distributed by email. For some readers, a PDF is perfect. If they are used to reading on screen or a large format tablet such as an iPad, they will appreciate the PDF. For others, print will always be preferred.

What, then, is the easiest way to prepare a book for sale? The easiest way is to create an eBook and use an eBook aggregator to convert it to the different electronic formats for you. The aggregator will also submit the files to the various sales outlets online, collect the sales price minus the online bookstore's fee, and pay you a royalty from the sale. Creating an eBook is simpler than creating a book for print because there are a few simple formatting and image placement rules to follow. The reader can change the font or type size to suit his or her needs, so the formatting must remain fluid. There is a fee to have an eBook aggregator prepare and submit your manuscript, but for those readers who are used to a dedicated eReader, this option will delight them.

Publishing a book online and in print are a bit more challenging than publishing PDFs and eBooks.

Publishing online has organizational challenges, but most options are without cost. Online publishing has the risk of all other electronic products—obsolescence. If the company hosting your website folds, or the social media site becomes unpopular, or your blog is lost in a server crash, the book is lost.

The best, most permanent way to preserve your research and writing is to publish in print. A book printed today, given the technology and materials, should last one hundred years or more. If preserved well, a modern book will last much longer. In the event of natural or personal disaster, giving a few copies of your book to the major libraries around the country will preserve your research and writing for generations to come.

Chapter 5

The Right Tool for the Right Job

To make your way from idea to finished book, using the right tool for the right job will save you time and frustration.

In a perfect world, you would use an organizational tool to set up the table of contents and organize your notes, a word processor to draft your manuscript, an image capture program to scan documents and other printed materials, an image editor to crop, size and alter images, a page layout program to typeset the book so that it reads and looks its best, and backup tools to keep your manuscript and image files safe from disaster.

In general, organizational tools are not the best place to format text correctly, word processors are not the best place to lay out book pages, and page layout programs are not the best word processors.

Realistically, you may not want to invest your time and money in all of this software. You may not need to. What you do need is an understanding of the rules of readability for books; and either, the willingness to learn how to create a layout, typeset the text, and prepare images in the software you already own, or recognition that the software you have will not do the job well. If the latter is the case, you can engage professional help or invest in software better suited to the job.

Organizing

In the preliminary stages, you may want software to keep you organized. Scrivener (www.literatureandlatte.com/scrivener.php) is a powerful organizing tool to gather your notes, pictures, video clips, or thoughts. It is available for both PC and Mac.

If you use an outline, the left-hand panel shows your outline in a menu that you can use to rearrange files, and expand or collapse depending upon what you want to see while you are working. You can split files into pieces to create a more detailed outline.

If you organize in a more visual way, you can see your notes, organized on a cork board. If you want to keep your sources attached to each note, you can do so either in the body of the text or off to the side in a panel designed to document source material.

At any time, you can move notes from one place to another using the drag and drop features in the cork board or outline, helping to organize your information into a cohesive whole.

Other organizing software includes: Microsoft OneNote (www.onenote.com) and Evernote (evernote.com). Both of these organizing tools have the advantage of being available on your desktop and by app on mobile devices with the ability to sync files. I use these apps to add notes or ideas when I am out and about, but when I am in the office writing, I use Scrivener to organize.

Word Processing

At some point, move your notes from an organizing tool into a word processor. Whether you are at the stage to add formatting, or you are still writing and want to collect your material chapter by chapter, a word processor is a better tool than organizing software to create a complete manuscript.

Word processors are ideal for creating eBooks. Unfortunately, most word processing software falls short when creating layouts and correct typesetting for print books because they lack the sophistication to create the best-looking pages.

Word processors often hyphenate incorrectly or add space between words to avoid hyphenating that can create rivers of white or blank areas through the type. Word processors do not have nearly the kind of control over how tight or how loose text is typeset that also can result in dense or dark areas of text on the page. Most word processors do not have as much control over margins, columns and text wrap around images, as page layout programs do.

Unfortunately, page layout software can be expensive, so you may opt to lay-out and typeset your final manuscript in your word processing software. If you do, be prepared to learn about the advanced features. Fortunately, some word processors have helpful time-saving features to create a table of contents, an index, and footnotes, for example.

There are numerous word processing programs available including:

- Microsoft Word (office.microsoft.com)
- Pages for Mac (www.apple.com)
- Word Perfect (www.wordperfect.com)
- OpenOffice Writer (www.openoffice.org)
- LibreOffice (www.libreoffice.org)
- Google Docs (docs.google.com)

Microsoft Word has become the standard among book designers and packagers, professional editors, some eBook aggregators, and online resellers. For book designers and book packagers, Word files can be imported directly into more sophisticated page layout software without much trouble. For editors, Word has a "Track Changes" feature that allows you to see and accept or reject an editor's changes. Most eBook aggregators prefer Word files because they can convert the file for the requirements of the different eBook readers easily. And, some online resellers will accept Word files from which to create print and electronic books.

Page Layout

When typesetting print books, you will achieve the best results from a page layout program. The two major powerhouses are:

- Adobe InDesign (www.adobe.com)
- QuarkXPress (www.quark.com)

Pages for the Mac (www.apple.com) was designed as a word processor but has many of the same features as the best page layout programs.

Page layout programs are designed to put the finishing touches on book-length manuscripts using the same tools professional typesetters use. These programs also can handle full-color books and, for the time being, are best for converting word-processed text into good looking eBooks in the EPUB format used by many eReaders.

PDF is another popular electronic format, and page layout programs create beautiful PDFs with settings to create the appropriate file sizes and quality for printing, emailing or posting online.

The biggest advantage to using a page layout program is the control you have over where items are placed on the page in relationship to other items, the ability to create precise text formatting styles (rules) for different needs, and the flexible layouts possible with master pages with different grids for different page styles.

The sophistication of these programs is a big step up from even the best word processors. Unfortunately, most page layout programs come with both a hefty price tag and a hefty learning curve. For some, using a book designer or packager to take your final manuscript from as good as a word processor can do, to as good as a New York publisher could do, may be a better trade-off than buying and learning a page layout program.

Image Capture

There are two ways to turn a printed photograph or document into a digital image—you can photograph it, or you can scan it. For items such as photographs pasted into a scrapbook, artwork, three-dimensional objects or photographs with textured surfaces, re-photographing the item may give you the best results.

For most flat items, however, scanning will give you a good digital image. Producing a good, print-ready scan will save you time and effort later.

There is more information about scanning in Chapter 8: Scanning and Optical Character Recognition.

Image Editing

The best way to prepare images in the correct physical size and resolution is to use an image editing program.

There are hundreds of image editors, including online tools, free downloads, apps for mobile devices, pre-installed software, and those designed for professional photographers. One of the best is Adobe Photoshop. For most people, the consumer version called Photoshop Elements (www.adobe.com) will do everything you need to complete your book project.

Illustration

While it is possible to create a book cover in a word processor or a page layout program, to create the best-looking images and type, you may want to use illustration software, also called vector editing programs. The most popular among graphic designers is Adobe Illustrator (www.adobe.com).

There are many others available, including:

- CorelDraw Graphics Suite (www.coreldraw.com)
- Xara Designer Pro (www.xara.com)
- Inkscape (www.inkscape.org)

Illustration programs are another case where the cost of buying the program (and the time required to learn it) may be better spent hiring a cover designer.

Utilities and Backup

While you are writing, make backups—frequently. You never know when your hard drive will crash, or some other calamity may come your way. One way to create on-going backups is to use one of the cloud services such as:

- Carbonite (www.carbonite.com)
- MyPCBackup (www.mypcbackup.com)
- Mozy (www.mozy.com)
- SugarSync (www.sugarsync.com)

If you keep good backups and something happens, you can always retrieve the most recent backup of your manuscript once you are up and running again.

If you also want to share files with colleagues or editors, think about using a file sharing service such as:

- Dropbox (www.dropbox.com)
- Hightail (formerly YouSendIt) (www.hightail.com)
- Box.com (www.box.com)
- Google Drive (drive.google.com)
- Microsoft OneDrive (onedrive.live.com)

These services are perfect for sharing copies of your manuscript, even if the file is large. Do not keep your only copy on one of these services, however, because anyone who shares the folder with you has the power to delete it.

The most secure place to keep backups is in the cloud, or on a portable hard drive, stored away from your home in a safe deposit box.

❧❧❧

How many or how few of these tools you utilize is up to you. You may find that the right tool for the right job is easiest. Or, you may prefer hiring someone to handle the tasks you would rather not tackle. Thankfully, most how-books or instructional guides are successfully published without spending a king's ransom on software or professional help.

SECTION 2

The goal in this section is for you to review your research and gather anything else you need before you begin writing.

Everyone should:

- Identify your target audience—the people for whom you are writing the book.
- Conduct a research review.
- Put your citations in order.
- Read the chapter on scanning and optical character recognition.
- Read the tips for conquering writer's block.
- Make completing your book project a priority by scheduling time on your calendar to devote to it.

Baby Steps

If, after conducting a research review, you are ready to proceed with the writing, draft a good outline, and start. If the task of digitizing your images feels overwhelming, look for a scanning company to help you.

Next Steps

After your research review, plan an additional round of research to fill in any holes. Digitize the images you have and organize them in files.

Giant Leaps

After your research review, plan an additional round of research to gather any additional information you may need to fully explain your specialty.

Even though it may seem that I am suggesting you retire and devote your life to writing your book, I am not. I want you to be realistic about the preparation phase, however, because it can take longer than the writing.

Because this section has so many tasks, there are additional Baby Steps, Next Steps and Giant Leaps within some chapters.

Chapter 6

Identifying Your Target Market

Your target market—who you are writing for—matters. According to *Elements of Style*, "The true writer always plays to an audience of one." To keep your perfect audience in mind as you write, place a photograph on the wall or near the desk as a constant reminder.

Having a clear idea of the people who will appreciate your book will influence what to include and what to leave out. If you write to meet your audience's needs and expectations, you will naturally answer their questions, and use the images and information needed to make explanations clear.

Who is Your Audience?

Other people with similar interests, of course, is the natural audience for your book. Even though you should write primarily to satisfy the curiosity of your core audience—most books have more than one natural audience.

Without knowing the subject of your book, it is difficult for me to determine who else may be interested in your expertise. The following list may contain natural members of your subject's audience, or may give you additional ideas.

Genealogical Researchers

If you are writing about your genealogical expertise, other genealogists will be interested in reading the book to help them with their research.

What level of expertise will your audience need in order to make the best use of your book? This is an important question to answer early on so that you will write to meet your audience's needs. If you are planning a comprehensive book to meet the needs of all levels of experience, you may need simple, clear explanations rudimentary enough for a beginner but also detailed enough information to interest a fellow expert. It can be a challenge to avoid writing over the heads of half the audience while satisfying the needs of readers with more experience.

One of my goals with this book and the others in the series has been to give the beginners enough information to be successful without becoming overwhelmed, while giving more experienced researchers a challenge to make their books the best they can be.

Local Historians

If your expertise has to do with a type of record, research methodology or what types of records are available locally, there may be local historians or hobbyists interested in the subject. Local libraries may be interested in any information you have about a community or local people.

The General Public

Your expertise may appeal to the general public. A how-to guide for a craft, whether modern or historical, could interest the general public, for example.

Museum Shops

If your specialty interests local historians, then a museum shop in the area may be interested in selling your book.

Libraries

Libraries are full of reference materials of all types. If your specialty has not been covered well by other books, that may be a good selling point to add your book to a library's collection.

Bookstores

Bookstores are great places. As a bibliophile, I love bookstores, but the pressure on bookstores is to move inventory. Unfortunately, how-to books, even those with broad, general public appeal, are a risk for bookstores unless the subject of your book is a hot topic. Unless you can generate traffic into the bookstore, do not count on bookstores to sell many of your books. There are ways to entice interested readers through the bookstore door, but that discussion is later in Section 5: Getting the Word Out.

While you are researching and writing, consider what your target market(s) may need to get the best experience while reading your book.

What Does Your Audience Need?

The goal while writing is to spend your energy making the book the best it can be, given the time you have to finish the research and write the book. Give the reader everything he or she needs to understand the subject or the directions.

Subject Matter

How much information you include may depend upon how much information you believe the audience needs to fully understand your specialty. The level of detail is up to you and how much research are willing to do.

Format

The format or style of a how-to or instructional guide should fit the nature of the information and the reader's needs. A step-by-step instructional guide, for example, may consist of numbered sentences followed by illustrations rather than a lengthy narrative. The format is up to you.

Documentation

I will never suggest that you compromise your scholarship in order to write an easy-to-understand how-to or instructional guide. The manner of your documentation, however, could be different than that of a genealogy or local history where other researchers expect to recreate your research steps, than a how-to, where readers want simple instructions. No, I am not giving you permission to leave out the citations. The audience will use your evidence to evaluate the credibility of the book. You can, however, choose a format for documentation that is easier to accomplish than one of the more rigorous or formal genealogical styles.

Images

Images help guide readers. Illustrations are a good example of this. Illustrations can help readers imagine skills, places or events they are unfamiliar with, such as what a typical inner-city tenement looked like, how cattle were branded, or how machinery was used to create textiles, even if the illustration is only representative of the experience. Think of how many kids have never used a rotary phone.

In addition, a beautifully illustrated book may be more appealing to a bookstore or a museum shop than a book with text only.

Index

An index is indispensable. Experienced readers may want to go directly to a subject that interests them. Other readers may need to return to a subject to gain a better understanding. Additionally, librarians hesitate to stock books without indexes unless they are fiction.

Keep the following ideas in mind while you are researching and writing:

- How much does the reader need to envision a complete and understandable picture of what you are explaining?
- How much detail is needed to give the reader a complete understanding of the subject matter?

- Could an image clarify what is difficult to describe?
- For those who may want to do additional research based upon your book, what level of documentation will be the most helpful?

What Will You Need to Explain the Subject?

The next step is to figure out what *you* will need to explain your specialty in the best, easiest-to-understand way.

Description

Your challenge is to learn enough about the subject to be able to describe that a complete novice may need to know to get started, and what more experienced readers will want to further their knowledge.

Detail

The credibility of your book may hang upon the details. What level of detail will you need to give the reader the best understanding of the subject?

❧❧

Your next step is to conduct a research review. A research review will help you organize what you already have, and develop a plan for gathering what else you may need before you can begin writing.

Chapter 7

Conducting a Research Review

The purpose of a research review is to discover and organize what you have, but more importantly, to create lists of what you do not have. This exercise will help you to form a research plan focused solely on the information you need for this book and not to wander into other interesting areas of research. After you conduct a thorough research review, you will develop a new research plan to gather additional information to help you pass along your expertise to others.

For now, take a look at the research you have.

If you are starting from the beginning, and have not written anything, nor developed the outline or organization for a book, keep reading. You may be surprised by what you do have. What follows will also help you structure your materials and to form a plan for any new research necessary.

Preliminary Organization

Even the best-researched book is unreadable if not well organized. You do not have to follow precisely one of the following organization forms, but you do have to layout your case logically so that the reader can follow what is happening.

There are a number of way to organize a how-to or instructional guide. The following organizational styles may give you a few ideas, not only for how to organize your book, but for what additional research you may need.

Step-by-Step

By far the most common way to organize a how-to book is step-by-step. You give the reader the instructions for how to accomplish a task by leading him or her through the process, step by step. Cookbooks are the most common example of this, but there are many examples from genealogy, as well. A quick look through Amazon came up with these how-to titles (or subtitles): *How to Do Everything:*

Genealogy; *How to Put the Past on Paper*; *How to Archive Family Keepsakes*; *How to Use FamilySearch.org*; *How to Trace Your Germanic Ancestry in Europe*; and *How to Identify Ancestors ... through DNA*, and the list goes on.

Chronologically

For some subjects, organizing from the past to the present makes the most sense to readers because it follows a natural timeline. A book about using court records would be a good example because what happens in the courtroom in the present is often influenced by what has been determined by legal precedent in the past. Giving the reader a chance to follow the progression of why the law is carried out the way it is, may be helpful.

Reverse Chronology

For other subjects, it may be easier to start in the present and work backward into the past. This is often the way we use census records. We start with the latest census records where a family is found and work backward to discover where the family was in earlier times. A reverse chronology may suit your subject better than a past to the present approach.

By Topic

Land records are a good example of how structuring a book by topic may be most appropriate because the rules for recording land was different under different colonial, federal or state systems. Within each topic, you may find that a chronological or step-by-step method for explaining how to locate a land record would work best. Conducting research in a specific location is another example of how a book could be arranged by topic, whether you are describing conducting research in a city, county, state or a major repository.

Building Blocks

There are some subjects for which the reader needs to gain understanding a little bit a time before moving on to the next, more complicated or difficult concept. Within this type of organization there are some elements of the step-by-step approach and some elements of the topical approach.

Degree of Difficulty

Degree of difficulty is similar to building blocks, although tasks could be organized from easiest to hardest or hardest to easiest, depending upon the lesson you wish to impart to the reader.

Problem-Solution or Question-Answer

In some cases, you could organize by outlining common problems (questions) along with suggested solutions (answers) for each case.

It is not necessary to determine what organizational style you will use for the final manuscript right now, but thinking about how you could organize may generate additional research ideas.

Taking Stock of What You Have

For me, before I consider writing a book about a subject, I take a look at my own bibliography and notes. Or, I compile one. In some cases, that has meant taking a bunch of dusty books off the shelf and evaluating each one for what I have to offer that is different than what has been written already. In other cases, it means taking a trip through Amazon's online catalog to determine whether I have conducted an exhaustive enough search to begin writing. I ask myself whether my own knowledge of the subject is complete enough to offer my expertise. There may be new material written and published in your field that you should read before you begin writing.

Thinking Through What You May Need

There are a some areas where you may need more information to be able to explain your specialty to people who are new to the field. While you are reviewing your research, consider the following:

Latest Research

How up to date is your knowledge of the topic? With approximately 200,000 books being published every year, it is easy to fall behind on some subjects, especially those that a great number of people have become interested in such as the use of DNA with genealogy. Far more books have been written about this subject in the last few years than have books about census records, that is for certain.

Examples

Do you have representative examples that will help the reader understand the subject? In some cases, your examples should be images. There is nothing quite like seeing an example for some readers. In other cases, not only may you want an image, but a complete translation or transcription, if that is what the reader will need to make sense of what they are seeing in the image.

Instructions

If you are planning a step-by-step guide with instructions, have you tested out your instructions on people with different levels of experience in the subject? There is nothing like a few test runs to illuminate the flaws in a set of instructions. It does no good to test out a recipe using a master chef, either. Test the recipe and the cooking instructions on someone who uses the kitchen as the shortest route to the garage. Then you will know how complete your instructions are.

Case Studies

There are times when a good case study is the best way show readers how you got from point A to point B, and what kind of sources or resources you needed to get there. Are there areas of your specialty where a case study or two would help?

Social History

Genealogical research establishes relationships. Social history research reveals details about daily life—*how* people lived and worked. Are there areas of social history that would help to explain your subject? Depending upon the subject of your specialty, you may have some of the following items, or you may need to look in an archive or repository for them.

The following are items rich in social history:

Personal Papers. Letters, diaries, journals, recipe cards, scrapbooks, greeting cards, birth announcements, wedding invitations or funeral cards. Look for anything that may have been written, compiled or saved as a remembrance.

Photographs. Get out the photo albums, look through the slides, and collect the negatives. See if you can spot evidence of the social history—the way they dressed, a new car, houses or land, a barn or farm animals. See what you spot in the background. It may be more than you think.

Newspaper Clippings. Look for obituaries, birth, wedding or engagement announcements, feature stories or advertising. Advertising also can be a quick, visual way to get ideas of what fashions and prices were like during an era. You may find newspaper clippings loose or within other bound volumes such as bibles, photo albums or scrapbooks.

School Records. Gather up anything school related, such as report cards, diplomas, academic achievements, group activities, club or sports awards, theater or music programs, personal or class photographs, and yearbooks.

Business Records. Look for anything that may indicate how people were employed or conducted business, such as employment records, pay stubs, account books, store ledgers, client lists, professional awards, guides or books, licenses or certificates.

Military Service. Look for service records, discharge papers, uniforms, commendations, medals, photographs, or identification papers.

Religious Records. Religious institutions were often the place where ceremonies were recorded, such as baptisms, confirmations, weddings, deaths or burials. You may find a certificate of the event. Also look for bibles or other religious texts, evidence of religious education, religious magazines or bulletins, general magazines or newspapers.

Association Records. Look for handbooks, costumes, awards, jewelry, rules or bylaws, group photographs or membership lists.

Court Records. Look for court rulings or judgments, lawsuits, probates, divorces, and civil or criminal cases.

Administrative Records. Locate any papers filed with a government clerk or other administrator such as deeds, taxes, licenses, utilities, voter registration, or auto registration.

Collections. Many people are collectors of objects such as stamps, coins, spoons, salt and pepper shakers, images, statuettes or photographs. There is almost no limit to the things people collect and where (or to what lengths) they may go to add to their collections.

Enthusiasts. The same is true of fans who keep or collect photographs of stars, autographs, tickets, posters, playbills, albums, memorabilia, or sports jerseys.

Ephemera or Memorabilia. Ephemera is a catch-all term for items that were meant to be temporary such as tickets, menus, playbills, posters, or advertising. Memorabilia is a slightly larger category that may include items such as snow globes, travel posters, postcards, souvenirs, reunion books, mugs, or t-shirts.

Any of these items will help you to understand how people live, their activities and who their associates are. Analyze whether elements of social history will help you explain your specialty to readers of all levels of experience.

Traditions

There are many areas where traditions play a role in what people do, or how people do things—family traditions, for example, may govern how to celebrate weddings or holidays. Occupational traditions may explain beliefs, such as miner's superstitions about women in mines. The military has its own set of traditions which may explain how medals are awarded, for example. Examine traditions within your field of expertise.

If your specialty is Swedish research, for example, are there things about Swedish family traditions that would help your reader understand how to be a better researcher? Or are there clues within family traditions that would point to Swedish ancestry? For some readers, figuring out *which* family traditions came from their ethnic heritage may be a challenge because so few of us are 100 percent this or that. And, it can be difficult to distinguish which traditions are ethnic, and which are religious, regional, or unique to a family.

Traditions are one area where people may be so familiar with the tradition that they do not give it much thought, or have never considered how or why the tradition began. Revealing the source of a tradition may be interesting, even as part of your introduction or background information about your specialty.

Analyze whether traditions play a role in understanding your specialty.

Historical Context

You may want to add historical context to help the reader understand the significance of your specialty. Take railroad records as an example. Showing other researchers how to use railroad records may necessitate a lesson in railroading history to understand the time frame of the records and location of where railroad records would be found.

Analyze what historical context you may need to fully explain your specialty.

A Picture is Worth a Thousand Words

Most how-to or instructional books benefit by adding images. Not only do images help break up daunting pages of dense text, they help the reader see what you are explaining. While you may be familiar with a process, a place or an era because of your research, your reader may need visual clues to put the pieces together.

You may have images within your own collection or you may need to acquire images in the next round of research. While you are reviewing your research, consider the following types of images:

Photographs

Depending upon your subject, you may want both modern and historical photographs to help illustrate your book. For example, if you are explaining the records available in a specific location, you could show the courthouse as it looked when it was first built, a second courthouse that has been made into a local museum, and the modern courthouse where the records are stored. Look through your own photographs to see what could be used to illustrate your book. Chapter 8 has advice if you need to digitize or alter photographs.

Artwork and objects deserve a special mention because these items should be photographed under studio conditions and not scanned, so that they will display well in a book. You will find information about photographing these items in Chapter 9 along with tips for obtaining permission to use historical photographs, having photographs taken by a professional, or taking new photographs yourself.

Documents

If the subject of your specialty includes original source documents, you may need images of different types. Assess what documents or document images you already have, and how they could be used in your book.

Illustrations

There are times when an illustration conveys a clearer message than either a document or a photograph. The following are a few examples:

An Ancestor Chart. If you want the reader to see who descends from whom quickly, a multi-generation ancestor chart may be the easiest way.

Timeline. A timeline is an effective way to show small bits of information in a logical way. You could show a military unit's participation in different battles, for example, using a timeline.

Diagrams. An architectural drawing, for example, may help give readers an idea of what a typical house would have looked like. I particularly enjoy artists' renderings of what a place may have looked like, or how buildings may have been constructed in the past, especially when there are only ruins left today. Diagrams are often a good way to show a process. Step-by-step instructions are often accompanied by diagrams.

One caution about using illustrations for the sake of having something to look at on the page—adding ClipArt is tempting because it is easy, but not, perhaps, what is best. Beautiful line art published in 19th century newspapers, books or magazines is now in the public domain. It is worth your time to find a good image to illustrate an old farming technique, for example, or to have a good image created by an artist rather than settling for a low-quality image.

Maps

Many of your readers will not be familiar with a local setting. Context maps show the reader what part of a state or country covered in the records. The map of Kentucky shows Bath County up in the northeastern part of the state. The second map shows Caldwell County in relation to Bath County on the same map.

A map can also help the reader find a location to visit. The topo map shows the roads leading to the cemetery, marks where the cemetery is, and shows the topography—all helpful information for a visit.

County map showing Bath County, KY

County map showing Bath and Caldwell Counties

Road map showing directions for readers to follow.

Maps help describe movement from place to place as you would if you were describing a battle scene, for example. A battlefield map would help the reader visualize where the opposing forces met, how far troops had to go from one battle to the next, and so on.

The possibilities for including maps are nearly endless: plats, roads, historic, political, battlefield, migration, topographical, economic, climate, coastline, survey, nautical, soil, trails, and so on. If you cannot find a map of exactly what you need, you can create one using Google Maps using the My Maps feature (mapsengine.google.com). Google Maps has a generous Terms of Use agreement that includes creating and sharing individualized maps with proper credit. Make sure to read the Terms of Use before you include a Google Map in your book.

Gather a list of places readers may need to see a map for context, clarification, or to visit for themselves.

Newspapers and Memorabilia

You may have newspaper clippings or other items of memorabilia among your research and fortunately, there are projects across the country devoted to saving and preserving old newspapers.

58

Look for newspaper clippings and other items of memorabilia or ephemera that you could make good use of—either to help you write the book or as an illustration for the benefit of readers.

Write a Bit

While you are analyzing each piece of your existing research, write a short bit about it. This exercise is similar to a good warm up stretch before running. Do not worry about the quality of the writing at this point. Even if you write only a synopsis of each book in your bibliography, you will be writing and giving yourself a quick reminder of what each book contains that will be useful later.

There are good tools for recording little bits of writing so that you can not only keep track of them, but rearrange them easily once you start writing the manuscript. In particular, I like the following software:

- Scrivener (www.literatureandlatte.com/scrivener.php)
- Evernote (www.evernote.com)
- OneNote (www.onenote.com)

OneNote and Evernote also have application versions that you can download to a tablet or smartphone so your notes are available to you even when you are away from your computer.

Take Care of the Housekeeping

While it is possible for you to relate your expertise without a single reference to a source, a well-documented book about your specialty will be more respected. As a part of your research review, put your citations in order, guard against any inference of plagiarism and gather any permissions and usage fees you may need to pay in order to use materials belonging to others.

Citing Sources

Create good citations as a part of your research review. Decide how you will cite each piece of factual information in your book. Include the name of the article, book, image or document, and the location where you found it so that other researchers can weigh the strength of your sources and recreate your research steps, if necessary.

I do not recommend waiting to create citations until you are ready to add footnotes or endnotes to your book. At that point, the task will seem daunting. It is better to figure out what method you want to use now, and stick to that method as you write and perform additional research. There is no need to decide whether you will include your sources as footnotes or endnotes yet, as long as you have the citations ready to work with when you start writing.

I understand that the mere mention of the Elizabeth Shown Mills book, *Evidence Explained*, sends some genealogists into fits of pique, but she offers a way to document every conceivable source type systematically. Friend, fellow genealogist (and a good gentleman of Kentucky), Kirk Woosley Patten, likens formal citations to setting a formal table. He explains that "once you understand where everything goes, you never have to guess which utensil to use." I agree, but I also shudder at the thought of having to correctly pick out the lobster fork. Formal citations may cause you the same anxiety.

There are ways around the fear of formal citations without compromising the scholarship of your book. The two major formulas for proper source citation in genealogies are *The Chicago Manual of Style* or *Evidence Explained* by Elizabeth Shown Mills. These same styles may serve your book well.

The Chicago Manual of Style type:
1. 1800 U.S. Census, Second Census of the United States, New York, Essex County, Crown Point, pg 192-A, line 7, Daniel Smith household; NARA microfilm 1804, roll 1.

Evidence Explained type:
1. Daniel Smith household, p. 192-A, Crown Point, Essex County, New York; Second Census of the United States, 1800, vol. 2, New York: Clinton-Green Counties; Manuscript Schedules of Decennial Population Census, 1790–1870. Records of the Bureau of the Census, Record Group 29, National Archives, Washington, D.C. [Evidence Explained (2007), p. 238].

Here is a third option.
2. **"beguiled ... rifling around in the past"**: Alice Munro, *The View from Castle Rock* (New York: Knopf, 2006), p. 347.

I found this example in David Laskin's book, *The Family*, (New York: Viking, 2013), p. 342. The book is well documented. He and his publisher have chosen to place their source citations in endnotes rather than in footnotes, and although they do not strictly follow either formal style, it gets the job done.

There is software as well as downloadable templates that make creating good citations easy. If you have not discovered the software *Evidentia*, now may be the time. This software leads you through the process—first choosing your preferred style as either *Evidence Explained* or *The Chicago Manual of Style*, then giving you a template in the chosen style for most of the common sources. There is also a way to create a template for sources that do not fit the existing templates.

If you are determined to create citations in a unique way, the following are the basic elements necessary for a good citation:

- Who created the source
- What the source is
- Where the source was created
- When the source was created
- How to find the source (where the source is held or where you saw it as a digital image)
- The form (original, a copy such as a microfilm or a digitized original)
- Why the source is useful

For a complete explanation of these elements, consult *Mastering Genealogical Proof,* by Thomas W. Jones. Consult Robert Raymond's article, *Citation Baby Steps*, in the FamilySearch wiki online for more information about why effective citations are necessary.

Plagiarism and Copyright Reminder

Avoid using another writer's words—no matter how beautiful they are or how tempting they are to repeat.

Facts and ideas cannot be copyrighted, but the way they are expressed belong to the author from the minute the words are recorded in any tangible form. The most common form of plagiarism is inadvertent. If you repeat more than three words in a row or use words in a distinct combination or with a distinct emphasis copied directly from another author, you must give that author credit.

Note: Writing a helpful how-to book without trying to make money does not absolve you from plagiarism or copyright violations. Give credit where credit is due and ask permission to use words, images or illustrations that do not belong to you, even if you plan to change them in some way. A derivative of an original belongs to the copyright holder, as well. If an original is not yours, ask permission. A good source for information about copyrights and genealogy is Judy Russell, the Legal Genealogist (www.legalgenealogist.com).

Permissions and Usage Fees

You may encounter repositories or collections that require permission to transcribe or display images of source materials in their possession. The terms of use and fees vary from repository to repository, so it is important to check before you make an image or a transcription an integral part of your book.

Oftentimes, permissions are nothing more than citing your source in a particular way acknowledging the repository or collection. In many cases, if you explain the nature of your book or that you are not planning a commercial run of thousands of books, you may be able to get fees waived.

As you are conducting this research review and as you expand your research in the next round, gather any permissions you may need, and keep a good record of any fees that you may need to pay. As you write, you will be able to evaluate whether it is worth the fee to include the image or source in the book.

ৰ৶ঌ৹

A research review should be fun. There are no rules about how much you need to do each day or each week as long as you keep the project moving forward. If you have a trunk full of photographs, start with a few dozen. Accomplish what you can in an hour and come back to the rest later. If you have a filing cabinet full of information you have been meaning to scan or enter—get it started, a few sheets at a time.

And write. When you evaluate a source, write a little bit about it. When you find a great image, write about it. Write about what you see, what you do not, and the questions it may raise that you would like to answer later.

The biggest problem I see with people who are starting a book project is becoming overwhelmed. It is easy to do, even for an experienced author. If you are busy with other activities and only have fifteen minutes a day to devote to the project, so be it. Do your fifteen minutes and go on to other things. Those fifteen minutes will add up over time.

If you make out a plan, and put the pieces of your plan onto your calendar, you greatly improve your chances for getting what you intend to accomplish, actually accomplished.

This is the time for making good notes about what you know for sure, how you know it, and where the next round of research must go before you begin writing.

At the end of your research review, you should have:

- A good bibliography
- A list of sources
- A list of permissions you may need
- A list of images you have and those you desire
- A list of elements from social history, traditions or historical context you wish to investigate further
- Simple, written summaries of each item you already have

In the next round of research, you will fill in the gaps.

Chapter 8

Scanning and Optical Character Recognition

You may want to use images—photographs, documents, maps and more—to help explain your specialty. If you have many images to scan, it pays to begin by learning about your scanner and scanning software. You will save a lot of time and effort making your images ready for print if you get a good scan from the start.

Scanning Basics

From the scanner's point of view, there are only three types of items it can scan—reflective items (photographs or documents), negative transparencies (film negatives), or positive transparencies (slides). Because the scanner will treat each of these types differently, you may need different software settings or different equipment to obtain the best scan.

The goal while scanning is to create an image large enough to look good in print, at the size you want to display the image. Once you have the largest scan you will need, you can scale, downsample or resize the image for other uses such as a website, an electronic book, or to share on social media.

Scanners

There are many different types of scanners including dedicated flatbed, all-in-one, photo, film, slide, hand-held, and microfilm/microfiche. Each has advantages and disadvantages.

Dedicated Flatbed Scanners

For most book projects, a dedicated flatbed scanner is what you need. The major scanner manufacturers such as HP, Epson, Canon or Xerox (among others) include software, most of which will work for your book project. Some dedicated flatbed scanners are designed to scan photographs primarily, so the software may include Digital ICE (digital image correction and enhancement). Most photo-priority flatbed scanners allow you to make corrections to the image as it is scanned.

Not all dedicated flatbed scanners are equipped to scan transparencies, either film negatives or slides. Transparencies require a dual light source and an adapter to hold the film or negative during scanning, allowing the light source to shine through the transparency. Because of the small size of the transparency (usually one inch square or less), the software must be able to scan at much higher resolution to obtain a print-ready digital image. (More about resolution shortly.)

Film or Slide Scanners

Dedicated film or slide scanners have no glass between the light source and the transparency to prevent distortion. These scanners also use a cool light source to keep from warping the film or slide, and the software included will be capable of high resolutions. Some of these scanners have a feeder for 35mm film strips or a stacking tray for slides. If you have older, large-format negatives, you will need a flatbed scanner with adapter trays to hold those negative sizes.

Hand-Held Scanners

Hand-held scanners (or wand scanners) are convenient, but often it is difficult to produce a good scan if your hands are not steady or the object is not perfectly flat.

One hand-held scanner I like, however, is the FlipPal (flip-pal.com). This mini-scanner was designed with the researcher in mind. It is small, light-weight, and is approved for use in repositories such as the National Archives. Even though the surface area of the FlipPal cannot scan a full piece of standard U.S. paper in a single scan, the software that comes with the FlipPal has a stitching function to put documents back together after they have been scanned in pieces. The one disadvantage to the FlipPal is how little control you have over making corrections as the scan is being made. It is a trade off—the ease and convenience of being able to scan photographs or documents at a repository, versus producing the best scan possible. Better to obtain the image while you can and make corrections in your image editing software later.

Microfilm/Microfiche Scanners

You may run into a microfilm or a microfiche scanner while conducting research. Many Family History Centers and libraries across the country have them. It may be more convenient to save your scanned images as PDFs while you are researching because they are easy to read on your computer later using the free Adobe Acrobat Reader software. If you know, however, that you want to use an image of a document, obtain a higher resolution JPG (.jpg) while you are at the library. Take both. Look for the settings in the scanning software to change back and forth from JPG to PDF.

Most word processors and page layout programs will not treat a PDF the same way they will a JPG. Most will not allow you to place a PDF directly into a document. You will need an image editing program to convert the PDF to a JPG, PNG (.png) or TIFF (.tiff).

All-in-One Scanners

For those of you who own 3-in-1 or 4-in-1 scanners (scan, copy, print, fax), the scanning software that came with the machine may be fairly rudimentary. Dedicated flatbed scanners tend to come with better software including:

- SilverFast (www.silverfast.com)
- VueScan (www.hamrick.com)

You may purchase this software as stand-alone products. You may find that once you have better software, an all-in-one will do what you need it to, as long as you do not have transparencies. In my research to date, I have not found a 3-in-1 or 4-in-1 scanner that includes a transparency adapter.

Resolution

First, let us be clear about some terminology. You may see the acronyms dpi and lpi and ppi used interchangeably. They are not exactly the same, however. Dots per inch (dpi) is an old printer's term that refers to the number of horizontal dots per inch in a halftone. If you look closely at a photographic image in a pre-digital-era newspaper, you will see the dots used to make up the photograph. Printing dots was a clever way to simulate the effect of a solid image. Commercial printers used the same technology to produce magazines, maps or brochures.

Lines per inch (lpi) is another way to measure the number of dots per inch in a halftone, although this is a vertical measurement. The more lines per inch, the sharper the image. Magazines have more lines per inch than newspapers.

Pixels per inch (ppi) is the proper way to describe resolution in the digital era. If you zoom in to a digital photograph closely enough, you will be able to see each pixel. Pixels are square, whereas dots are round. The higher the number of pixels per inch, the higher the resolution in the image, and the better it will look when printed.

What resolution you need depends upon the physical size of the image you want to display, and how you will display it.

Scan high and use low, meaning that you want a scan that is as big physically—in inches—as you will display in print. Most books are (physically) 8.5" x 11" or smaller. If you subtract room for margins, about the biggest image you will need is 8" x 10." If you go wild with the print size for a coffee table book, you may need a larger image.

For print, the resolution must be at least 300 ppi for photographs. Line art (think handwriting in a document) may look better at 600 ppi because the edges of the lines will be crisper.

Many of the older photographs you will encounter may be physically small. It was not until the 1990s that photography became so much cheaper. Today, you can buy a poster-sized print for less than what a small school portrait cost in the 1940s.

Take a 1" x 1.5" slide or school portrait as an example. In order to create a proportionally equivalent 8" x 12" digital image at 300 ppi, the final file size must be 2400 x 3600 pixels (8" x 300 ppi and 12" x 300 ppi). If you are scanning a 1" x 1.5" slide, in order to end up with a file at 2400 x 3600 pixels, you will need to scan at 2400 ppi (1" x 2400 ppi = 2400 pixels wide and 1.5" x 2400 ppi = 3600 pixels long).

A common pre-1950s photograph size was 3" x 4.5," so let us use that as an example. If we want to use a photograph that size in print at 6" x 9," then we will need a final file size of 1800 pixels x 2700 pixels. In order to achieve that resolution, you must scan at 600 ppi (3" x 600 ppi = 1800 pixels wide and 4.5" x 600 ppi = 2700 pixels long).

If you are planning to acquire images from a stock photography company, a library or an archive, ask for the image resolution needed to print at 300 ppi in the physical size you want for the page or the book cover.

There may be other uses for your photographs at much lower resolution, such as an eBook, to email, or to post on social media sites. As long as you start with an image large enough to look good in print, scaling down is easy with good results. Scaling up is not. An image that has been scaled up may look fine on the screen because your computer screen can only display an image at 72–96 ppi. A scaled-up photograph may look fine in your word processing program viewed on a screen, but pixelated or blurry when printed in a book.

There is also a difference between scaling a photograph and stretching it. Your word processing program will allow you to take an image, insert it into the text, and then adjust the display size by pulling the corners. Pulling the corners is not scaling the photograph; it is stretching it. Stretching causes even worse results in print than scaling the image up to a larger size.

Scaling a photograph means opening it in an image editing program and changing the physical size of the image. You will achieve far more consistent results on the press if you scan the image to the correct size first, and then place the image into the layout in the correct size and resolution.

File Size

Do not over-scan your images, either. To keep the file size of the final book manageable, create images at a size that will look good in print, but not any bigger. In other words, scan your image so that you could print an 16" x 24" photograph to use as a marketing piece (the biggest use you may have for the image), but adjust it down proportionally before placing it into your book layout.

To adjust the image down proportionally, determine the final size you want the image to be on the page, for example 3" x 3.75," and use your image editing program to make the physical size of the image smaller.

What you do not want to do, is place the largest size image into your manuscript, and squeeze it into its final size by dragging the corners. Dragging the corners will make the physical size smaller, but it will not alter the file size. If your original image is 8" x 10" at 300 ppi, it will have a physical size of 2400 pixels x 3000 pixels. If you squish those pixels closer together to make them fit into a 3" x 3.75" space, your resolution will go up from 300 ppi to 800 ppi (2400 pixels divided by 3" = 800 ppi and 3000 pixels divided by 3.75" is 800 ppi).

Print publication requires a final image resolution at 300 ppi. Use your image editing program to reduce the physical size of the photograph to 3" x 3.75" which is a proportional reduction, while maintaining the resolution of 300 ppi, giving you a final image size of 900 pixels (3" x 300 ppi) x 1125 pixels (3.75" x 300 ppi).

Color Depth

Color depth affects file size. The greater the color depth, the more color possibilities there are and the larger the file size. A black-and-white image (e.g. a printed document) has only 1 bit of color depth because there is only one color—black. The other color, white, is the paper color. A black-and-white photograph is made up of shades of black—an 8-bit black-and-white file would contain 256 shades of gray. A 24-bit color file could contain up to 16.7 million colors and so on up to 36-bit and 48-bit files.

Scanning a photograph to display on the side of a bus, would need as much color information as possible because the image is so large, and too little color information can cause banding rather than smooth transitions between shades.

Many of the newer scanners offer greater than 24-bit depth. The biggest difference between 24-bit and 48-bit scans is in the file size. Reserve the 48-bit setting for scanning negatives and slides. Anything you want to scan for a printed book (and even less so for an eBook or digital file) can be scanned at 24-bit color depth and look great. There is no need to over-scan color depth.

Color Density

To achieve the blackest blacks and the whitest whites—the greatest possible dynamic range for color in your images—you may want a scanner that captures the greatest image density, not necessarily the greatest bit depth. Be forewarned, however, the higher the image density, the higher the cost of the scanner, and realistically, unless you are planning a high-end, glossy photo book, the end results on the page will not be any better.

Color Space

Color space matters to some printers for some print jobs. Chances are good that you will not have to mess much with the color space during your book project, but, just in case, here is a quick explanation of what color space means.

RGB

Computer monitors and other digital screens use the RBG color space (red, green, blue). RGB is also fine for printing photographs. RGB is preferred for images in eBooks that will be displayed on digital screens. The most common file format for RGB images is JPG. When you are scanning photographs, it is acceptable to scan them as RGB images and save them as JPGs.

CMYK

The CMYK color space (cyan, magenta, yellow, black) is necessary to use an off-set press and print in full color. Cyan, magenta, yellow and black are the four process colors that are combined to create full-color images. For most books, you do not need to worry about the CMYK color space. It is acceptable to leave your images in their original RGB color space when creating your final file. Let the printer convert the images to CMYK based upon the equipment they have, to generate the best results.

Grayscale

Become familiar with the grayscale color space. For books with black-and-white images in the interior (forget the covers for right now, almost all covers will have full-color), convert your images to grayscale before you place them into the layout. Another reason to do this is to see how the image will look when printed in black-and-white. Not all color images make good black-and-whites. If there are not enough shades of gray, the finer details will be lost.

Convert black-and-white originals to grayscale. It is possible to scan directly into grayscale, and some scanners have good grayscale settings. Most of the time you will achieve better results if you scan black-and-white photographs in full color, and then use your image editing program to convert the image to grayscale.

Bitmap

The bitmap color space is one that you may use, but infrequently. On occasion, you will find that a document or line drawing is easier to read if scanned as a bitmap. The bitmap color space only contains black and white; there are no shades of gray. The scanner will force each pixel in the image to be one color or the other.

Sometimes, especially if there is a noisy background on a document, the type or handwriting is clearer when scanned as a bitmap image.

File Formats

Digital image file formats are either compressed or non-compressed. A non-compressed format will retain the most information and will create larger file sizes than a compressed format.

TIFF or RAW

Two non-compressed formats are TIFF (or TIF) (.tiff or .tif) and RAW (.raw). RAW image files can be especially large because they are not compressed in any way. To compare, an image taken in my 16 MP (megapixel) camera and saved as a TIFF is about 5 MB (megabytes) in size, whereas the same image saved in RAW format runs 16 MB or more. Saving images in the RAW format is an option in high-end cameras. Some scanning software will create RAW files, but unless you are planning to use your image on the cover of a high-end magazine, there is no compelling reason to create RAW files while you scan.

JPG

The most common file format for photographs is JPG (or JPEG) (.jpg or .jpeg). JPG is a compressed file format, and yes, you will lose information every time you open, alter and save the file, somewhat like making a photocopy of a photocopy. But, unless you alter the file hundreds of times and then blow the photo up to something large enough for the flaws to become obvious to the naked eye, do not worry about whether you scan and save your photographs as compressed or uncompressed files. Save them as TIF or JPG, whatever is easiest for you to use with your image editing software.

Producing a Good Scan

Before you begin scanning, clean the glass on the scanner. Unless there are smudges, compressed air or a good microcloth will do the trick. If there are smudges or fingerprints, use a good glass cleaner. Read the instructions for your scanner to make sure an alcohol-based glass cleaner is safe. Then, spray the cloth, not the scanner glass and clean the glass often. Small specks of dust will show up in the scans (magnified if you are scanning film or slides) and it takes much more time to fix the dust particle flaws in your image editing program, than it does to eliminate them from the scanner.

Do not damage originals in order to scan them. Do not cut them or try to make repairs, and please *do not* clean the photograph unless you know what you are doing. Any effort to alter the surface of a photograph can damage or destroy it. If you are in doubt, seek the help of a photo restoration company. If you have delicate photographs, it is always safer to re-photograph, than to put them on the scanner exposed to a strong light source.

Photographing a Photograph

The trick to photographing a photograph is to use a macro setting on your digital camera that allows the lens to be close to the photograph while keeping it in focus. Fill the frame with the photograph to take as large an image as possible.

Keep the angles consistent so the photograph does not become distorted in the digital image. Place the photograph on a level surface (wall or table) and set the camera up to shoot straight on. If the camera is angled in any way, the original photograph will not look square in the new image. You can fix distortions later in your image editing program, but you will save a great deal of time if you take a good photograph to begin with.

If your old photograph has curled or has warped, introduce a little humidity before unrolling it. I have had good luck with my own photographs by steaming up the bathroom and taking the photograph into the bathroom away from the faucet where the hot water is running. I have only tried this on modern photographs (less than 50 years old). I would not attempt this on any photograph made before modern fixatives were used. If you are at all in doubt, take the photograph to a photo restoration company for help before you begin. Never try to force a photograph to unroll. Once the emulsion on a photograph cracks, you cannot undo the damage.

For photographs that uncurl easily, placing a piece of non-glare glass over the top may help to hold it down while you photograph. Even non-glare glass can yield reflections, though, so watch for flares from light sources such as lamps, overhead lighting or windows.

If you are not a steady hand, use a tripod. In fact, a tripod with a scientific arm that allows the camera to point straight down, is the easiest way to obtain great digital images of photographs or documents.

Scanning Slides or Film Negatives

Before you scan slides or film negatives, use compressed air to clean them. If you remove a slide or negative from a plastic film sleeve or run a microcloth over it, static electricity can attract even more dust. Be careful not to use the spray air too close to the slide or negative because of the moisture that comes from the spray.

Scanner Software

Get to know your scanner and its software. Locate the feature that allows you to change the physical file size and resolution while scanning. It will not take you long to be able to calculate what you will need to achieve a 300 ppi resolution for images at the maximum size you will display them in your book. Remember to scan high, use low. It is better to create an image that is bigger than what you will ever need and scale it down to fit the page, than to scan an image too small and scale it up to size.

Some scanning software features will correct image flaws while scanning. Some software has good automatic settings for color, contrast, brightness, sharpness, and saturation or neutralization. Others do not. Experiment with a few flawed images to find out what your software is capable of correcting well.

Save Time Scanning

Most scanning software allows you to preview the image before you scan it. In the beginning, this feature will save you a lot of time having to look back and forth between the scanning software and your image editing program to make sure you captured the image you wanted in the scan. After a time, especially if you are scanning the same types of items that are also the same size, you may be able to skip the preview to save time. The trick is to keep similar items together, the black-and-white photographs, for example, or the images with fading tints.

While it is tempting to place as many photographs on the plate as possible and scan them all at once as one big photograph, avoid this. Not only will you spend more time turning them into separate photographs later in your image editing program, but the scanner will take readings across many different photographs which will give the automatic correction settings a difficult time determining what should be corrected. The results are often bad scans.

Some scanning software allows you to batch scan everything on the plate with separate settings for each item. This feature will save time because each object on the plate is being analyzed and scanned individually.

The straighten and flip settings can save time. Even if you place a photograph on the plate perfectly, closing the lid may cause it to move. Allowing the scanner to straighten the photograph will save time. Same for flipping photographs—especially flipping slides and film negatives. It can be difficult to slip the slides and film strips into the holders exactly the right way each time. Look at the preview, and then let the scanner turn the image right-side up or flip it on the vertical axis to make the scan match the direction of the original.

Photographs

While it would seem that scanning photographs will have fewer challenges than other types of material, it all depends upon the type of photographs you need. If you have the time, consider scanning everything you have and creating backups on external hard drives or DVDs just in case. You never know when originals will be lost or damaged.

Older photographs that have curled over the years can yield Newton Rings when scanning—distortion caused when there is distance between the photograph and the glass. If a photograph is particularly delicate, taking a new photograph of the old photograph is always safer than putting it on the scanner and exposing it to an intense light source. If you cannot re-photograph the item, look for a studio photographer who has the right setup and lighting to do so.

Occasionally, scanning a black-and-white photograph in full color will leave tinges of yellow, cyan or magenta in the picture. You can use your image editing program to eliminate unwanted tints. Or, try scanning in grayscale to see if you achieve a better result.

If your book will contain only black-and-white images, it may take some experimentation not only with your scanner, but also in your image editing program to make each photograph look its best when printed in black-and-white.

It was popular for a time to print photographs on textured paper so that they looked more like a painted canvas. These photographs (mostly from the 1970s) can be a challenge to scan because the texture can cause shadows on the scan. Taking a new photograph may be a better option.

Matte prints often scan with fewer streaks or glare than glossy prints. Modern glossy prints are not as difficult as older glossies mounted on thick paper, such as those from instant cameras such as Polaroids. If you see streaks in scanned images from glare off the glossy print, taking new photographs may be easier than fixing the digital images.

When a digital image is printed on uncoated paper, such as what will be used on the interior pages of your book, dot gain (ink absorbed by the paper) causes photographs to become darker than expected. You may need to lighten the shadows and mid-tones of photographs in order to make them look their best in print. This is true whether the photographs are in black-and-white or color.

One way to create a digital image from a slide is to scan it; another is to project it onto a screen and photograph it using a digital camera. While the projector version works quite well for images that will be shown on a computer monitor, often the result in print is flat, soft or dark images that do not look as good as if you had scanned the slide directly. If a slide is particularly important to you and you cannot produce a good scan, print the slide at the size you need for the book, then scan the new photograph. Printing slides is an expensive option, however, if you have more than a few vital slides.

Documents and Illustrations

For the most part, documents and illustrations (line art) are easier to scan and achieve good results, than photographs. Line art such as lithographs look best when scanned at 600 to 1200 ppi to keep the edges and lines crisp. Many of these images will be black-and-white, so scanning as bitmaps (BMP) that forces the image into black-and-white, may give you the best results. If the line art is in color such as a logo or sign, scan in at least 24-bit color depth to keep gradients smooth. Scanning at lower bit depths may cause banding in the colored areas.

One challenge may be the paper the item is printed on, however since thin paper can allow printing on the reverse side to show through. If bleed through is a problem, one option is to photocopy the originals using light settings to lessen what shows through, and then scan the lightened photocopy using settings that make the document darker.

Using Optical Character Recognition

Most scanners come with optical character recognition (OCR) software. While it may be tempting to OCR documents or passages from printed sources so that you do not have to transcribe each and every one, be careful with the results. The software works best with printed, standard font text (nothing script-like or hand-writing-like) in point sizes between six (6) (very small but still readable) and 72 (about 1 inch high) on laser or inkjet quality print or better.

Mocavo (www.mocavo.com) the online genealogy search engine, is experimenting with OCR that works on handwriting. They are the first, and they have not perfected it yet. You will not find commercially available scanner-based OCR software that can help you with handwritten documents just yet.

No matter how sophisticated your OCR software, you must proofread the results. It is difficult for the software to tell the difference between a "1" that looks like an "l" that looks like a "]."

The easiest OCR programs to use are those that let you correct the copy while the software is creating the text. Many of the best programs show the image in one window with the text results in another window side by side so that you can look at the original as you edit.

If your scanner did not come with OCR software, OmniPage (www.nuance. com/for-individuals/by-product/omnipage/index.htm) consistently receives high accuracy ratings and is easy to use.

Maps, Newspapers, and Memorabilia

If you have maps, newspaper clippings or memorabilia, such as a theater program that was printed using halftones (bunches of little dots rather than a solid image like a photograph), you may have some challenges when scanning items printed on older presses.

Halftones may create moire patterns (common in black-and-white images from newspapers) or rosette patterns (common in color images due to the CMYK colors used on the press). The result of scanning may be images with irregular areas, or areas that are much darker or lighter than other areas.

A special feature in some scanning software allows you to de-screen as you scan. Software that comes with a de-screening feature will have the following settings for different types of print: art print (175 lpi), magazines (133 lpi) and newspapers (85 lpi). You will achieve the best results with the setting closest to what was used to create the original image on the press. Sometimes de-screening can soften an image too much. Sharpening can help restore the edges.

If your software does not have a de-screening feature, try scanning at a 45-degree angle. Turn the object so that it is not straight up or down (90 degrees), but at an angle (45 degrees) on the plate. Another option is to scan at twice the size you are planning to use in the book, and then downsize the image so that the dots or dot patterns are not so obvious.

Objects

It is much easier to photograph objects, such as heirlooms, against a neutral background than it is to scan them. It is almost impossible to make a teacup look good sitting on a scanner. Instead of scanning dog tags, a uniform, needlework, or a picture in its frame, take a photograph.

For less than $50, you can buy a small studio lighting kit that sets up as a two-foot square box, with neutral backgrounds of several different colors, a couple of lights, and a table-top tripod. For around $200, you can buy a similar studio lighting setup to photograph larger objects such as quilts or furniture.

Art

Photograph artwork rather than scan it, especially if the art is in a soft media such as pastels or charcoal. Pencil sketches can smudge. Oil paintings or watercolor paintings can be a challenge because of the texture of the paint or the unevenness of the canvas.

Film Negatives and Slides

The biggest issue with scanning film negatives and slides is cleaning them before you scan to minimize the dust and particle debris in the digital image and scanning at high enough resolution for your planned use.

A standard 35mm negative is not square. It measures approximately 1" x 1.5" or at a 2 x 3 ratio. If you want the digital image to fill an 8.5" x 11" page, you will need a digital image of 2550 pixels (8.5" x 300 pixels) by 3300 pixels (11" x 300 ppi). So, the resolution for a 1" x 1.5" 35mm film negative is 2550 ppi. The ratio of standard American paper at 8.5" x 11" is not quite 2 to 3, however, so your scan at 2550 ppi will be perfect across the 8.5" top, but too long for the 11" length. Even when you adjust for the margins, cropping may be necessary. If you are thinking about printing from your digital image and want a good 12" x 18" print, scanning a 35mm negative at 4000 ppi will work.

Curled filmstrips can result in blurry scans. If necessary, the individual negatives can be cut and mounted into slide mounts, but once you cut the negatives, they can no longer be printed at a standard photo lab. You will need a specialty lab that often charges more. If you are going to cut a filmstrip, make prints first.

Scan film negatives with the emulsion (duller side) down. The emulsion side should be closest to the glass on a flatbed scanner. You can tell if you are looking at the emulsion side if the film numbers along the edge are backward.

Before you scan slides, check to see if your scanning software has adjustments for different slide types. Kodachrome slides, for example, should be scanned on a Kodachrome color setting for best results. If you have no idea what type of film was used to create your slides, you may have to play with the color adjustment settings to create the best digital image during the scan.

Tip: Although it may be tempting, once you have finished scanning, never discard the originals. Newer scanners may do a better job in the future, and digital images can be lost or become corrupted.

Enhance, Repair, Retouch

Even if you achieve great scans, you may want to open each image in an image editor to take a look close up. Before you place any image into your layout, fix flaws, sharpen softly-focused images, adjust the contrast, or crop to enhance the composition. Repair damage from bends, breaks or mold on the surface. Restore the faded color. Fill in the scratches and correct over- or underexposed areas.

There is controversy surrounding editing or enhancing images that alters *in any way* the historical accuracy of the image. Because you are using the image to explain your specialty, it should be historically accurate. Having said that, there is no reason not to repair or retouch photographs so that they look their best.

When does restoration become alteration? That is a matter of opinion, but I think it is fine to use a little grain reduction to make a person's skin look smooth and beautiful, or to remove red-eyes, or to whiten teeth. It is fine to crop an image to enhance the composition, or to merge two images to create a more complete picture of what a place looked like. I know I am stepping into controversial waters here, but it is acceptable to remove distracting elements from the picture even if it alters the historical accuracy of the photograph a bit. I am not advocating that you digitally cut out your ex, or blur the face of someone you do not like. Oftentimes, however, amateur photographers take pictures without paying attention to the background, resulting in images that appear as if a telephone pole, for example, is growing from a person's head. I find it historically acceptable to remove the telephone pole.

There are many options for editing your digital images. Most computers come with simple image editing software pre-installed. There are also many websites or photo sharing sites that offer image editing tools. Some of them, such as Pixlr (pixlr.com) or Picasa (picasa.google.com), have impressive features. There are also apps by the dozen for tablets or smartphones that edit, enhance or create funky artwork from digital images. Another option is to buy a stand-alone image editor such as Corel PaintShop Pro or Adobe Photoshop (the full version is pricey, but Photoshop Elements, the consumer edition, is not).

Before you alter any digital image, make a copy and keep the original scan in a safe place. Work off the copy in case you make an alteration that you regret.

This book is not the place for a complete primer on digital image restoration. Consult, *Digital Restoration from Start to Finish* by Ctein or other works on digital photography repair and retouching.

Anyone can learn to make simple adjustments to damaged photographs. If you are not interested in learning how to make complex repairs, a photo restoration firm can make your damaged images look almost new. Save this step for the images that are so faded or so broken that fixing them yourself may be nearly impossible without a lot of investment in time and effort, because digital restoration can be expensive.

Final File Preparation

The first step in the final preparation of your digital images is to create a backup that can be stored somewhere safely off-site. A backup drive, a flash drive or a DVD can be given to another family member, or stored in a safe deposit box. It breaks my heart every time there is a natural disaster, not only for the lives that are lost or endangered and the property destroyed, but for the memories that cannot be recovered in a tangible way.

At this stage, you may not be ready to choose the final images for the book. You may have far more images than what you could possibly use, so the next step is to implement an organizational system that makes sense—not just for this book project, but for future projects.

For some projects, naming each digital image with the subject and approximate year will make sense. For other projects, you may have so many images that keeping folders by topic may make more sense.

I also keep originals in folders and work only from copies. I give my copies different file names with an indicator of what type of correction I have made. As an example, a file that has been color corrected will have its file name changed from IMG2036.jpg to IMG2036cc.jpg. That way, the files still alphabetize together, but I can tell without having to open the file which is the original and which has been altered.

Consider adding borders to keep images with light edges, for example, from fading into the page. There is no need to apply any final touches, however until you are ready to place the images into the page layout.

Share

While you are scanning, share to build interest in the book. Send a few interesting images by email, post them on Facebook or Twitter. If you have a smartphone, send a few by Snapchat or Instagram. Create a few albums or slideshows at websites such as Photobucket (photobucket.com) or Flickr (www.flickr.com).

Sign up for one of the multitudes of online picture sharing sites such as Snapfish (www.snapfish.com), Shutterfly (www.shutterfly.com) or DotPhoto (www.dotphoto.com). Then send an announcement that you have created a photo album for interested readers to see.

Create interesting gifts for purchase on sites such as CafePress (www.cafepress.com) or Zazzle (www.zazzle.com). You can even design fabric using photographs at websites such as Spoonflower (www.spoonflower.com) or Fabric on Demand (www.fabricondemand.com).

Learning a few simple techniques for scanning your images will give you an abundance of options for how to use them, and will guarantee the images will look their best in your book.

ക്ക

If you find yourself overwhelmed by the prospect of scanning an abundance of photographs, film negatives or slides, you may want to engage a scanning company to help you.

Working with a Scanning Company

Contact one of the many companies listed on the Memory Preservation Coalition's website (memorypreservationcoalition.org). The coalition is a non-profit group dedicated to helping individuals preserve, protect and archive documents and photographs.

One idea I particularly like is having a scanning service come to you. Scangaroo launched this idea. The company has since been acquired by Gen-Arc Digital Estate Scanning (www.gen-arc.com). They use mobile scanning labs to come to your home so that important photographs, documents, scrapbooks or video never leave your possession. They also offer cloud-based digital asset management meaning you can store your documents and photographs so that they can be accessed for years to come (assuming the company stays in business).

Another option is to contact FamilySearch about their Worldwide Photo Scanning and Preservation Initiative. The Mormon Church has teamed up with Kodak and E-Z Photo Scan (ezphotoscan.com) to equip a few of their Family History Centers, their central library in Salt Lake City as well as a center in Riverton, UT with high-speed, high-resolution scanners. Look for one of their "photopalooza" events or find out whether the Family History Center in your area offers photo scanning.

There are also local companies who can scan photographs, or convert older forms of analog film into modern digital video. A company that specializes in memory preservation, however, may be better than the local photo shop.

National Archives Standards

Before you hire a scanning company, ask whether they follow the guidelines prescribed by the National Archives for handling your photographs or delicate documents. You would not want an item damaged by careless handling.

File Size and Format

Make sure you have the images scanned at the largest size you will need to make a reprint or to include in your printed book. You may have images of different sizes to scan, so if you want all digital images large enough to create a full-page image in your book or a large photo reprint, be specific about that requirement.

Be clear about what file format (JPG or TIFF) you need. Most scanning companies will return files as JPGs. Unless you have a compelling need for TIFF images, JPGs will work for a printed book, an eBook, and any use you can think of online.

Bound Items

Ask about scanning photographs that are bound such as those glued into photo albums. Photo albums often require special handling in order to scan, so these items may cost more. If your photo albums are bound or such that they will not lay flat on the glass for scanning, ask whether the company could re-photograph, or whether they have the kind of equipment used to scan open books. Book scanning equipment may be better for the uneven surfaces in a scrapbook than a flat, plate scanner.

Slides and Film Negatives

Ask about scanning slides and film negatives. Make sure the slides or film will be scanned at a resolution high enough to create a digital image large enough for your biggest need. Often slides and negatives are scanned at a standard 4000 dpi resolution which will yield an image of 3622 pixels by 5320 pixels for the average slide that measures 23mm x 34mm. This image size is large enough to produce a photograph of 12" x 17" at 300 dpi, which is large enough for most book projects unless you are planning an oversized coffee-table book.

Video Transfer

You may have other media that you want made into digital images or transferred to a modern DVD—VHS, VHS-C, 8mm, Hi8, Super8, mini-DV or other formats.

Most film- or tape-to-digital video transfer is done at a standard resolution, and the transfer is done in one piece—the length of the original film to a single video clip.

If you need still digital images from your video, work with the technician to create a list based upon time stamps. You also may need to ask for frame-by-frame images over several seconds in order to obtain the best still from video where the subjects are moving. Obtaining multiple images may cost a bit more, but is more likely to generate one usable image than a single attempt.

If you need stills at higher resolution, that process is more difficult because the film must be marked and stopped in order to adjust the resolution upward. The technician will likely make the complete transfer, then rewind the film and start and stop at each place where you requested a digital still from the film. Again, this may cost a bit more, but if you need a high-quality, high-resolution digital image from a video, it may be worth the money.

Restoration or Retouching Services

Ask about photo retouching services. Most scanning companies offer basic re-touching services, and some offer advanced retouching services for photographs that are badly faded or damaged. For most old photographs, even a bit of dust and scratch removal, color correction, sharpening, saturation adjustment or over- or under-exposure correction is well worth the trouble and expense. Much of this, however, can be done in your image editing software. If the photograph requires extensive digital restoration, such as fixing tears across people's faces, or removing color shifting caused from mold, expect to pay more. If the only photograph you have needs major restoration, the cost may be less important than having a restored, usable image.

Write a Formal Proposal or Contract

Write a formal agreement detailing the work you want to have done, the cost, when you are to deliver the items to the company (or the date the company's scanning equipment will come to you), and when the scanning will be complete. Include the file type and how the images will be given to you—thumb drive, external hard drive, archival DVD, through a file sharing service, or in permanent cloud storage that you can access at any time.

❧❧

The primary goal for scanning is to create a digital image large enough and at the correct resolution to look good in whatever format you plan to use it. Once you have a print-quality digital image, you can reduce the image size for other uses such as sending by email or posting on the Internet. A secondary goal is to preserve documentary evidence. Preserving your images is important, but try not to let the task of scanning sideline your book project. For those of you with hundreds or thousands of images to scan, it could.

Chapter 9

Developing a New Research Plan

In this round of research, gather as much information as you need to begin writing. You may find, as you work through the organization of the book and the material you will present in each chapter, that you will return to research to gather more information. Writing and research go hand in hand. There is rarely a clear line where research should halt and writing begin.

The rest of this chapter contains tips for collecting as much factual evidence and visual representations as you may need to explain your expertise in detail to researchers of different levels of experience.

Before You Begin the Next Round of Research

Let us step back to the book project for a moment to make sure you have a clear idea of the scope of the project, because you will not want to spend time researching elements that you will not use for this book.

Do you have a clear vision of the project? Think about writing the introduction. The reader will want to know what you will cover, what level of experience the reader should have, and what level of detail you plan to provide.

Before you can explain it to your reader, however, you have to be clear about it yourself. About how long will the book be? Did your research review answer all of your questions, or will you need this round of research to make final decisions about how much will be included? If you do, that is all right. You may more information to make the book well-rounded and complete.

Try not to get too bogged down by expanding the project unnecessarily. In this round of research, gather enough material to write a cohesive book aimed at your preferred audience.

Reviewing Old Sources

Even after a thorough research review, there may have been changes to databases or archives you have searched in the past. In the age of digitization, much is changing, and changing rapidly. It pays to take another look.

Locating New Sources

There are times when old dogs must learn new tricks, and if you are going to pass along your research expertise to the next generation, become familiar with the tools younger researchers are using.

Use the Search Engines to Full Advantage

Learn the advanced features of search engines such as Google or Bing to search for the subject and topics in your book. There are good tips and tricks for conducting efficient searches in *Google Your Family Tree* by Daniel Lynch, *50 Google Hints, Tips & Tricks for Online Researchers* by David Bradford (available free on Rootsweb through Ancestry) or *Google Genealogy Style* by Kimberly Powell (genealogy.about.com). These tips work whether you are searching for people or subject matter. Many of the tips for Google also work on Bing, Yahoo!, Ask or search engine aggregators such as Dogpile.

Search Blog Posts

There are hundreds of thousands of bloggers online who are posting useful information. Many of them use the blogging software rather than website building software simply because it is easier to setup and use. There are blog search engines, such as the BlogSearchEngine (www.blogsearchengine.org). There are also subject aggregators such as Alltop (www.alltop.com) that pull information on different subjects into a single easy-to-browse directory.

Search Social Media

Hashtags, Twitter's way of indicating subject matter, has been adopted across other social media platforms, and you can search for relevant content using the pound symbol (#) plus a subject (e.g. #genealogy). There are hashtag search engines such as Tagboard (www.tagboard.com), Hashatit (www.hashatit.com), Hashtags.org (www.hashtags.org) and Hashtagifyme (www.hashtagify.me). Twitter, of course, has its own hashtag search feature (www.twitter.com/search-home).

Facebook has updated its search feature so that you can search for information within individual posts using keywords (e.g. picture of 1930 Springfield). Other social media sites have similar features.

Watch the AutoComplete Work

As you search using Google, for example, watch the keywords that begin to form underneath the box where you are typing. These are keywords that have been used by other people to locate content. You may find keywords you had not thought of to locate relevant content.

Search the Wiki Sites

Wiki sites, because they have the potential for presenting undocumented or false information, are often looked upon as less valuable than other more "legitimate" websites. In fact, the wiki sites, because the best of them are managed by people with not only expertise in their subjects but a passion for them, keep any bogus information posted by malicious or clueless people to a minimum by monitoring what is posted. The major genealogical websites have their own wikis. These are a few of the top general wiki sites: Wikipedia (www.wikipedia.org), About (www. about.com), eHow (www.ehow.com), and WikiHow (www.wikihow.com).

To be thorough, search every place that could yield new information or more robust content for your book.

If you are an experienced researcher, you can skip the next section and proceed to gathering social history, historical context or images, whichever is most appropriate to your subject. What follows is information for discovering new source material and location-specific research that may or may not apply to the subject of your expertise.

Repositories List

Start a list of repositories you want to visit or have someone else visit on your behalf (e.g. courthouses, libraries, archives or private collections). If you are unable to take a trip to do the research yourself, there are both professional and amateur genealogists who are willing to do research for you. For more information about hiring someone, see Working with a Professional Historian or Genealogist below.

Within your repositories list keep the title, author and call number of every item you want to search at each repository. If you find a book at more than one repository, put the book on the list for each place. You never know when a book may have been lost or misplaced. Leave a place to add new sources you run across while at the repository, and keep a log of what you were expecting to find, what you found, and what you did not find so that you know to keep looking.

Library and archives staff can be helpful since they may be more familiar with the items in their collection than you are, and can point you to sources you may not have considered.

The National Archives and Records Administration (NARA)

NARA (www.archives.gov) is the U.S. depository for records compiled on behalf of the Federal Government. View filmed records at one of the regional NARA centers. Other records such as the census records and many land records have been digitized and are available through one of the major genealogical databases. The most requested records from NARA are military service records, immigration and naturalization records, passport applications, land records and bankruptcy records. But NARA has much, much more. If you are unable to travel to the main facility in the Washington, D.C. area or to a regional center, a professional researcher who specializes in gathering records at NARA can help you.

State Governments

State government records may be found at a state archive or within governmental agencies. Examples of state governmental records available for research are: local military units or national guards, vital records (births, deaths, marriages and divorces), state courts (appeals courts and the supreme court of the state), penitentiaries, business incorporations, health and agricultural agencies.

Not every state has a statewide archive. Illinois, for example, keeps some records at their central facility in Springfield but also has records spread out through their Regional Archives Depository.

Local Governments

Local governments are also a rich source of records. Local governments include cities, counties, school districts, water and sewer districts, fire and police protection districts as well as the local courts. You may find records by city, county or township including: board minutes and proceedings, land deeds, mortgages and tax sale records, poll books, voter registrations, early naturalization records, civil and criminal court cases, coroner's inquests, school and probate records.

Before searching, establish whether the borders of the counties changed during the period of your research expertise. Software such as AniMap (goldbug. com/animap/) shows county border changes, as does the Newberry Library's Atlas of Historical County Boundaries (publications.newberry.org/ahcbp/).

The National Association of Counties has a nice database of counties along with addresses for each county's courthouse or administration building plus links to county websites (www.naco.org/counties/pages/findacounty.aspx).

Discovering the location of older local records may be a challenge. Some local governments keep all of their records; others give the older records to a university or local archive. The only way to find out is to call and ask. Retention policies change over time. What is precious to one administration may be "clutter in the way" to the next.

Many local government records have been filmed and may be available at a local library (or through interlibrary loan), or available through one of the major genealogical websites. FamilySearch.org has an incredible list of film available. You can have film sent to a Family History Center, and to a few public libraries.

Local Libraries

There are many databases of public libraries available online including the Find a Library feature at WorldCat.org (see the online libraries section below). Check the catalog of any local libraries that may have materials important to your research. Even the smallest library may have a good local history collection and may be the only place where you will find limited-edition or privately published histories of the area. You may be able to borrow these books through interlibrary loan, or if they do not circulate, you may be able to call the reference librarian and describe what kind of information you are interested in and ask that they copy the pages that would be helpful to you.

University or College Libraries

Oftentimes individuals will leave their personal and business papers to their alma mater for inclusion in the school's archival collections. Or, local people, even if they did not attend the school, may choose to leave their materials to the local college. Check the catalogs of any local college, university or community college in the area important to your research. You may also find well-researched masters or Ph.D. theses about the local area in the university library.

Online Library Catalogs

Worldcat.org is the largest online library catalog in the world. A helpful feature on WorldCat is the repository location feature. When you search for a book (or article, DVD or CD), it will locate that item and tell you the closest libraries that have a copy of the item. It is worth signing up for a free account so that you can keep lists of books or articles, so you do not have to repeat searches. WorldCat also has a "Find a Library" link that will give you a list of public, school, corporate, academic, or specialized libraries within a city, state, province or zip code. Some of the specialized libraries will be helpful for social history research or adding historical context. Another source for finding libraries is PublicLibraries. com. This website has a searchable database of public, college, presidential and state libraries.

Archives

WorldCat is also expanding as ArchiveGrid to include archival material from around the world. ArchiveGrid (beta.worldcat.org/archivegrid/) is similar to the old National Union Catalog of Manuscript Collections (NUCMC) on steroids. NUCMC still exists through the Library of Congress (www.loc.gov/coll/nucmc/).

Online Libraries

Many institutions are making out-of-print materials available as electronic books. You can find them for sale in print at online bookstores such as Amazon.com, or as free electronic downloads at sites such as Google Books (books.google.com) or HathiTrust (www.hathitrust.org)—a consortium of research institutions that have made millions of titles available as digital books.

Some universities are also making books available electronically, good news if you are looking for one of the many county histories written in the late 19th or early 20th century. Some of these "mug books" as they are called (because people paid to have information included about themselves) are useful when researching a location.

William Filby's *A Bibliography of American County Histories* is also a helpful resource for locating local histories.

Archive.org, the Internet Archive, deserves special mention since it has the WayBack Machine—an archive of billions of web pages. If the information you seek is on a website that has been taken down, a copy may still exist on the Way-Back Machine.

Many of the records to help you write your book are available online, but not all. Some research must be conducted on site—the old-fashioned way.

Add Social History

If adding social history will help explain your expertise, do so. Social history is more about *how* people lived rather than where or when and provides context. If social history is not relevant to your expertise, skip ahead to historical context or gathering images.

The following are categories of social history you may want to look into during this round of research:

Heirlooms. What items that belonged to ancestors were kept by family members? Household goods? Books? China or silver? Jewelry? Watches or clocks? Clothing or quilts? Some of the rarest items in Americana museums are the everyday household items or utensils because so few still exist. Everyday items were used, worn out or broken and thrown away.

Household. Who was in the household? How many family members were in the household and when? Were there young children coming along after older children moved away? How many generations lived together? Were there friends, boarders or servants along with the family? Who were the neighbors?

Homes. What type of houses were common? How were they built and by whom? What type of furniture did people have? How big were houses? What did the floor plan look like? How was each room used? Did the house have plumbing and electricity? Was there central heat? Did people use fireplaces or stoves to heat the house? What type of fuel was used?

Ethnic Heritage. Even though America is the world's great melting pot, many people maintain their ethnic heritage. Look for ethnic differences in language, customs, cooking, clothing, music, theater, building styles and the way holidays or other special occasions are celebrated. Are there obvious ethnic influences in family traditions? Have they changed over time?

Customs. Birth, marriage, and death have customs that differ by location, ethnic influences and era. Did births take place at home? Who would have attended the birth? How many pregnancies were typical for women of the era? What was the infant mortality rate? How did couples meet? What was courtship like? How were marriages celebrated? Did the couple honeymoon? What was a typical age at marriage? Was it different for men than for women? How were burials handled? What happened during a funeral? What customs or laws governed inheritances? Are there unusual names in your family? Were names passed down from generation to generation?

Beliefs. Religion, superstition, education, politics and social standing influence beliefs. Beliefs affect the decisions people make. Could beliefs have influenced events important to your specialty? Did wives tales or folk wisdom play a role?

Health. What kind of illnesses were common? Did people live to be old? What percentage of children died young? What kind of home remedies were there? Were there doctors in the area?

Religion. Was there a predominant religion? Did that change over time? What religious beliefs did most people follow, or not? Did people attend services regularly? Who was the head of the church? Who held leadership roles? What type of music would congregants have heard? What messages were given? What other social activities were associated with the house of worship—weddings, funerals, church suppers, revivals?

Politics. Who participated in the political process? Were there public debates? Who ran for office? Who was the first woman in the community to vote? In small towns, you may be surprised by how many ordinary people held offices. Think beyond who was mayor—there were also roads overseers, school district superintendents, fire department members and utility organizers and builders.

Education. How much schooling did the average person have? What was taught? How did children get to school? Were the girls taught? How long was the school day? Did children bring their lunches? What type of lunch? Did kids use a lunch box or a bucket? How did children carry their books? What circumstances influenced the school year? Who were the teachers? How big was the schoolhouse? How did the children dress for school? How was money raised to pay the teachers and build the school houses?

Social Standing. Did an individual's social standing affect where he or she lived? Did it affect the associations one joined or the people one knew? Were there customs people adhered to because of their social standing?

Economic Standing. How well did people live? Was every day a struggle, or were people generally well off? Can you tell by the possessions in probate files how well families lived? Can you tell by the neighborhood? Is there other evidence of the average person's standard of living?

Employment or Profession. Did families pass businesses down from generation to generation? What type of schooling or apprenticeship did one need in order to practice a profession? How many times did the average person change jobs and why? Who were the bosses, the managers and employees? Who were the customers? Who were the wholesalers? What businesses traded with each other? What techniques did people use? What made businesses thrive or fail? What other economic influences affected business? Did an invention revolutionize businesses or eliminate the need for them? How were employees paid? Did they earn salaries or were they paid hourly or were they paid hourly? Did businesses supply goods or services on credit?

Roles. Who were the primary bread winners? What was expected of women and children? Did that change over time or due to circumstances such as war? In what kind of situation did women and children work? At what age were children considered old enough to work during? What were common childrearing practices? Who cared for the sick or the aged? Who handled the family finances?

Entertainment. What type of leisure activities did people have? How much leisure time was there? Did people play music? Attend concerts? What was the popular music? Did people own musical instruments? Did people play games or sports? Were there theaters or playhouses? What kind of art would people have seen or created? Was there photography?

What did people read? Did people own books? What were the popular magazines? What were the blockbuster novels? (**Note:** Magazines in the 19th century often serialized popular novels).

Did families go on vacations or travel? Did they visit resorts or go camping? Were there popular local destinations or did they travel abroad? What would people have packed in a suitcase? How did they get to their destinations?

Holidays. What holidays did people celebrate? Are they the same holidays as today? Are the customs the same? What type of food was served? Who participated? Who gathered for each holiday? Why or why not?

Neighbors. Did neighbors live in the next apartment or a few miles away? What kind of relationships did neighbors have?

Neighborhoods. What types of businesses were in each neighborhood? What ethnic, economic or religious influences were there? Which neighborhoods have been declared historic districts?

Animals. Did people own work animals? How were the animals cared for? How were the animals marked or branded? Were brands registered? Did most properties have animal shelters or barns? Did people raise animals for sale? What type of market was there for animals? What kind of taxes were imposed on people who owned animals?

Building Styles. Did people build their own houses or barns? Were building styles influenced by local building materials? Were there ethnic influences? A good reference of building styles is *A Field Guide to American Houses* by Virginia McAlester.

Clothing. How did people dress? How many sets of clothing did the average person have? Were there customs to be followed such as wearing black after the death of a loved one? How practical were the styles of the day? What kind of clothes were worn for special occasions? What material was used to make clothing? How did people come by the material—linen woven at home or fabric purchased at a dry goods store? Did most people purchase manufactured clothes?

Transportation. What type of transportation was available? Were there trains, boats, barges or cars? Were the street cars horse drawn or electric? Were there sailing ships or steamships? How about personal transportation? Did people own buggies or wagons? Motorcycles or motor cars? Bicycles?

Cooking. What type of diet did people have? Who did the cooking? How did people cook? How much time was spent cooking? Did people shop or grow food? What was on a typical household menu? Can you find period recipes that you could try?

Communication. How did people keep in touch with each other? Are there period letters or journals? How would people have sent a letter? Was there a postal service, or did one have to wait until someone else from the community made a trip? Was there a telegraph? Who owned telephones? Did the town or area have a newspaper? How often was the newspaper published?

Inventions. What inventions changed how people lived or worked? How long was it between the time a new invention came along and the average person had access to it or could afford it? How did people hear about new inventions? How did inventions or changes in productivity or efficiency change what people could own or buy?

Relocation. Did people move from one place to another? From one country to another? How did people move? Did one member of a family move first? Did the family move together? Were family members left behind? Could people return to visit, or was a move a final goodbye?

There is a lot to think about in terms of social history, but learning about these things may help you better describe your specialty.

Where to Locate Social History

To study social history, you will use many traditional genealogical sources. To gather rich, detailed information consult eyewitness testimony—through interviews, diaries, journals and letters; expert research found in academic books and journals; museums where artifacts of daily living have been preserved; and memorabilia or ephemera—those items meant to be used and thrown away.

Manuscript Collections

I have discussed the value of WorldCat and ArchiveGrid in finding manuscript collections. These search engines can also be used to locate letters, diaries, journals or other community history appropriate to your research. Do not limit your search to personal accounts, either. Business records can give you an idea of what it was like both to own a business or to be a customer of the business.

Every archive is different. Some archives keep only original sources created by governmental institutions while others keep personal papers. It pays to search major and local archives.

Oral History Collections

You may want to consult an oral history collection if your research is primarily in the 20th century. The Oral History Association (www.oralhistory.org) has a good list of links to oral history collections across the country. Probably the greatest collection of oral histories is Stephen Spielberg's Shoah Project hosted at the University of Southern California (sfi.usc.edu).

Scholarly Articles

Journals address nearly every historical niche, and the people who write articles for these journals are experts in their own fields. You may find the physical journals at your local university and some public libraries. Most universities have access to JSTOR's online collection (www.jstor.org). One category not often consulted for well-researched material are the thesis collections of colleges and universities. Even though not all theses are published, their bibliographies are often treasure troves of original source material.

Museums

One of the best ways to experience how people lived during a particular era is to visit a historic house, living or open air museum of that time. There, you can get a feel for the size of the living space, items that were in the home and, in some cases, the land that surrounded the home. There are museums for nearly every type of living space from ships that transported people to the new world, to tenements in the inner city, to sprawling plantation homes. The trick is to find one from the right era, in the area because building styles varied so greatly from place to place.

Another way to experience an era is to attend a re-enactment. Re-enactors pride themselves on their ability to create exact replicas, and they often create temporary museums using items such as Civil War-era tents filled with era-appropriate items.

Collectors clubs and their events are another source of temporary museums. There are collectors clubs for farm equipment, automobiles, costumes—name it; there are people who collect it. When they gather together to show off their collections, you will have an abundance of objects to look at, and enthusiastic experts to answer your questions.

Inns and hotels are additional sources of period information. Think of these structures as working museums. Some have been restored to their original look, although most have modern conveniences such as indoor plumbing and electricity. Nor will you likely have the experience of sleeping in a feather bed, as most inns and hotels opt for modern mattresses. In order to restore their buildings accurately, however, many inn owners have become experts in period furniture, building techniques and other information in which you may be interested.

Look for specialized museums if you want to get an idea of how people worked. There are too many types of specialized museums to name them all here, but consider some of these possibilities: school house, transportation, medical office, agricultural, newspaper office, courthouse, mining, and railroad depots.

Art museums may be a source for landscape paintings that could show you what an area looked like before photographs were available. Art is are also a source of images of period dress or events, such as battle scenes.

A good source for finding historical museums is the *Directory of Genealogical and Historical Societies, Libraries and Museums in the U.S. and Canada.* If your local library does not have a copy, ask that they purchase it.

Many museums, if they do not also have a full library, have a collection of books and journals to help the staff answer questions about their collection. These highly specialized collections could save you countless hours of research. Ask if the museum has a working bibliography of their books and journals, or a list of their archival items. Make an appointment with the staff member who has expertise in what you are researching. He or she may know of additional sources.

Ethnic Associations

Use the search engines to find associations or journals that honor an ethnic heritage. Some have active memberships and websites devoted to the history of immigrant populations and the customs that make each culture unique. Many ethnic societies maintain libraries, archives or museums, as well.

Neighborhoods

Look for a history of the neighborhood. You may find that archaeologists or field historians have studied the area. You may find a neighborhood association that maintains a website, or that has historical information about the neighborhood. Determine whether the neighborhood been declared a historic district. The National Park Service maintains a database of buildings on the National Register of Historic Places (nrhp.focus.nps.gov).

Religious Institutions

Houses of worship are not only rich sources of original documents, they often keep a local library for congregants that may include more than religious texts. It is common to find histories of the institution written on anniversary dates, such as centennials, sesquicentennials or bicentennials.

Search Engines

Use the search engines to find niche sites to help answer specific questions. Try searching for "coal mining in 19th century Pennsylvania" or "marriage customs in 17th century Massachusetts." You never know what you may find. Check out demonstration or re-enactment videos on YouTube; hard to find books on Google Books or the HathiTrust; and the incredible collection of digitized images at the Library of Congress.

Cyndi's List (www.cyndislist.com) is a collection of active links to websites of interest to genealogists and includes many links to places to search for social history. Use the search engine on her site, but also browse the list of links within the category you are interested in. You may discover search terms you have not considered.

Specialty Books

Many modern specialty books are full of social history such as cookbooks, travel guides, business or industry histories, histories of events or tragedies, and institutional or neighborhood histories. The two largest publishers of this type of material are:

- Arcadia Publishing (www.arcadiapublishing.com)
- The History Press (www.historypress.net)

Publishers Global (www.publishersglobal.com) Publishers Global has a directory of publishers by subject including military and history publishers.

eBay

eBay is a rich source of ephemera and archival material. I never know whether to be sad or glad when archival items come up for sale on eBay. I guess it is better that the material be sold to a collector who will preserve it, than not. Search for items on eBay that may pertain to your specialty, an area or an era of interest. If you cannot afford to purchase the item(s) of interest, perhaps the seller would give permission to use their photographs.

Setting up an eBay email alert is simple and helpful to ongoing research. Create a free eBay account and sign in. In the big search box enter a term you are interested in (e.g. court records clay county) and hit search. Click on the button at the top of the results labeled "+ Follow this search." Search terms will be saved, and you will have the option to receive a daily email showing you the results.

To help narrow the listings, use the categories in the left-hand navigation bar. Adding dates will also narrow the results. For example, I have searches running for Colorado for each year from 1859 through 1876, the territorial period. If you were to add "Colorado 1859–1876" to your search rather than individual listings for Colorado plus a single year, the search results would only return an item that had the whole phrase "Colorado 1859–1876" in it exactly. That could limit your search too much. It is better, in this case, to have a greater number of individual search terms than one covering a range of years.

One of the challenges of investigating social history is not in how hard it is to find it, it is how easy it is, and how much of it there is. I could easily become distracted on Google Books or eBay for days. The best advice I can give you is to avoid the temptation to become a collector. You do not need every possible book or item available before you begin to write. Use the tools above to answer specific questions, rather than an excuse to go fishing or collecting.

Include Historical Context

If historical context will help explain your specialty, include it. If not, skip ahead to the next section on gathering images.

Historical context is as much about placing people within their communities as it is analyzing what historic events may have changed the course of their lives.

To write about a subject within historical context means to understand not only the era (much of which is social history), but also the location. It means researching the politics and events that affected *how* people lived. It means investigating the forces in the economy that determined how *well* they lived. And, it means looking at why some people stayed, why others left, and how they got where they were going.

Research the Locations

When you research locations, your goal is to discover how important the location is to the story in order to "set the scene" for your readers. Can you describe what people in the community would have seen every day? Can you name the landmarks they would have known—the lakes, hills, waterways, springs, the public buildings, housing styles, the business district, the neighborhoods? What was the community like? How far apart were the neighbors? What were the weather and the terrain like? What challenges did they face when settling in the area or running a business there? What were the sounds and smells? How was it different at night or during the winter? The biggest challenge is not to describe, for example, the New Orleans of today, but to describe the New Orleans *of the era*.

County Histories

County histories are a good place to begin. Search the online catalog of a library in the area. Most library catalogs allow you to search either by keyword or subject. Using the subject category may return a better list. Look for a history written during the time covered by your research. You may find lithographs or photographs in the book that will help you describe the area. Google Books (books. google.com) and the Internet Archive (www.archive.org) are also good sources of early county histories available to read online or for download.

City Directories

Browsing through a city directory from the right era is another good way to get a sense of the businesses operating in the area. City Directories often have street maps. While it is easier to find a city directory for larger towns, some directories include the rural areas nearby. Ancestry.com has a good collection of digitized city directories, although many thousands are available on microfilm through:

- The Family History Library (www.familysearch.org)
- The American Antiquarian Society (www.americanantiquarian.org)
- The Library of Congress (www.loc.gov)

Bird's Eye View Maps

Bird's eye view maps were popular in the 19th and early 20th Centuries and if you can find one with a publication date within the era your research covers, you can get an idea of how the town was laid out, what buildings were prominent, and the terrain. The best sources for these maps are:

- The David Rumsey Map Collection (www.davidrumsey.com)
- Art Source International (rare-maps.com)
- eBay (www.ebay.com)

Fire Insurance Maps

Starting in 1867, the Sanborn Company made fire insurance maps of more than 12,000 cities and towns to help insurance companies assess the risk of insuring buildings. There are many digitized Sanborn maps available online, and major universities and libraries also have collections of these maps. The Sanborn maps will give you an idea of what each building was constructed of and how many structures were on the property (barn, carriage house, garage, or coal bin).

DVD Extras

Modern day filmmakers often go to great lengths to achieve historical accuracy in their films, and often the DVD extras will describe their research or how they created different aspects of the film. If a film was set in the area you are researching, watch the DVD extras, as well as the commentary tracks, for background information. Although I would not use films as the only source of location research, there is something to be said for being able to see what a location would have looked like for yourself.

Places Where People Lived

In addition to reading about the community, your readers will likely want to know more intimate details, such as what homes were like. Was they made of logs or brick? How were they furnished? Did people read by candlelight or oil lamp? Were there rag rugs on the floor and quilts on the beds? Were there fireplaces or furnaces? Answering these kinds of questions will give you an abundance of detail. *Houses and Homes: Exploring Their History* by Barbara Howe, Delores A. Fleming and Ruth Ann Overbeck is an excellent study of the role that homes play in local history.

Deed, tax, and homestead records along with plat maps can help pinpoint where individual homes were. If the houses no longer stand, look for personal accounts, photographs, or a historic home museum representative of homes in the area (or the era) to gather more detailed information.

You may find representative floor plans in the following publications. Beginning in 1846, *Godey's Lady's Book* published house plans, and *Ladies Home Journal* offered early Frank Lloyd Wright home designs for $5. Sears, Roebuck and Co. sold entire houses as kits to build. You will find back issues of these magazines and catalogs at major libraries.

If you find a legal description using the Public Land Survey System (Range, Township and Section) and need to plot a location, here is a site for doing so: Earth Point Tools for Google Earth (www.earthpoint.us/TownshipsSearchByDescription.aspx).

If your land description uses the metes and bounds system, you may want to purchase one of the many software programs available to help you plot out the property. Cyndi's List has more than a dozen software programs listed for both Windows and Mac. Or, here is a website that will generate a map for you using metes and bounds data (genealogytools.net/deeds/index.php).

Places Where People Worked

The places where people worked are also important because they are the other locations where people spent a great deal of time. Details of people's work lives may be as interesting as details of their home lives. Did people work on farms or in factories? What local conditions influenced what businesses developed or died? Did they own the business or were they employees? What products or services did the business sell? Who were their customers? How did they raise the money to get the business going and keep it going? What was it like to spend a day or a shift in the workplace?

Look to the census for information about local professions, including the manufacturing censuses. The manufacturing census was a part of the population census from 1810 to 1840, and as a separate census from 1850 to 1880. Many of these are becoming available online through sites such as FamilySearch (www.familysearch.org) and Ancestry (www.ancestry.com). The National Archives and Records Administration (www.archives.gov) has microfilm copies of the census of building trades, neighborhood industries and factories, taken every five years from 1904 to 1919, every two years from 1921 to 1939, and every year since 1949.

Look to the newspapers of the era for business advertising. Search a local archive for items with company logos and sales brochures, or a local museum for examples of product packaging.

Specialized, living, or open air museums may be the best way to experience what it was like to work as people once did. If the museum has docents or re-enactors, see if you can spend an entire day working as the people of the era worked. Rent a costume and wear what they wore. Try your hand at operating the machinery, pressing the linen or cooking the meals.

In addition to homes and workplaces, consider a little research on places people attended school, shopped, attended religious services or other public buildings in the community that would have been frequently visited, such as the local library or courthouse.

Identify Events

Get a feel for the politics of the time and the area. What were the political issues of the day? Was the area lawless or well established? Did political boundaries in the area change? What events took place? Events could be almost anything that was newsworthy—as simple as a new bell for the school to the crime of the century, natural disasters, or conflict of any sort.

Events that affected the nation affected the people within the nation. How events affected local people, however, is subjective. One of the difficulties with including historical context is accurately identifying the events that had an influence without conflating the importance of events to individuals or their communities. For example, the assassination of President Lincoln affected the entire nation. But, it did not affect each individual in the same way. It had a much different effect on an eyewitness in the Ford Theater than it would have to a family who had lost their land and their sons because they were on the losing side of the Civil War.

If historical events play a role in explaining your specialty, it is a good exercise to create a timeline of local, regional, national and world historical events covering the period your book covers. Look at any historical events you have already identified from your research review, and plot these events within your historical timeline, along with a note about what item in your possession yielded the information (e.g. newspaper clipping, scrapbook page, photograph, etc.).

The following are good, general sources to help you gather world, national and regional events. Local events will more likely come from local newspapers covered in the next section. *The Genealogist's U.S. History Pocket Reference: Quick Facts & Timelines of American History to Help Understand Your Ancestors* by Nancy Henderson (San Diego, CA: Family Tree Books: 2013). *In Their Time: A Timeline Journal for Placing Family Events into Historical Context, 1000-2076* by Roger L. Dudley (Denver, CO: Warfield Press, 2013).

Eyewitness to History (www.eyewitnesstohistory.com) is a good source of first-person accounts. They describe themselves as "History through the eyes of those who lived it."

New York Times TimesMachine (timesmachine.nytimes.com/browser) has digital issues of the *New York Times* from its beginning in 1851 until 1980, although you have to be a subscriber to the newspaper. Some libraries have subscriptions to this database through ProQuest.

At this point, include any event you think may have had an impact. Later, we will take steps to make sure that you do not include events merely for the sake of including them. It is much easier to winnow down too much information once you begin writing than to stop and conduct another round of research.

Read What People Read

One of the best ways to become acquainted with local events as well as how people spoke, thought and felt in the past, is to read the newspapers and magazines that people read then.

Newspapers

Reading a local newspaper will give you a good feel for the language of the era, albeit sometimes a bit flowery or over-dramatized by today's standards.

Look at the headlines. Headlines then, as headlines today, are designed to attract the reader's attention and tend to follow the hot news. The headlines will help you fill out your timeline with historical context.

The best part of early newspapers is often the gossipy type of news about the comings and goings of local people—who has come to visit whom; who is taking a business trip; who has returned with what kinds of goods—fabulous stuff for authentic detail. Many newspapers also have lists of groups, such as the Masons or the Temperance Society and when they met.

Take a look at the advertisements. The ads are much more about social history than historical context, but they will give you an idea of what items cost, what goods were available locally, and what kind of items a family may have had to scrimp and save for in order to purchase.

To find out whether there was a newspaper published in the town or area, consult the U.S. Newspaper Directory, 1690-Present, found at the Chronicling America section of the Library of Congress website (chroniclingamerica.loc.gov/search/titles/). The Library of Congress also has a large number of digitized newspapers available. If you want to know more about a specific paper or about the early newspaper industry, consult *The History and Present Condition of the Newspaper and Periodical Press of the United States*, produced by the Census Office of the Department of the Interior. This book is available as a free download at Google Books (books.google.com).

The following free sites have links to digitized newspapers:

- The Ancestor Hunt (www.ancestorhunt.com/newspapers.html)
- Elefind (www.elefind.com)
- Google News Archive (news.google.com)
- Old Fulton New York Post Cards (fultonhistory.com/Fulton.html)

There are also many local or state-wide newspaper preservation projects. Consult the area's major universities as well as the state historical society, as they often either have original copies or microfilm copies of newspapers significant to the area. The Ancestor Hunt (www.theancestorhunt.com/newspapers.html) also has a state-by-state list of historic newspaper projects as well as helpful articles on searching historic newspapers.

There are several subscription websites devoted to newspapers where you can either search by name or keyword. The name search can be frustrating, especially if you are searching common names. Use the advanced search features that allow you to narrow the search by date and location. Use the keyword search to locate information on towns near where the newspaper was published. Local newspapers often carried columns of information from surrounding towns as a regular feature.

The following are the leading newspaper subscription sites:

- Newspapers.com
- NewspaperArchive.com
- GenealogyBank.com
- PaperofRecord.com

One of the best features of the subscription newspaper sites is the ability to search across multitudes of papers. Letters home were popular especially during times when masses of people were leaving an area, such as during the many gold rushes, economic downturns or land giveaways. Keep the date ranges narrow to limit the number of results.

Magazines

Finding an era-appropriate magazine often is more difficult than finding a local newspaper. The American Periodicals Series, 1741–1900 is a database available through a ProQuest library subscription. There are not nearly as many digitized early magazines as there digitized newspapers, but there are a few universities undertaking magazine digitization projects.

The most popular national magazines of the 19th century were *Harper's Weekly* (established 1857), *Frank Leslie's Illustrated Newspaper* (established 1852), and *Godey's Lady's Book* (established 1830). Many major libraries have copies of these magazines. The Alexander Street Press (www.alexanderstreet. com) sells library-based subscriptions and has digital copies of *Harper's Weekly* from 1857 to 1912. Your local library may have access to these databases. The Internet Archive (archive.org) has copies of *Frank Leslie's Illustrated Newspaper*, and *Godey's Lady's Book* is available by individual or institutional subscription through Accessible Archives (www.accessible-archives.com).

One of the best ways to get an idea of what people would have been familiar with, or events they may have reacted to, is to read what they read. While national magazines are helpful in following major events or subjects such as fashion trends, finding a local newspaper can provide priceless, personal information about individuals and the people they knew.

Follow the Money

If you want to know how well people lived, you will get some clues from records such as the census or land deeds, but you should also see what was happening in the region or country that could have affected the choices people made. The "Panic of 1857," for example, that began with a few bank and railroad failures left many people looking for any opportunity to make money when gold was discovered in the Rockies a year later. More than 100,000 people risked everything for a get-rich-quick opportunity in the gold fields of what is now Colorado.

How did people in the area make a living? Did they trade with other local communities or only among themselves? How did they conduct transactions—in cash, barter or on credit? What inventions influenced the way people made money? What economic forces were the drivers, either upward to booms or downward to busts?

One of the easiest places to start researching economic events is on Wikipedia (www.wikipedia.org). They host a page for each decade that includes science and technology (including new inventions), commerce, and notable misfortunes such as natural disasters and epidemics. There is also quite a bit of social history on these decade pages, including literature, theater, music, sports, fashion, and art.

Where Did People Go?

Did local people move from place to place? How did they do so? How did people get where they were going within the area? Did transportation change over an average lifetime? Did groups of people either emigrate or immigrate? Did the ethnic makeup of the community change when they moved? Groups of people moving from place to place can be a source of frustration in finding original source material, but figuring out where they moved may be the best way of establishing *why* they moved.

Migration or Immigration

Did people make substantial moves? To a different region? A different country? In most cases, people were either pushed from one place by difficulty or conflict or they were pulled to another place by opportunity.

People often emigrated in groups, settling in areas where others from their homeland had already gone, others who practiced the same religion and spoke the same language. Naturalization records are one way to track movements. Naturalizations consist of two parts—the intention to naturalize and the final papers. There are exceptions to this, of course. Many people filed their first and second papers in different places. Naturalizations before 1906 took place in local courts, after 1906 in the Federal courts. After 1906, look at the National Archives and Records Administration (www.archives.gov). If you need a naturalization before 1906, search local courthouses.

Maps are essential if you are tracing the routes people took. The climate and terrain had enormous influences on which way people traveled, and the methods they used to get there. Historical atlases will help with migration routes. Climate maps, as well as era-relevant paintings, can tell you a lot about whether the land was flat, dry and hot or overgrown, swampy and steamy. The Perry-Castaneda Library Map Collection at the University of Texas (www.lib.utexas.edu/maps/), has a huge number of thematic, climate and historical maps available online.

A good topographical map is helpful in determining how difficult the terrain may have been during a move. The DeLorme Company has software with modern topographical maps of North America and a subscription database of older USGS maps that will overlay the modern maps. These older maps can be helpful for locating places by name that no longer exist. Additionally, cemeteries sometimes are shown on older maps, but not on the newer versions. The U.S. Geological Survey also has a great number of historical maps available for free download (nationalmap.gov/historical/). USGS maps are not copyright restricted.

Transportation

How did people get where they were going? Did they float along the Ohio River or join a wagon train? The experience of making a move is material rich in detail, and luckily there are many first-hand accounts of what it was like to travel by sailing ship, steamship, river barge, wagon train or steam train. Transportation museums are another good source of information.

In order to explain your specialty well, you may need the kind of details you will get from researching social history and the historical context the era. And, along with the written details, a few good images are a must.

Get the Graphics

In this round of research, gather the images to help your readers see what you are explaining. Use charts, if necessary, to show relationships or to help keep names straight. Use photographs if you have them. Use illustrations to demonstrate concepts or maps to give directions, or show routes and distances. Gather any visual clues you think the reader may need to fully understand your information.

Charts

Generation charts or pedigree charts are good visual references if you need to show relationships. Generation charts show three or more generations at a glance. Most genealogy software will produce a generation chart at the push of a button. Keep the charts as simple as possible so that they are easy to read on a single book page. It is difficult to include more than four to five generations on an 8.5" x 11" page.

Another useful visual reference is a family group sheet showing a nuclear family—a couple and their children in the order in which the children were born. Genealogy software creates these charts, as well. The charts can be modified to show multiple marriages with all of the children (full and half-siblings), as well as the children's spouses. Family group sheets are another simple way for readers to see who belongs to the family at a glance.

Photographs

Include photographs of people, places or objects if they will help the reader visualize what you are explaining in the text.

Historical Photographs

You may want to include historical photographs of the region or era. Even if you do not use all of the photographs you may find in your book, they may be helpful to you while writing when describing scenes or objects.

Searching the Internet

While it is easy to locate images by using the "Images" feature on a search engine, the Internet is not the best place to find digital files with resolutions high enough to look good in print. For print production, you need an image at 300 ppi at the size you want to display it. You will need a higher resolution image than most of what you will find on the Internet because websites use images that have been down-sampled to 72 ppi for quick retrieval and display.

You can use the search engines to locate collections that contain the images you want, some free from copyright restrictions, others require a fee.

Locating Photograph Collections

Use the "Images" feature on Google or Bing to search for a location or an event. For example, I searched for the "Battle of Vera Cruz, Mexican War" and came up with dozens of digital images of paintings of that battle including one that came from the War Memorial page at Columbia University's website (warmemorial. columbia.edu). Clicking on the link to the original image took me to the Roll of Honor for the Mexican War. From there I was able to obtain the address for the

Office of the Provost at Columbia University to contact for permission to use the image, as well as to obtain a better, higher-resolution version to use in my book.

Bing has an interesting feature on its Images page called "Image Match." By clicking on an image, then using the Image Match feature, the search engine will list other places online where that image exists. In this case, I found the same Mexican War image on the Library of Congress website in several varieties including a digitized version from color film, another from a color slide, and a black-and-white version, all with links to images with resolutions high enough to use in a book. The information about the image indicated that there are no known restrictions on publication. Good news, indeed.

Sources of Royalty Free Images

The following are websites where you may find photographs or illustrations free from copyright restrictions so that you can include them in your book without permission or fees. Proper attribution, however, is a must.

Library of Congress Photographs. Each image within the pictures collection at the Library of Congress (www.loc.gov/pictures/) has an indicator of whether the image has any known rights restrictions. The images in the American Memory Project within the Library of Congress are gathered from other collections, so be sure to check with the image's owner for permission.

Flickr: The Commons. Flickr (www.flickr.com/commons) is a photo sharing site that has a section of images that owners have agreed to allow others to use without copyright restriction. Flickr is also the host of many museum and archive photographic collections. Unless you find the image you want among The Commons, ask permission to use it.

Getty Images Stock Photos. While Getty (www.gettyimages.com/creativeimages/royaltyfree) mostly sells images, it has made a collection available without copyright restrictions. Please do not be tempted to use an image that is rights restricted, however, without paying for use. Getty is known for its hardball tactics to extract compensation if you use an image without permission.

Ancestry. Ancestry (www.ancestry.com) has a postcard collection consisting of thousands of images from around the world. Old postcards are a great source of location and event images.

Wikimedia Commons. Wikimedia Commons (commons.wikimedia.org) has millions of images without licensing restrictions contributed by the individuals who own them.

Again, proper attribution is a must.

Sources of Rights-Managed Images

Rights-managed images are those that you may license for use. The following are sources of low-cost, rights-managed images:

- Shutterstock (www.shutterstock.com)
- Dreamstime (www.dreamstime.com)
- MorgueFile (www.morguefile.com)

Historical Societies

Many local historical societies have photographic prints, slides or negatives in their collections that have not been digitized or cataloged online. The same is true of some local libraries. It pays to call and ask. Explain that you want the image for a how-to book. If the institution will not make the images available to you without cost, negotiate the fee. You may have to pay only for the staff time to scan the image for you. You could offer to help scan images in return for waiving a fee. What the historical society may lack is staff to scan their images.

Ideas for Images

The following sites have millions of images of everything imaginable. If you need ideas, consult one of these sites.

ClickAmericana. Click Americana (www.clickamericana.com) has images covering every decade from the 1820s to the 1980s. ClickAmericana has such a good collection of images that you are certain to get a few ideas, and the site encourages sharing to Facebook, Twitter or Pinterest.

Retronaut. Retronaut (www.retronaut.com) describes itself as a photographic time machine. Retronaut has partnered with museums and archives around the world to create this digital collection.

Mountain West Digital Library. Mountain West Digital Library (www.mwdl.org) is a portal to the image resources of several historical societies and universities in the western states.

Panoramio. Panoramio (www.panoramio.com) is a user-generated Wiki site where photographers post their images. Panoramio is a good resource for modern photographs of locations. Ask for permission. Often, the photographer is flattered that you want to use the image and asks only for proper photo credit.

You may find uses for modern photographs. The sites above are also sources for images of what places look like today, for people in period clothing; objects found in museums or full-color images of historic places. In fact, you may find better images taken with modern equipment, than historical photographs.

Digitally Altering Photographs

Most photographs could use a little touching up, to lighten areas that are a little too dark, sharpen edges or increase the contrast. Most image editing programs allow you to make these corrections easily. The corrections that are not quite as easy are those that help re-build parts of a damaged photograph or those that eliminate unwanted or distracting elements (see Enhance, Repair and Retouch in Chapter 8).

Color or Black & White?

Not all photographs look their best when reprinted in a book. You can test how each photograph will look by creating a digital scrapbook, of sorts, with all of the images you are considering. Use Lulu (www.lulu.com) to print a private book as a proof. That way, you will see each image as it will look printed in black-and-white so that you can reject some images or fix others that look washed out or too dark.

Taking Photographs During a Research Trip

If you are taking a research trip, schedule enough time to take an abundance of photographs. Digital photography is cheap, so shoot away. You may not use all of them in this book project, but they will be available for lectures or future projects.

Bracket Your Shots

Most digital cameras will allow you to alter the speed or the aperture from shot to shot. Some cameras do so in a three-shot burst. By bracketing, the camera will use different settings to alter the amount of light in the photograph. By bracketing, you are likely to take at least one usable shot from the three-shot group without having to alter it in your photo editing program.

Take Establishing Shots

The best example I can give of an establishing shot is to take a picture of the sign at a cemetery entrance, and then a few shots of the view within the cemetery to give readers an idea of what the landscape is like. In a town, take a few photographs of the landscape as you come into the town, and a few of the town square and surrounding neighborhoods.

Take Encapsulating Shots

An encapsulating shot is a complete picture. At a grave site, take a photograph of the entire stone. In the town square, take a shot of the whole courthouse.

Take Close-ups

On tombstones, for example, take close-ups to make sure you can read names and dates when you get home with the photographs. Taking close-ups will also remind you to look carefully at the entire tombstone from all sides, so you do not miss anything. In town, take photographs of any historic markers. Shoot close enough so that you can read the marker when you return home.

Take Both Vertical and Horizontal Shots

You will not know how a photograph may fit best into the book's layout until much later, so shooting from both directions is helpful.

Panoramas

Panoramic photographs sometimes tell the story better than a single photograph can, and they are easy to create. If you want readers to experience how wide open the area is, how close together homes are, or where buildings are in relation to other buildings, panoramic photographs are the way to go.

There are many image-editing programs, such as Photoshop (or Photoshop Elements) that will stitch together different shots to create a single image. It can be tricky to stitch together two historical photographs if the horizon lines or focal distances are different. Editing prior to stitching can help.

If you are taking new photographs to create a panorama, overlap the shots by about thirty percent. Do not change the focal distance while you are shooting the series, and try to keep the horizon line at the same position in the viewfinder as you shoot. If you are not a steady hand, a tripod can help with this.

For panorama purposes, I shoot a scene first going from left to right, and then repeat the series going the other direction. Sometimes, shots taken going one direction come out better than the other.

Most people take photographs according to long-established personal habits. We shoot from the same standing position, from the same distance, from the same angle or from the same direction (e.g. horizontal). Your book may be more interesting, however, with a few out-of-the-ordinary photographs.

Documents and Memorabilia

If your specialty is a type of research methodology, include at least a few documents so that readers can see for themselves the type of source material they can expect to find.

Some items are considered ephemera or memorabilia rather than documents, but may work for your specialty. Ephemera or memorability includes items such as letterhead from a business, newspaper clippings, funeral cards, playbills, school report cards, and so on.

Think about the real estate on the page. What should make the cut for the book are those images that help explain your specialty *and* are visually interesting. In fact, photographs or illustrations may be better than documents, memorability or ephemera for that purpose.

Illustrations

There are times when an illustration is better than a photograph. Before photography, paintings were used to illustrate an event or to capture the likeness of a person. At ruins, for example, you are likely to find an artist's rendering of what a place probably looked like, since there may be no paintings or drawings from the era to show the place as it once looked.

There are times when a line drawing is better than a photograph to illustrate an event. Think about how you use maps online today. If you want to see what a place looks like, you may prefer the street view (a photograph), but if you need to drive there, a standard street map (an illustration) would be easier to follow.

There are rich sources of illustrations online. The key, again, is finding files with sufficient resolution to look good in print.

You may find an image that is out of copyright, such as a line drawing or lithograph from a 19th century magazine or book. The trick is locating an original and producing a good scan or photograph. There are stock photography companies that also offer line art free, but in most cases, you must pay to use the image.

If you are looking for house plans, Architectural Designs (www.architecturaldesigns.com) has plans with photographs and floor plan illustrations as PDFs for download. These plans are for houses to build today, but are based upon historical designs. The floor plans in the PDFs may not be of sufficient quality for re-print, but you could re-create one as a simple pen and ink drawing to use in its stead.

Another option is to find an illustrator who can create original drawings. (See Working with an Illustrator below.)

Maps

If appropriate, create a list of places for which a map may help readers get their bearings. Locating an era-appropriate map is an invaluable source of accurate information. Such a map enables you and your readers to see what streets existed, or how far the town extended, for example.

Fortunately, there are many places that have good map collections. Check with the major universities (e.g. Harvard and Yale), large libraries (e.g. Newberry Library and the Free Library of Philadelphia) and the local college or university in the area of your expertise.

Historical Maps

The following is a list of good map collections online:

- Library of Congress Maps Collection (www.loc.gov/maps/)
- David Rumsey Map Collection (www.davidrumsey.com/)
- Perry-Castaneda Library Map Collection at the University of Texas (www.lib.utexas.edu/maps/)
- American Geographical Society Digital Map Collection (collections.lib. uwm.edu/cdm/landingpage/collection/agdm)

Modern Maps

There are instances when a modern map is best, such as showing relationships between places. Modern maps can be useful for this type of demonstration.

There are easily searchable modern maps at:

- MapQuest (www.mapquest.com)
- Bing (www.bing.com)
- Google (www.google.com)

Each has fairly generous Terms of Use that allow you to capture a screenshot of a map and reproduce it elsewhere as long as you are not using the map, itself, for commercial gain. Check the terms on the site before you spend too much time gathering maps as screenshots.

Google, Bing and MapQuest each offer street maps, topographical features, and satellite views. All three offer directions and information about local services such as restaurants, hotels, and local attractions.

Google and Bing offer GPS coordinates and closeup views—Google calls it Street View, Bing calls it Bird's Eye and Streetside. These features are helpful in determining what exists at a location currently. Not all areas are updated by Bing or Google frequently, so looking at the date watermarked on the map will give you an idea of how long ago the view was captured.

Google allows you to sign in to your Google account and create maps with your own map points, to save or share by email. They also offer developer tools to create your own maps and place them on your website or blog. The Community Walk feature allows you to create a map with personalized points, and add photos, videos, and comments.

Google Maps will give you the outline of an entire county by searching for the county and state. Since so much genealogical research is conducted county by county, showing an outline of a county with the cities visible may be helpful.

Screen Captures

Screen captures are not an issue if you are planning to publish only in an electronic form. They can be an issue, however if you want them to look good in print.

Your computer, whether a PC or a Mac, probably has a screen capture feature. On the PC, press Control + Alt + PrtScrn, then paste the image into another program such as Word or Photoshop. Unfortunately, standard screen capture software does not always create an image that looks good in print because the software is only able to capture what is on the screen displayed at 72 to 96 ppi.

To obtain the best possible screen capture, increase the size of an image displayed on screen by zooming in (Control+Shift+[+] on a PC), which makes the image bigger on the screen when you capture it. Ideally, you will end up with a screen capture at a size large enough to create a 300 ppi image at the size you want for the book. For example, if you were to capture an image on screen at 16" x 12" at 72 ppi, that would translate into a pixel size of 1152 x 864. The largest 300 ppi image you could create from that pixel size would be 3.84" (1152 divided by 300) x 2.88" (864 divided by 300).

SnagIt (www.techsmith.com/snagit.html) has been the industry leader in screen capture for years. It has the most options for gathering screen captures from different sources such as websites or video, and the ability to edit and enhance captured images. The cost is around $50, but if screen captures are important to your printed book, it may be worth the purchase.

Use as many images as you think you need to explain your expertise. If the book is too big because it is beautifully illustrated, you can always split it into more than one volume.

Asking for Help

You should have an idea of what your additional research needs are, and what you may need help with—either from other researchers, or perhaps the professional assistance of photographers, illustrators, researchers or companies who will help you make your images look their best.

Help from Strangers

Reference librarians are my favorite "complete strangers" to ask if I need help with research. Many libraries offer an "Ask a Librarian" feature which is essentially an online chat between you and someone in the library who may be able to obtain quick answers to your questions.

PUBLISH YOUR SPECIALTY

Social Media

Mobilize an army of researchers at the click of a mouse using social media. Throw your question out on one of the big genealogical blogs and see if one of the blog's authors can answer you, or put you in touch with someone who can. See if a museum you are interested in has a Facebook page.

Photo Sharing Sites

There are helpful photographers on Findagrave.com, Flickr.com or Panoramio.com. Oftentimes, a credit for taking the photograph is enough for the photographer to give you permission to use their photo.

If you cannot find exactly the right photograph online, sometimes you need only ask. If you want a photograph of a landmark, for example, you may find a helpful stranger associated with one of the websites above, willing to make a trip over to the place to take the picture. The staff at the local library or historical society may also know of a volunteer willing to help you.

For the best results, be specific about what you want. Explain that the photograph will be used in a printed book, so you need a high-resolution image. If you need a photograph of a building with enough clear blue sky above it to accommodate your title and subtitle, say so. Ask for both horizontal and vertical images if you do not know yet what you need for the layout. You are more likely to receive exactly what you need if you are specific when you ask.

Wikis

Consult the wikis. Wikis are websites containing user-created content. It pays to use the best wikis such as the *FamilySearch Research Wiki* or Dick Eastman's *Encyclopedia of Genealogy*, which are written about genealogy by genealogists. Helpful people post articles on these sites about experiences they have had with records, locations and genealogical research methods you may find helpful.

After getting what you need from a helpful volunteer, a nice thank you goes a long way. Send a hand-written note or a small gift card for someone who has gone the extra mile for you.

Help from Other Experts

There may be certain aspects of your own expertise where consulting another expert may help you with your book project. Experts can be most helpful if you can sum up succinctly what you need and why, to get on and off the phone quickly, or to come to the point in a few paragraphs in an email.

If you need more than a quick question answered, schedule an interview. You must tell the expert why you are consulting them and what types of questions you want to have answered before they will agree to an interview. Most experts, will not allow you to waste their time dithering about. Prepare a list of questions before you make the call. You never know, the expert may be available right then if you are ready to go. Other experts may prefer you to send the questions ahead of time or to answer by email.

Expert advice can be invaluable and can cut your research time down dramatically. He or she may know of other resources available or other authorities who could help. Most experts in their field know which books are the definitive guides and which are best to gain background information. An expert should be able to explain the jargon common to their field of expertise to you in an easy-to-understand way.

Some experts will give you quick answers freely; others may charge for their time. Others may turn you over to a research assistant. With any expert you hire; it is worth the effort to negotiate. To get the best deal possible, it does not hurt to have a good counter-offer ready, or something that would suffice, say ... a nice meal. You will not know until you ask.

Working with a Photographer

You may need photographs for the book that you are unable to take for yourself, obtain from a collection, or from a helpful local volunteer. In this case, hire a photographer or license a photograph taken for other commercial uses.

Find the right photographer for the job. If you need location photos, look for someone who shoots photographs for advertisements in the area. That photographer may have images not previously sold to clients that he or she would make available to you, for a nominal fee or photo credit. If the photographer has to go somewhere on your behalf, however, be prepared to pay for their travel time as well as shooting time.

If you need an event photographer to capture a re-enactment, for example, hire someone who has experience taking candids rather than a portrait photographer who is more skilled at staged pictures of people.

Studio Photography

If you need good studio photographs of objects such as heirlooms, consider using a professional. A commercial photographer should be able to shoot objects in their own studios, or take their equipment to a location if the heirlooms are too fragile or too big to be moved to the studio.

Portfolio

Before you hire, ask to see a portfolio. Many photographers have their portfolios online, so you may be able to find exactly the right photographer before placing a call.

Fees

Ask about fees and whether they include travel, time at the location and any cropping or alterations before the photographs are given to you. You will not need prints unless you want them. Some photographers expect to make their money on packages of prints, although many photographers are willing to take a higher event fee in exchange for giving you the digital images outright.

Most event photographers will charge for the time they spend at the location, not by the number of images they take. Be clear about this, however. You will not want to pay for time and two hundred images you cannot use, just because the photographer took them. You also do not want the photographer to limit the number of photographs taken. Even with a good photographer, one-quarter to one-third of the shots taken will not be great photographs.

File Type and Resolution

Most photographers today shoot in resolutions much higher than what is needed for print production, so resolution should not be an issue. Ensure, however, that the photographer will deliver images in the largest resolution and size you need. In most book projects, that is the book cover image.

Location Images

If you want location shots, give the photographer the names of the local landmarks you are interested in, for example. A good photographer will know to take shots from different angles, but it does not hurt to be specific. If you want a blue sky in the background in order to put your title in that space, say so. If possible, show the photographer a book cover with an image similar to what you want, so the concept for your cover is clear.

Capturing an Event

If the photographer is to capture an event, be specific about the images you want. Give the photographer a schedule of activities and a list of the people you want photographed. You may need to provide a spotter—someone who is familiar enough with the people to point out who is who on the shot sheet.

Consider asking for establishing shots—shots of the location where the event is taking place. Ask for close-ups as well as group shots, candids as well as staged or portrait shots.

Make sure the photographer is familiar with the event location. Schedule a site inspection with the photographer to discover any lighting issues, obstacles or distracting backgrounds to avoid.

Deadlines

Set clear deadlines. Unless you have an upcoming event where you would want the photographer to be present, wait until the manuscript is nearly finished to send a photographer to take location photographs for you. The only exception to this rule is if the time of the year makes a great difference to the quality (or subject) of the images. If you want a clear shot of a building, for example, you may want the photograph taken in winter.

Copyrights

Do not make a big issue about copyrights unless you are willing to pay more to make the photographer give them up entirely. Negotiate the uses you want for the photographs instead. If you plan to use the photographs for more than your book project, obtain the rights for other uses—on your website, in your eBook, on an event t-shirt or journal cover, on photo souvenirs, and any other use you can think of. It is unlikely that a photographer will deny you any extended uses of their photographs within reason. But, it does not hurt to be thorough.

Note: If you have permission to use a volunteer's photo for your book (from sites such as Findagrave or Panoramio), but want to use it for some of the extended uses listed above, ask permission from the photographer for those uses as well.

Payment

Ask about any extra charges, so there are no surprises and clarify how you are expected to make payment and when. Half of the total fee is common for a down payment to secure the booking, with the final half due upon delivery of the photographs. Ask about album fees, overtime charges, or any special handling of the images not included in the quoted price.

Cancellations

Cancellations can be problematic. If you have to cancel, be prepared to pay at least part of the photographer's booking fee unless you cancel well ahead of time. Unfortunately, there may be a reason for the photographer to cancel. To protect yourself, require that the photographer has a similarly qualified backup colleague to fill in, in the event of a cancellation, or that he or she pay any additional charges you may encounter in order to hire someone at the last minute.

Write a Formal Proposal or Contract

Use a formal proposal to indicate the photographs you want and how you want them delivered to you—on a thumb drive, an external hard drive, an archival DVD, or through a file sharing service. Make sure deadlines, and dates of events are clear. Include all prices and payment terms. State what uses the photogra-

113

pher is allowing you, and be specific about what happens if either you or the photographer cancel.

Working with an Illustrator

Working with an illustrator is a bit different than working with a photographer. Because of the artistic nature of the work involved, illustrating often takes far longer than taking photographs. If you want one-of-a-kind illustrations, build extra time into your publishing timeline.

Hire the right illustrator for the job. Illustrators have their own styles, although many illustrators can work in different media, such as pencil, pen and ink, or watercolor. Some illustrators create only computer-generated images. Find a style that you prefer, and then choose an illustrator who can create the images you want. Use the same illustrator throughout the book so that the style is consistent.

Portfolio

Ask to see a portfolio. Many illustrators have their portfolios online, or they can point you to other books they have illustrated. The illustrator may have worked on a book that is available commercially, and has an online preview.

Fees

Ask about fees and be specific about the size and resolution of the digital images you need. A professional illustrator should be able to advise you how their artwork will look best in a print publication, whether by scanning the originals or photographing them. There may be additional fees if the illustrator must engage a studio photographer to create a digital image of their art.

Deadlines

As with hiring other professionals, be specific about what you want and make your deadlines clear. Ask for a set price per illustration, and inquire about any extra charges, so there are no surprises. Clarify how you are expected to make payment and when. Illustrators often require payment in installments as the illustrations are in progress, rather than half before and the balance after an event as you would pay a photographer.

Copyrights

Copyrights may be a more complicated issue with an illustrator than with a photographer. Because of the time it takes to create illustrations, illustrators may not be as eager to give up their copyrights. Negotiate any other uses at the same time you negotiate for your book. You may wish to use the illustrations on social media, on your website or in an electronic book. If you have an event coming up, you could use the illustrations on giveaway items such as t-shirts, tote bags or mugs. Negotiate the rights to use the illustrations in other ways or at least leave open the possibility for uses in the future.

Cancellations

If you must cancel, be prepared to pay at least part of the fee unless you cancel well ahead of time. If the illustrator cancels, you can expect a full refund of any fees you have paid. In your agreement, ask that the illustrator pay any additional fees you encounter as a result of his or her cancellation if you are up against a deadline to finish the book.

Write a Formal Proposal or Contract

Use a formal proposal to indicate the illustrations you want and how you want them delivered to you—on a thumb drive, an external hard drive, an archival DVD, or through a file sharing service. Make sure deadlines are clear. Include all prices and payment terms. State what uses the illustrator is allowing, and be specific about what happens if either you or the illustrator cancel.

eLancers and Freelancers

One place to find an illustrator online is to use one of the freelance services, such as Elance (www.elance.com), oDesk (www.odesk.com) or Freelancer (www.freelancer.com). At any of these sites, you will find illustrators listed under designers or graphic design and the person you hire may be from another country. You post the project details and your budget. Freelancers will bid on your project. You accept a bid from the person who offers the best price and has the portfolio you think is best. You will be able to see their ratings from other clients before you choose.

They do the work. You approve the work or ask for revisions. They submit final versions, and you pay them through the website, not directly. The sites will take care of the funds transfer and any taxes that apply.

Another place to find freelance illustrators or photographers are at local schools. There are plenty of high school or college students who want to build their portfolios, and who may work for a recommendation or fees far less than a professional would charge.

Working with a Professional Historian or Genealogist

Even though you are an expert in your subject, there are times when it pays to hire a professional historian or genealogist to help you finish your research. Although there is some crossover between the work that professional genealogists and historians do, before you hire someone make sure you have the right type of professional for the job. Genealogists tend to focus on establishing relationships, whereas historians tend to focus on location-based research.

Initial Consultation

The initial job consultation should be free. A phone call of 30 minutes or more is not unusual, but you should have your homework done before you call. In some cases, you may need to describe the research problem in detail in order to get a professional researcher's opinion of what it will take to obtain what you need and how much that may cost.

Portfolio

Ask to see examples of their previous work, and check the researcher out online at their personal website, and on social media sites. If there are no testimonials listed, ask for the names of a few previous clients. Look for credentials and certifications. In the U.S., membership in the Association of Professional Genealogists (APG) is a good indication of their experience. In the UK, look for membership in the Association of Genealogists and Researchers in Archives (AGRA).

Deadlines

Be clear about your expectations and deadlines. State how many hours you agree to pay for and the completion date for the work. If the researcher must travel to a repository, be prepared to pay for their time even if they do not find anything.

Fees

Fees vary greatly and you can negotiate. Shop around and get a sense of the going rate for researchers in the area. Clarify how and when you will make payment(s).

Ask about additional fees for copying or the use of a digital camera at different repositories. The researcher will expect you to cover these expenses. Spell out fees for travel. Expect to pay a retainer, and have the researcher explain how the retainer will be applied to the balance.

Research Report

Expect a full research report and that the researcher will maintain the copyrights to the report. If you want to use any part of the researcher's report in your book, obtain permission. Then quote and adequately attribute the researcher.

Digital Images

If you want the researcher to obtain digital images of documents or other evidence, explain the digital image size and resolution needed.

Where to Find a Professional Researcher

The Association of Professional Genealogists (www.apgen.org) has a database of genealogists for hire by location or specialty. They also have a good checklist for hiring a professional genealogist, (www.apgen.org/articles/hire.html). You will find the code of ethics members agree to abide by on their website.

Progenealogists (www.progenealogists.com) is Ancestry's official research firm. You can get an estimate online and talk with a researcher before agreeing to hire anyone. Genlighten (www.genlighten.com) lists researchers and their specialties.

You may find freelance research historians among the members of the American Society of State and Local History (www.aaslh.org) or the Society of American Archivists (www.statearchivists.org). Your local historical museum may also have suggestions.

The following private firms have employees who may take on freelance jobs:

- History Associates (www.historyassociates.com)
- History Factory (www.historyfactory.com)
- Historical Research Associates (hrassoc.com)

At the end of this round of research, you should have most of what you need to start writing the book. Writing and research are a cyclical process. There may be times when you will need to return to research momentarily in order to flesh out details of a story or two.

Hopefully, you have been organizing information and images as you have been researching so that you have all of the following:

- Written notes about each piece of documentary evidence you plan to use in the book along with full citations
- Notes taken from your social history and historical context research
- A list of images
- A list of any remaining holes or outstanding items

෬෪෨

It is time to leave the comfort of research for a time, and start the process of writing. Do not worry. Like golf, you can take a few practice swings before you are expected to make it count. Just in case you are worried about staring down a blank page, the next chapter is full of tips to conquer writer's block.

Chapter 10

Writer's Block: Staring Down a Blank Page

Most writers experience a bit of anxiety when beginning a new project, and the prospect of having to stare down a blank page may seem daunting. Do not let it stop you. In this chapter, you will find exercises to stimulate the creative juices, and if you have been writing about your sources, you already have some bits and pieces started. In other words, you conquered the blank page without even knowing you had.

Baby Steps

For novice writers, fear is often the biggest obstacle. Fear of making mistakes or of not finding the right words. Fear of getting started or fear of never finishing, are common complaints.

> The goal when you begin to write should be foremost to increase your confidence in yourself as a writer.
>
> **—Heather Sellers**
> *Page After Page*

The best way to gain confidence is to practice, practice, practice. Becoming a better writer is similar to becoming a better skier. You cannot merely imagine yourself skiing. You have to go to the mountain, ride to the top and come all the way back to the lodge, even if you fall a few times along the way. Writing is no different. Your first draft may not be perfect. In fact, it may not even be readable. Fear not! Put a section or a set of instructions down on paper. You can revise it all later.

Next Steps

One way to get started is to study how others have tackled similar subjects. The following series are built upon showing readers how to do something, or imparting the latest, greatest information about a subject:

- The Everything [Subject] Book (www.everything.com)
- The [Subject] Book for Dummies (www.dummies.com)

Look for books with "A Beginner's Guide," "Bible," Everything You Need to Know," or the like in the title to see how different authors address an audience of beginners, or those wanting a complete look at a subject. Look for "insider's" guides or personal narratives to gain ideas for telling your own story of getting to know and love your specialty. Look at the bestsellers within the business section. These books are often a good guideline for how to impart expertise.

Giant Leaps

Stop and evaluate each of the existing books for genealogists (or local historians) in your area of expertise. Let us take the subject of DNA for example. I found more than a dozen listed on Amazon.com going back to 2005, but most written within the past two years. Evaluating each of the books already published in your area of research expertise will help you eliminate overlap from existing books while offering something new or different to potential readers.

The rest of this chapter will give you a few issues to consider and story starters you can use to gain experience before you begin writing.

Before You Write

It is better to learn some lessons before you begin writing than after you finish a first draft. The following is a bit of collective wisdom from books, editors, and writing courses.

Give Yourself a Round of Applause

Not everyone is willing to undertake a project as big as writing a book, so congratulations. If you are still reading this book, then you have more tenacity than ninety percent of the thirty million genealogists out there who will never get beyond the idea that they will write ... someday.

Discover What Motivates You

It is not enough to start a book project; you must complete it if anyone is to benefit from it. Focus instead on how much other researchers will appreciate reading it. Remind yourself that you are adding to the broader knowledge within the genealogical community. Know that all of your precious expertise will not end up in the dumpster after you are gone, because there will be a book with your hard-earned research sitting on the shelves of researchers and libraries across the country.

Analyze What Makes You Doubt

If you are an inexperienced writer, you are not alone. There are relatively few genealogists who have written about their own families let alone their expertise. What is the worst that could happen? Nobody dies from a badly written book. There are no lives on the line. If you finish your manuscript and are unhappy with it, there is always an opportunity to fix it. That version can be a practice run. The next version will be better.

Set a Schedule

To finish your book project, you must write. The most common advice in the writing community is: "butt in chair." That pretty much says it all. You must *choose* to write and be there to do so. If you write one page a day, at the end of the year, you will have a 365-page book. You do not have to write in marathon sessions. You can write for fifteen minutes a day or one hour a week.

One caution, however. If you leave too much time between when you write, you may spend most of your time trying to remember what you wrote and what you had planned to write next. Schedule your dedicated writing time close together to get more actual writing done. Continuity is important, both to the substance of the book and to your ability to keep the project moving forward.

Just Say No

For many writers, a cloud passing over is excuse enough to abandon writing for some other task or activity. You may have to tell the people in your life that when you are writing, they are responsible for entertaining, or cooking, or cleaning, or driving—themselves. The withdrawal symptoms (for you and your family) will subside eventually.

Do Not Wait for Inspiration

You cannot wait for the right inspiration or perfect conditions if you expect to complete your book. There will always be laundry to fold, kids to pick up, and additional research that may be interesting. If you wait for perfect conditions, you may as well wait for perfect weather—72 degrees and sunny with a slight breeze blowing gently from the east, but not enough to rustle your papers or muss your hair. You cannot wait for a miracle either—nor a flash of genius—nor divine intervention.

Be Careful Who You Ask for Advice

Think twice about showing your manuscript to friends, family members and particularly to other genealogists—especially those without nearly your level of expertise. I wish it were the case that everyone was not only *capable* of offering beneficial advice, but also *willing* to offer constructive criticism. Jack Bickham hits the nail on the head in his book, *The 38 Most Common Fiction Writing Mistakes (And How to Avoid Them)*, when he explains, "There are know-it-alls and know-nothings. If your work is good, many of them will be jealous. If your work is bad, few, if any, of them will know how to point out your mistakes in a constructive manner." If you need an editor, hire a professional. Exchange manuscripts with another expert, or join a writer's group where you can get constructive feedback from other people who write.

Consider ...

> Consider the possibility that you may be an excellent writer who simply needs to sit down and write.
>
> **—Mary Embree**
> *The Author's Toolkit: A Step-by-Step Guide to Writing and Publishing Your Work*

Enough said.

Choose Your Words

The following advice is universal. It applies to fiction, non-fiction, family histories and how-to or instructional guides.

Write for Your Reader

You have identified your target market. You are most likely writing for other researchers. If you keep your target audience in mind as you write, you are much more likely to write the kind of book that your readers will thoroughly enjoy. If you try to write for an audience of everyone, you are writing for no one in particular, and the book will suffer for it.

Too Clever by Half

It is better to be understood than not, so familiar words are better than more erudite-sounding words. If you are unfamiliar with the meaning of a word, consult a dictionary. Lose the shorthand used in email or text messages. Clarity is the key to communication. Do not try to reinvent English grammar, either. It is enough trouble to follow the rules as they exist. Write so the reader will understand you.

Three Words You Can Stop Using Today

Forget using the words very, just or really. While common in conversation for emphasis, they are unnecessary clutter in a book. A global search through your manuscript will tell you if these words have become so much a habit that you do not notice when they slip into your writing.

Verbs, Nouns, Adjectives, and Adverbs

If you ask editors what makes them spot a novice writer, most will point to the overuse of adjectives and adverbs. If you use a strong verb, you may not need an adverb to modify it. For example, state that he sprinted, not that he ran quickly.

Use strong nouns as well. Do not use the word container, if you mean a wicker basket. State that she owned a tilt-top table made of mahogany, rather than a round-topped, spindly-legged, deep brown table. Strong verbs and precise nouns get the job done better.

Active Voice is Better

Use the active rather than the passive voice. In the active voice, the subject is doing the whatever the verb indicates. Marvin mailed the letter. In the passive voice, the object is being acted on. The letter was mailed by Marvin.

There are times when the passive voice fits the situation best, but those instances are far fewer than opportunities to use a strong verb that describes exactly what is happening in the narrative.

> The habitual use of the active voice ... makes for forcible writing. ... [W]hen a sentence is made stronger, it usually becomes shorter.
>
> **—William Strunk, Jr. and E.B. White**
> *The Elements of Style*

The following is the conjugation of the verb, to be. If you find these verbs in combination with other verbs, you are using the passive voice (e.g. the letter was mailed, the letter was being mailed, the letter had been mailed).

Indicative	Past	Future
I am	was	will be
You are	were	will be
He is	was	will be
We are	were	will be
You are	were	will be
They are	were	will be

Perfect	PluPerfect	Indicative
I have been	had been	am being
You have been	had been	are being
He has been	had been	is being
We have been	had been	are being
You have been	had been	are being
They have been	had been	are being

It is best to use the most active, direct and succinct way to describe the action.

Neither Hedge Nor Wheedle

If you have a point to make, make it. There is no sense running around a subject until the reader is exhausted or confused. Hedging around a subject or wheedling your way into one is most common when addressing sensitive subjects. Try direct first. Then adjust or soften the tone, if need be.

Pick and Choose

Be discerning about what you include. No one wants to read unnecessary minutiae. Readers only want the good stuff. If the details are something useful to the reader in their own research, include it. If not, leave it out.

Do Not Get Graphic

Describing the reality of war wounds is one thing. If, in the back of your mind, you can see your mother squinching up her face and saying, "Ewwww." Leave it out. Everybody poops. There is no reason to describe it for your readers. That is not edgy. That is icky.

Writing Should Have Rhythm

You are not writing an expository essay for school. Each paragraph does not require a topic sentence followed by neatly regimented supporting evidence. Overly long paragraphs will slow the rhythm. Keep the paragraphs short and the narrative moving.

Imitation is the Finest Form of Flattery

If you are going to emulate another writer's style, choose someone who is still alive and writing. What readers were used to in the 19th century is not what readers expect today. You are better off imitating the style of Jack Canfield or Mark Victor Hansen than Napoleon Hill.

Perfect Is Not Possible

You do not have to squeeze your style or the authenticity out of the story to achieve perfect words or grammar. A conversational tone is fine for a how-to or instructional guide. It is easy on both the writer and the reader. There is no need to twist yourself into a knot over every word, as did Oscar Wilde, who once said about himself, "I have spent most of the day putting in a comma and the rest of the day taking it out."

Do Not Edit as You Write

Stopping to re-write a small section over and over again, is an easy excuse not to move on. Get it all down, and then worry about the re-writing. You are more likely to see structural flaws in the larger manuscript than you may in a small section.

Items to Have on Hand

The following are handy items if you get stuck.

A Good Dictionary

The best is probably the *Merriam-Webster's English Usage Dictionary*, available in print or online (merriam-webster.com). If you prefer something different, you will find this online dictionary helpful (www.onelook.com). And Google, of course, will give you a definition if you put a word or phrase into the search box.

Thesaurus or a Synonym Finder

The *Merriam-Webster Dictionary* (and website) includes a thesaurus. Another good thesaurus is Thesaurus.com (www.thesaurus.com). *The Synonym Finder* by J.I. Rodale has not been updated in years but is still useful. And, there is a synonym finder online at Synonym.com (synonym.com). This website also has antonyms and definitions.

Word Usage Guide

If you need to know the etymology of a word (how the use of a word developed), the best source is the *Morris Dictionary of Word and Phrase Origins*. If you would rather use an online guide, consult Richard Lederer's *Verbivore* (www.verbivore.com) or Evan Morris's *Word Detective* (www.word-detective.com).

Editing Advice

If you find yourself in need of editing advice, consult The Editorium (www.editorium.com). They also provide useful tips for writers using Microsoft Word. Bill Walsh, editor and humorist, runs an advice site for copyeditors (www.theslot.com) or consult the following subscription site for copyeditors (www.copyediting.com).

A Wee Bit of Levity

Personally, I like to read something funny, especially when I am stuck for what to write next. It is often the only inspiration I need to keep going. The following are my favorites:

- *Eats, Shoots & Leaves: The Zero Tolerance Approach to Punctuation* by Lynne Truss
- *Sin and Syntax: How to Craft Wickedly Effective Prose* by Constance Hale
- *Lapsing into a Comma: A Curmudgeon's Guide to the Many Things that Can Go Wrong in Print—And How to Avoid Them* by Bill Walsh

Food for Thought

Every book project involves decisions about what to include and what not to include. You have done much of this already by how you guided your research. The following are a few more questions to ask yourself before you begin writing.

What Do You Want Your Readers to Know?

By the time the reader finishes the book, what is it you want the reader to understand about the subject? Is there an overarching theme or idea you want the reader to take away? How much in-depth knowledge to you want the reader to have? Will a beginner understand the subject? Will more experienced researchers gain something as well?

Is there Something You Want Readers to Do?

You may want other, interested researchers to contact you, or continue your work for the benefit of future researchers. If there is something you want readers to do as a result of reading the book, how will you communicate that?

How Will You Handle Sensitive Topics?

How much of what you have discovered do you want to reveal? You have an obligation to accuracy, but not at the expense of the feelings of living people. What happened a century ago is fair game, but revealing hurtful or potentially embarrassing, private details about living people is problematic.

Let Your Subconscious Help You

If you stop to think about your book project every night before you go to bed for even five minutes, your subconscious will help you see the bigger picture or tackle the material when you sit down to write next. Many writers swear by this simple technique.

Story Starters

While you may not be writing "stories" in your how-to or instructional guide, story starters such as what follows help get the juices flowing. Think of these exercises as the last practice swing before you have to face the pitcher. Tackle one exercise or all, or skip them entirely if you are ready to write.

Start Your Memoir

The best way to establish a habit is to commit to doing something each and every day for one month. At the end of that month, the activity will have become a habit. Write about yourself, for just ten minutes a day for thirty days. Not only will you make writing a habit, but you will have a good start on your memoir. The next generation may be more interested in your life than you think.

The following is a simple exercise to help you establish a habit for writing: pick a photograph and write what memories spring from the photograph. It does not matter whether you pick a photograph from your photo album or if you use a search engine to find an image of your hometown, first school or the car you drove in high school.

Help the Reader Feel the Experience

The best storytellers are those who use details to help the reader believe that they are experiencing what is happening in the story. Use your web browser to search for the following expressions as images, not news:

- And they're off. Kentucky Derby.
- Tornado. Joplin, Missouri.
- Pow Wow. Native American dancing.
- Teen Carries Younger Brother 40 Miles.
- Ferry sinks. 300 feared dead.

Now write a few paragraphs that make the reader feel as if they are experiencing the scene for themselves.

Personal Memory Joggers

The following is another way to stimulate memories. List your friends chronologically. Describe them how you remember them—their looks, their personality traits, the things they enjoyed doing, the foods they hated—whatever you can remember about them.

Do the same thing for the:

- Schools you attended
- Teams you played on
- Jobs you had

- Bands you followed
- Houses you lived in
- Associations you joined
- Cars you owned ... and so on

The following are books and a game full of memory joggers:

- *Mom [Dad], Share Your Life With Me* by Kathleen Lashier
- *Grandma [Grandpa], Tell Me Your Stories* by Kathleen Lashier
- *To the Best of My Recollection* by Kathleen Lashier
- *The Book of Myself: A Do-it-Yourself Autobiography in 201 Questions* by Carl and David Marshall
- *Q&A a Day: 5-Year Journal*
- *Reminiscing: 21st Century Master Edition*

Creative Writing Techniques

The following are exercises to inspire you to put words down on paper. The writing does not have to mean anything, and you do not have to use full sentences, although for some exercises it may be easier if you do. You do not have to limit yourself to only those things found in each suggestion. If you have a better idea, write about it.

Set the Table. Imagine yourself at the dinner table when you were young. Describe who was there, how the table was set, what was served and the conversation that took place.

Introductions. Think of two people well known to you but not known to each other and introduce them. How would you describe them to each other?

Make an Excuse. Make an excuse to your mom, to a teacher, to a police officer, to a friend—about anything.

Lost and Found. Describe how you got lost, and then the steps you took to find your way.

Folk Remedies. Make up a remedy for snoring, sneezing, chin stubble, tardiness, or stinky sneakers—imagine how it could work. Who knows? It may.

Oh No! Describe things you would do with a friend or sibling you would never do with a spouse or parent.

What Would You See? Describe the events you would witness if you lived across the street from a mortuary, police station, schoolhouse, livery stable, biker bar, or a newspaper office.

Land of Make Believe. If you could make up a place, what would it be like to live there? Or travel there?

Each of these exercises allows you to practice descriptive writing.

Instructional Writing Techniques

Use these exercises to practice thinking through a process step-by-step, and writing instructions for someone who is completely unfamiliar with the process. Then re-write each exercise with a more experience audience in mind. Notice what parts of the instructions you would leave out with a more experienced audience. One thing that is easy to do with an instructional guide is to assume the audience knows more than they do. When you begin to write your book, use these lessons as a guide for what to leave in, what to take out, or what introductory material will make it clear to readers the level of experience they must have before your book will be useful to them.

Give Directions. Choose one of your favorite research repositories, and give instructions for getting there by walking, driving, and using public transportation.

Cook a Favorite Meal. Choose one of your favorite home-cooked meals, and give instructions for shopping, preparation, and timing each dish so that the entire meal is ready to serve when guests take their places at the table.

Assemble a Toy. Find a toy that requires assembly from the box, and without reading the directions, write a set of your own directions for assembling the toy.

Quick Start. Write a quick-start guide that would get new researchers up to speed on the topic of your expertise. Use only short paragraphs and bullet points to capture the main ideas.

Practice Instructions. Write a set of guidelines and exercises for practice projects so that readers can gain experience.

Case Study. Use a case study to illustrate how your expertise could help others in their own research.

Detailed Instructions. Choose an aspect of your expertise and focus in on the small details to give readers a great depth of knowledge of the subject.

Once you finish each exercise, evaluate it for whether your instructions will meet your audience's needs, whether the purpose of the instructions are clear enough that the audience will know what they should be able to do once they have read the instructions, and whether the instructions are complete or could be missing steps.

❧❧

The only way to cure writer's block is to write. That does not mean you must tackle the intended project while you are feeling blocked, but it does mean you must write about something. If you will write every day, you will develop a habit of writing. Starting your book project will be easier, and once you begin, the words will come more naturally. When needed, step away from your book and write about something nonsensical, write about your activities the day before, or write down a memory. When you are back in the swing of things, begin again with your book.

Chapter 11

Project Management

Any project that has a multitude of "moving parts" can become bogged down. The following are suggestions for keeping your project moving forward.

Schedule When You Are at Your Best

Try not to fit your book project into scattered, unpredictable little pockets of time. Put the project on your schedule at a time when you are at your best and able to focus. If you are a morning person, for example, trying to stay up an hour later to work on the book may not be the best way to spend that hour.

Do not schedule yourself to the point where you are exhausted either. Down time is necessary. If you find that you are spending every spare minute working on the book, re-prioritize so that you have time for breaks and time for the book.

Commit to a Don't List

Manage the distractions, whether they be the phone, the kids, the laundry, Facebook or Twitter. Make yourself a list of don'ts—things you will not do during your scheduled project time. The most common excuse given for not finishing projects is unproductive tasks intruding on the business at hand.

Put multitasking in your list of don'ts while you are at it. Trying to be productive on multiple projects at once often nets poor results for all.

Organize Your Work Space

Nothing bogs a book project down faster than having to stop to search for something "vital." Before you begin compiling the book, take whatever time you need to organize your research into easy-to-locate folders and to prepare your method for extracting and compiling information from the source.

Break the Project Down into a Simple Outline

Start by creating a simple outline of the tasks that need to be accomplished. The following is an example of how a simple outline for a research guide could look:

Research Guide to the Colorado State Archives
    Making the Most of Your Day at the Archives
    Parking in Downtown Denver and Other Headaches
    Vital Records Held at the Archives
    Using State Agency Records
    The Courts
        Supreme Court, Appeals Court, District Courts,
        County Courts, Municipal Courts
    Territorial Records
    County Records
    Municipal Records
        Extinct Municipalities
    Special Districts and Their Records
    School District Records
    Publications and Microfilm
    A Guide to the Master Films

An outline gives you a simple overview of what needs to be done, so you can prepare a schedule that makes sense for the tasks.

Create a Checklist

Use your outline as a checklist. Mark off what you have done and what remains. If it makes more sense, reorganize your checklist into similar projects even if they occur in different parts of the book. For example:

Monday	Get photographs of the archives building and surrounding area
	Create a list of other research possibilities downtown
	Evaluate driving/public transportation directions
Thursday	Visit Supreme Court library to research history of the court
Saturday	Write the introduction to The Courts
Monday	Courts before the territorial period
	Laws governing the territorial courts
	The territorial Supreme Court
	Court districts during the territorial period

Estimate the Time it Will Take

Expect that everything will take longer than you think it will. Even the best book project managers can underestimate the time it can take to complete a project as long and complex as a book.

I set deadlines because they keep me on track. I also like the flexibility of being able to reschedule some tasks. If I have an hour scheduled for a task that only takes fifteen minutes, I add in another more difficult task in the remaining time. I also like to give myself an out—on occasion. If I am feeling tired or overwhelmed, I keep a list of "brainless" activities that I can accomplish without a lot of thinking that must be done to complete the book, anyway.

Be cautious with your "happy" tasks. We all have tasks we like more than others but if you burn up all of your happy tasks, then you are left with only the "must do" stuff. That can put a damper on the rest of your schedule. Balance out the difficult or rigorous with the fun or "brainless."

Question Perfectionism

I am all for producing the best, most accurate book possible, but if you consistently find yourself repeating the same task, or going over the same section again and again, put it aside and work on something else for awhile. Perfection can be an excuse to avoid finishing the project.

Keep the End in Mind

Every task you accomplish contributes to the whole, but sometimes it is hard to see the book when you are looking over a long checklist. Put a picture of a full bookshelf up somewhere you can see while you are working to remind you that someday your book will be proudly displayed on the shelf alongside others.

Celebrate the Milestones

Look at your task list and set a few milestones among the tasks. When you finish a section, celebrate. When you finish all of the book's front matter, celebrate. Give yourself permission to do something nice for yourself at each of the milestones. And reserve a really big bear hug, a nice dinner out, or a day at the spa (ball park, ski slope, cabin—whatever tickles your fancy) for the day you finish the book.

❧

The only way to go from idea to book is to keep the project moving forward until you finish. Schedule the time and commit to it. If you feel overwhelmed, pick a different aspect of the project temporarily. Come back to the part you left behind when you are feeling more refreshed.

Section 3

The goal in this section is for you to write a first draft, then edit and polish the manuscript.

Everyone should:

- Create a style guide. Style guides are big time savers.
- Edit. Every manuscript deserves editing.

Baby Steps

There is no getting around it—you have to tackle the first draft. If conducting a full edit seems overwhelming, once you have a draft, fact check it, make sure the captions on images are correct, and edit for typos. Every manuscript needs at least one good read through to catch mistakes.

Next Steps

Once you have a draft, *content edit*, fact check, edit the captions and look for typos. The content editing is an additional step, but your manuscript will be better for it. A good content edit will reveal whether you have included everything you had intended or whether some sections are more robust than others.

Giant Leaps

It can be difficult to judge one's own level of expertise and how well it is explained. For the benefit of the reader, if you have instructions or any kind of problem solving, test the material out on readers with different levels of experience.

Once you have a draft, conduct a full edit. Your hard work deserves nothing less.

Chapter 12

Engaging while Explaining

Long gone are the days when a dusty, boring tome was considered the pinnacle of academic achievement. Readers today want to be engaged. They want easy-to-understand information, presented in a way that is interesting. Writing in an engaging and interesting manner is also the best way to keep readers turning the pages from beginning to end.

Creative Nonfiction

Before discussing the techniques of engaging while explaining, I want to introduce you to a relatively new genre called creative non-fiction. Before we go any further—creative non-fiction is *not* fiction. You must build your book upon the facts, but the way you explain your specialty can benefit from the techniques journalists use to tell stories in a vivid way.

Non-fiction, traditionally, solves problems, gives advice or illustrates techniques. You can use creative non-fiction to do the same, while writing in a way that is more engaging than a strict, factual recitation.

Learn from the Best

Reading is, by far, the best tool to teach writing. The more well-written how-to books you read, the more likely you are to pick up the author's techniques without having to dissect each line to study how it was written. Not that you should imitate a favorite author's style *exactly*. Reading a talented author's work will help you discover how a good writer combines elements and information in the most effective way.

I turn to the following when I need help with techniques:

Comprehensive

- Loretto Dennis Szucs, The Source
- James C. Neagles, *U.S. Military Records*

Building Blocks

- Thomas W. Jones, *Mastering Genealogical Proof*

Problem-Solution

- George G. Morgan and Drew Smith, *Advanced Genealogy Research Techniques*

Topical

- Barbara J Howe, *Houses and Homes*
- William Thorndale and William Dollarhide, *Map Guide to the U.S. Federal Censuses, 1790-1920*

Geographic

- Judith Prowse Reid and Simon Fowler, *Genealogical Research in England's Public Record Office*
- Christina K. Shaefer, *The Center*

Classic How-To

- George G. Morgan, *How to Do Everything Genealogy*
- Denise May Levenik, *How to Archive Family Keepsakes*

I encourage you to pick up a few of these books, read them and keep them handy as you write, to refer to in case you have questions.

The Big Picture

Before I break down non-fiction writing into its finer elements and techniques, first let us look at the bigger picture. If you read writing guides or attend writing classes, you will hear the expressions, vision, focus and structure. All of these imply the "bigger picture."

Vision

Now that you have finished the latest round of research, you should have narrowed your vision from what is possible to what is practical based upon the research you have. You should be able to state your vision for the book in a short paragraph. For example: "The book details research material available in Boulder County, Colorado at four archival repositories, one university library and six public libraries."

Focus

Focus should describe the target audience for the book and how readers will get the most out of the information provided. For example: "Researchers new to Boulder County should start at the Carnegie Branch Library for Local History where they will find compiled genealogical and local history research, along with more than 500,000 items of archival material. More advanced researchers will find additional original source materials at the County Clerk's office, and the University of Colorado archives. Several local libraries have excellent local history reference collections. This book will detail the types of materials found in each Boulder County public library and repository."

Structure

The structure is more concrete and describes the organization of the book—how the information is presented to the reader. The following organizational styles were discussed in Chapter 7. Here is a brief recap:

Step-by-Step. By far the most common way to organize a how-to book is step-by-step. You give the reader the instructions for how to accomplish a task by leading him or her through the process, step by step.

Chronologically. For some subjects, organizing from the past to the present makes the most sense to readers because the subject follows a natural timeline.

Reverse Chronology. For other subjects, it may be easier to start in the present and work backward into the past such as the way we often use census records drawing on what was learned at each step to take the next step.

By Topic. Land records are a good example of how structuring a book by topic may be most appropriate because the rules for recording land was different under different colonial, federal or state systems.

Building Blocks. There are some subjects for which the reader needs to gain understanding a little bit a time before moving on to the next, more complicated or difficult concept. A book about using DNA for genealogy would fit this model.

Degree of Difficulty. Degree of difficulty is similar to building blocks, although tasks could be organized from easiest to hardest or hardest to easiest, depending upon the lesson you wish to impart to the reader.

Problem-Solution or Question-Answer. In some cases, you could organize by outlining common problems (questions) along with suggested solutions (answers) for each case.

Whichever style (or combination of styles) you choose should be whatever the reader needs to best understand and make use of the information.

Point of View

Before you start writing, you should decide how you will address the reader. In other words, from whose point of view will you be relaying the information? One of the biggest pitfalls for inexperienced writers is diving in without making this decision first. Without defining a point of view, it is easy to slip back and forth, which may make perfect sense to the writer who has a vast amount of research to call from, but it can be confusing to the reader. Choosing a point of view is a helpful writing tool for you also, letting you determine how the reader is going to experience the book.

The easiest way to visualize point of view is to imagine a camera on a tripod looking out over a vast landscape. The point of view is not the landscape, nor the camera, but the person looking through the lens.

If *you* are looking through the lens, then you will be describing your experiences in the first person: "I found this technique to be the most useful in my own research."

If the *reader* is looking through the lens, then you are describing their role (a bit tricky, I admit) in the second person: "You should begin your research at the land office located downtown."

The last possibility is that you, the *author*, are looking through the lens, but you are not describing your personal experience, rather your expertise with the subject. For example: "Homestead records are the building blocks of genealogical research in the West during the period 1865-1910."

On occasion, your opinion about the subject will come through in the writing: "The information available from records gathered in this manner is unreliable."

The point of view you choose *may* make the task of writing easier, but *should* make understanding the subject or achieving a level of competence with the subject easiest for the reader.

First Person Point of View

When writing in the first person, you are telling your story, from your point of view. The major personal pronoun used is "I."

Explaining your expertise through your experience researching is one option, however, be careful not to spend the entire book describing your achievements and no time telling the reader how he or she can be successful in their own research using your techniques.

The following is an example of giving instructions using the first person point of view:

> When I research at our local courthouse, I try to arrive by 8AM because the parking lot immediately adjacent to the courthouse fills up by 8:30AM when the building opens.

Second Person Point of View

When writing from the second person point of view, the reader is the central character, so the major personal pronoun used is "you." You address the reader directly, which is common in how-to books. I have done so throughout this book because it is an easy, conversational way to relay information. Creating a more formal distance between us by referring to myself as "this author" and to you as an abstraction (i.e. an author, a publisher, a genealogist, or a family historian) sounds stilted and awkward.

The following is the same example using the second person point of view:

> If you plan to research at the local courthouse, try to arrive by 8AM because the parking lot immediately adjacent to the courthouse fills up by 8:30AM when the building opens.

Third Person Point of View

Most non-fiction books are written in the third person. The major personal pronouns used are "he," "she" or "they." Information is relayed without reference to the author or the reader.

The following is the same example using the third person point of view:

> To make best use of the local courthouse, researchers should arrive by 8AM because the parking lot immediately adjacent to the courthouse fills up by 8:30AM when the building opens.

You may have a point of view in mind already, but have not identified it as such. Write a chapter or two and evaluate what you have written. You may have a natural inclination toward a point of view already. What is most important about choosing a point of view is that you stick to it for consistency. Slipping back and forth between points of view will confuse the reader.

Tone

Establishing the tone of your book is about relaying information in a consistent way. Will you take a conversational tone? A comedic or ironic tone? Academic? Most writers develop a natural style or tone, although it may not make itself apparent until you are well into a first draft, especially if you have not written much previously. Tone is not a decision to be made with absolute certainty before you begin writing. It is something to be aware of and to watch for when reviewing your first draft. The book will read more naturally if the tone is consistent throughout. Again, consistency is the key.

Voice

Voice is a little harder to describe. Voice depends upon whether you are writing objectively (not allowing your opinions to influence what information you include and how you relay that information to the reader) or subjectively (allowing your feelings about the subject to become known to the reader). Voice should also be consistent.

A subjective voice is easiest to slip into when writing about subjects that are emotional such as slavery or the Holocaust. It is natural to feel a range of strong emotions when writing about emotional subjects. Whether you inject your emotion and opinion into the text is up to you.

Whether to write with an objective or subjective voice is another area to evaluate for consistency.

Theme

A theme is the central idea or message of a book, and in storytelling is a way to bind together stories into a cohesive whole. Often, the theme is echoed throughout the book without explicitly stating what it is. In non-fiction, it may come through in what you choose to include, and what you do not. For example: "This is a book about being thorough." Being thorough, however, is only a topic. What you *express* about being thorough becomes the theme.

A theme may not become obvious until after you have a draft finished. At that point, you may find that there are ways to reinforce the theme by imparting some information a different way. For example, would creating a case study help the reader to see how following the instructions in the correct order made the difference between success and failure? Would quoting the latest research change the reader's mind about how things have always been done, in favor of something better? Would taking a series of photographs help demonstrate a concept that is otherwise difficult to explain?

Some authors start with a theme and adhere to it because it helps to narrow what will be included in the book, and others discover the theme after writing a first draft. Either way, a theme can be the unifying element that makes a book feel whole and complete.

Coherence

The final big picture item is coherence—imparting information logically—moving from element to element, or subject to subject, making sure the reader remains firmly grounded. For example, even though you have detailed knowledge of how a 19th century newspaper was created, your reader may not. In order for the reader to follow along, the explanation needs enough detail to show that the type was set letter by letter backwards, in rows followed by a strip of leading to separate one row from another and to hold the individual pieces of type in place as the full type case was inked and the paper pressed onto it—in that order.

I know this is a lot to think about, but I wanted to make you aware of each of these big picture issues—vision, focus, structure, point of view, tone, voice, theme and coherence—before you begin writing.

Non-Fiction Mechanics

The following are non-fiction mechanics to consider when deciding how to best present your material.

Structure

One of the first considerations, of course, is how you will structure your material to help the reader grasp the subject and make the best use of the book. Most of the decisions regarding structure are organizational (see above). Other decisions may have to do with format. For example, a workbook requires space for the user to take notes or make calculations in order to best use the book. You may have to play with the formatting to achieve the best combination of narrative and user-directed activity for your subject.

Selection of Detail

Selection of detail—how much to tell, the level of detail, how complete the coverage of the subject—depends partly on the subject, but mostly on your intended audience. In order to write an effective guide, deciding who you are writing for, is paramount. Take the subject of DNA as an example. In the last decade there have been huge advances in the understanding of DNA and what scientific uses there are for the complete genome map. To cover all of this material would be ambitious, but most likely useless for an audience who wants to understand where their ancestors came from, and how to prove a family tie to another person. In this case, too much detail is detrimental to the goal(s) of the book.

In other cases, a lack of detail could derail the usefulness of the book. Take a research guide for a county as an example. A research guide written as "a local" may completely mystify someone who is unfamiliar with the area. In this case, giving directions using familiar landmarks is a pitfall because someone from outside the area may have no idea where "old man Barker's farm" is, for example.

Sequence

For some subjects, the order in which you present the material is crucial. Here again, I raise the question of who your intended audience is. A beginning or in-experienced audience may need a more rigorous adherence to chronology, order or process than an experienced audience.

As you write, you may find that your subject, or your passion for the subject lies with a more experienced audience. That is fine. There is room for books of all levels, and readers out there anxious for the material.

Use of Facts

There are some subjects for which the use of data and statistics are necessary to provide evidence of a theory or assertion. In other cases, quoting authority figures will bolster your credibility as an author because it will demonstrate that you are well read in your subject, or that you are an active participant in a community of like-minded researchers.

Everything you write in a how-to or instructional guide should be factual. How much additional supporting evidence you include, is up to you.

Non-Fiction Techniques

The subject often determines the best techniques for non-fiction writing. A set of instructions, for example, may be best in short, numbered lists—a step-by-step approach. Other subjects—a case study, perhaps—are well served by narrative writing techniques—narration, exposition, action, description, and summary. When using narrative techniques, most writers need all five to impart information in a compelling way.

Whether or not you use narrative techniques is up to you and the subject in question. Consider for a moment, however, the following sets of directions. One is written in a strictly factual way, the other is more colorful. While you are writing, ask yourself whether adding a little "color" could liven up the information, or whether it would muddy up a perfectly good factual explanation.

> Example 1:
>
> To reach the courthouse, take Hwy 1 north. Turn left at 3rd Street. Go west seven (7) blocks to Maple Street and turn right. Proceed one (1) block into the town square. The courthouse is in the middle of town square. There is parking on either side of the streets surrounding the town square.
>
> Example 2:
>
> To reach the courthouse, take Hwy 1 north past the Towson Home—a large 1840s house with six white columns facing the

street. This home is open for tours most summer days between noon and 4PM.

One block past the Towson Home is 3rd Street where you will turn left and proceed seven (7) blocks to Maple Street. The neighborhood you will pass through is the oldest neighborhood in town and many historic homes dating back as early as 1810 still stand.

At Maple Street turn right. Maple Street is one-way and will enter the town square at the southeast corner. The streets surrounding the town square are also one-way going counterclockwise. The easiest way to park is to wait for traffic to clear so that you can enter traffic in the inner lane to look for a spot nearest the courthouse.

Same directions, different effect.

Beginnings

The book must have a beginning, a middle, and an end. The beginning may determine whether or not the reader becomes engaged and continues reading.

Oftentimes, it is easiest to tackle the beginning last. Write the guts of the book first, if need be. Afterward, you may be better able to encapsulate what is to come in a riveting opening line.

Middles

The middle fulfills the promise you made in the beginning. The middle supports, develops and sustains the reader through the book. In the middle, you should maintain a logical structure, but you do have more latitude to vary the pace, to introduce an interesting back story, describe conditions or fill out the setting.

Ends

End the book in a way that is satisfying. Cover the subject thoroughly and wind it up. If you end abruptly, or with nagging questions unanswered, the reader will feel cheated.

A common problem with endings is that they do not—that is—end. If you have more information you wish to include, look for a place in the middle to introduce it, do not wait until the end to throw in leftover pieces and parts.

Your last line, as your first, should give the reader something to ponder. Judy Garland's last line in *The Wizard of Oz*, "And oh, Auntie Em, there's no place like home," is satisfying because her troubles are over, and she got what she wanted. Paul Newman ends the film *Butch Cassidy and the Sundance Kid* with irony when he says, "Oh good. For a moment there, I thought we were in trouble," as Butch and Sundance charge into a hail of gunfire.

You get the last word, make the most of it.

Narration

If you will use narration as a technique, use it to reveal information in a way that stimulates the reader's imagination. It is through narration that you will "show, not tell." Telling is left to exposition. To *tell* is to give information. To *show* is more often to withhold it—to create an impression rather than making a flat statement.

> *Telling*: Traveling by stagecoach was uncomfortable.
>
> *Showing*: To make each route profitable, the stage coach company had to pack the interior with at least eight passengers, leaving each person approximately 14 inches of seat space. The cheapest airline today provides seats at least 18 inches wide.
>
> *Telling*: Homestead applications were filed at the land office.
>
> *Showing*: The process began when a suitable piece of land was located and an application was filed with the closest land office, often a full day's ride away. But an application did not guarantee ownership of the land. Much more was required.

Exposition

Use exposition to give information—to get to the point. Exposition will explain.

Sometimes, a quick statement of fact is all you need. For example: "In mountainous areas, switching from standard gauge to narrow gauge cut costs from $90,000 per mile of track to $20,000 per mile." Other times, a subject is so unfamiliar to the reader that it requires a more lengthy explanation.

Use exposition to help the reader become familiar with new information, old-fashioned expressions, foreign words, how tasks were accomplished in the past, and so on.

Action

Action is difficult to describe in non-fiction unless you are telling a story. On occasion, however, telling a good story is the best way to keep the reader engaged. In that case, action is where all of the drama is. It is where the story moves forward, one step after another.

Word choice is important in action, because the more precise and concise the words or expressions, the more vivid the action.

Rhythm or pacing can also influence the effect of action. Shorter sentences help create suspense. Longer sentences slow the action down. A combination of long and short sentences can create a sense of chaos or uncertainty in the action.

Action also has to be logical. There must be a stimulus before a response. Action on paper has to happen the way it would be experienced in real life.

If you will tell a story to illustrate a point, for example, use action to advance the story, to build tension, to reach a climax, and resolve the event.

Description

Description is another storytelling technique, but also can be used to enhance the way your expertise is explained. Description is used, typically, to inform or explain, set a mood, or give sensory details. An informative description may be what the reader needs to understand the subject, or any action taken and its consequences. For example: "Trading in their old 12-pound, smooth-bore Howitzer for a new Whitworth cannon, allowed the troops to remain across the river out of range of the enemy's guns, while firing deadly shots that landed within inches of their aim."

Description can be used to create a mood—to create a feeling of being at the scene. A suggestive description can evoke a feeling or suggest the atmosphere of the scene. For example: "The attacking force was estimated to have exceeded 15,000 men. Men, who in the moment before Longstreet signaled Pickett to charge, looked out over the unmarred slope of green, tall grass to a stand of trees on the crest of the ridge nearly a mile in the distance."

A dramatized description with good sensory details sprinkled into the narrative can help readers feel the experience, not just be told about it. For example: "As Major General George Pickett motioned his men forward, a massive Confederate artillery bombardment filled the air with acrid smoke and flying debris, but did little to quiet the Union artillery fired from the advantage of high ground."

Use description to help the reader experience events and feel the action. Accurate description also builds your authority as the author, and lends credibility to the subject.

Summary

Summaries are a way to fast forward past events that took place and should be acknowledged, but are not important enough to tell in full detail. Summaries can be informative, giving the reader a sense of moving through time by a sequence of events. For example: "Migration along the Hudson River surged with the opening of the Erie Canal in 1825. Migration surged again after the canal's expansion began in 1832."

Summaries can also be descriptive giving the reader the quality of the events taking place while advancing the narrative in time. For example: "With the opening of the Erie Canal in 1825, merchants gained access to new markets at a remarkably reduced cost. Moving goods by carts drawn by pack animals limited the volume and quality of supplies to anything that would not spoil during a three to five week trip to market. Moving goods by barge greatly increased the volume of goods shipped and shortened the trip to days which cut spoilage down considerably. By 1835, fresh produce grown near Albany was sold in markets as far away as Lake Erie, miles away from where it was grown."

Use summary to skip the boring stuff, and to move your narrative through time and space to where the next interesting tidbit begins.

Interpretation

Your subject may lend itself to interpretation. Historical events, for example, are open to interpretation. If your subject lends itself to discussion, controversy or opinion rather than a strict recitation of factual information, then argumentation, persuasion or rhetoric are methods used to influence opinions.

Argumentation. A genealogical proof statement, for example, is a form of argumentation where you lay out the evidence in a logical way and follow a set of rules that lead to a logical conclusion.

If you wish to posit a theory in your book, you certainly may. However, you should back up your theory with facts also addressing any evidence that points to a different conclusion than your own. In other words, both sides of the argument should be presented showing why greater credence should be given to your theory based upon relevant information.

Persuasion. Persuasion has a completely different role than argumentation. Persuasion is not so much about seeking the truth (or proof), as it is in changing minds. Using your book to change readers' minds about a subject can be a trap if you tailor the facts to shape the reader's opinion.

Rhetoric. Asking rhetorical questions can make readers think about your subject in different ways, although, as an expert, you should also be prepared to give the reader enough factual evidence upon which to make a reasoned argument.

Pitfalls

Anachronisms, misused colloquialisms, references and tenses are the pitfalls most common to writing about subjects having to do with the past.

An anachronism is an item appropriate to a period *other* than that in which it exists or is described. It is not enough, for example, to know that the typewriter was invented in 1869, if it was not commercially available except in a few major cities until the 1890s.

Colloquialisms—words or expressions specific to a place (or an era)—are another potential pitfall. Not all Southerners describe the exterior place where their rocking chair resides, for example, as a "veranda." And not all Northerners call the spot near the front door a "stoop."

Try to use timeless references, so that if someone reads your book twenty years from now, meaning will remain clear. Hardly anyone under 40 would understand a reference to the Betamax, for example. And forty years from today, a reference to an iPhone may be a head-scratcher.

Tense is another potential pitfall when it comes to records. If you are describing events that took place in the past, you can use the past tense. When describing records, however, you must use the present tense because the records still exist. For example: "DeLong *appears* in the Bourbon County court records as the Clerk of the District Court."

The bottom line on pitfalls—watch your tenses and fact check early and often. If you are at all unsure, check again before you add the description or use the expression.

Fiction Techniques Useful to Non-Fiction

The following are the fundamentals of fiction: setting (or scene), characters, dialogue (see mannerisms below), and action (see above). There are ways to employ fiction techniques in a way that is appropriate to non-fiction, depending upon your subject.

Setting

Setting grounds the reader in specifics—where and when. If your subject is Civil War medicine, for example, a list of surgical instruments may not be as engaging as a description of the field hospital in which they were used.

You can establish the setting by describing its qualities: the closeness or enormity of the space, whether the atmosphere was tension-filled or relaxed, as well as the texture, peculiarities or uniqueness of the place.

Character

If you are telling a story, people are the most important elements. The best stories are not about what happens but to whom it happens. In non-fiction, you do not have the luxury of forming the characters the way you want them to be. You can, however, characterize people—make them seem more real than words on a page, by what you reveal about them.

It is relatively easy to characterize people you have known. For example: "Grandma was fastidious in her appearance, and always wore her thick, salt and pepper hair swept up in the style she adopted as a young schoolteacher before the war."

It is a little more difficult to characterize someone you have never seen or heard. You can turn to images (if there are any) and documentary evidence. For example: "The two brothers could not have been more different. One followed the frontier, took risks, and established business after business. When he failed, he picked up, moved on and tried again. The other brother remained in New

England, got married, raised eleven children and worked his whole life making shoes, as his father had."

Your challenge is to describe people in a way that makes the reader feel something for them and want to know more about them, while revealing them in a way that is historically accurate and backed up by documentary evidence or by what you—yourself—have observed.

Note: When referring to a "character," I am always referring to a real person and not to a fictionalized character.

Characterization Techniques

One mistake inexperienced writers often make is to start off describing every detail about a person. While you do gain a sense of a person when you see them for the first time, you do not learn everything about them all at once. You get to know people over time. Sprinkle in character traits and descriptions as they fit naturally into the story.

Another way to work in character traits and descriptions is to alter the distance from which you view the character. A closeup view will yield more intimate details—a chipped tooth, a quirky laugh, or the smell of her favorite perfume. A middle-distance view will show things you could observe from across a room, such as his gait, her beautifully tailored suit, or the way he fiddles with his glasses. Elements from a long-distance view may come more from documentary evidence and from a bit of the reader's imagination—she worked in a turn-of-the-century textile factory; he was a gambler and a gunslinger; or, she opened a soup kitchen during the depression.

There are three ways to characterize people: directly, indirectly or by creating a general impression.

Create a General Impression. Create a general impression by using what the reader already knows about places, landscapes, professions, cities, neighborhoods and so on. The following example creates an impression based upon the description of the character's job: "He worked a hardscrabble farm of eighty acres in a place where rain was a ghost and the blowing wind a constant companion."

The following is a distinctly different impression based also upon a job: "He was a dentist, by trade, at a time when any local barber would offer to pull teeth."

Avoid stereotyping while creating a general impression. Not all New Englanders were Puritans, and not all Westerners were cowboys. Using specific words and phrases will help. The phrase "a hardscrabble farm of eighty acres" paints a more vivid picture than "he worked the land."

Direct Characterization. One way to reveal character traits is by doing so directly—to describe his or her personality. A direct description, of course, is your opinion formed either as an eyewitness or by drawing reasonable conclusions from the evidence.

Yes, you can draw reasonable conclusions from the documentary evidence. If a man lived on a farm, worked the farm his whole life and died on the same farm, you can conclude that he was steadfast. If a woman traveled to the West before other women, built a log cabin and climbed the tallest peak in the area, you can reasonably conclude that she was adventuresome.

There are multitudes of character-trait lists online. The following is a short list to get you started:

Able	Expert	Melancholy	Selfish
Adventurous	Faithful	Mischievous	Shy
Bossy	Generous	Organized	Stubborn
Brave	Helpful	Prim	Tireless

Recall the narration section above and the information about the concept of "show, don't tell." Direct characterization (telling) is to make a blanket statement about the person. For example: "He was organized." However, indirect characterization (showing) is often a more vivid way to describe the character. For example: "His office was so neat, there was never a book off the shelf or a paper out of place."

Indirect Characterization. Indirect characterization will reveal an individual's personality through their appearance, attributes, mannerisms, thoughts, or effect on other people.

Physical Appearance. It is natural to be curious about what people looked like. The farther back in time the subject of your book takes place, the less likely you are to have an image to show to your readers.

Physical description could include: race or ethnic group, height, weight, body type, age, physical condition, eye color, hair color, hair style, facial hair, distinguishing features or physical imperfections. Personal appearance goes along with physical description including clothing, clothing styles, grooming (neat or unkempt), and so on.

It is not impossible to find a physical description if you do not have an image, although you may have to look in many places to find one, and have a bit of luck on your side. You can find physical descriptions in the following record types:

- Military records
- Pension records
- Naturalization records
- Voter registrations
- Passenger lists
- Insurance files
- Draft cards
- Passport applications
- Prison records

One caution about introducing physical characteristics is to avoid making the character sound as if he appears on a wanted poster. "The suspect is five-feet, nine inches tall, with brown hair, brown eyes, wears a shoddy pea coat, and is known to frequent the saloons." You get the idea.

A better way to introduce a physical description is to combine it with action. For example: "He was a lumberjack. His six-foot, two-inch frame must have been honed like steel after a lifetime swinging an ax to cut notches on the area's ninety foot tall trees. Trees with trunks so thick it took crews on a sixteen foot long, two-man saw to bring them down." It is easier to envision the size and strength of a man who is swinging an ax than giving his height alone.

You will notice the use of a qualifier in this description. He "must have been" honed like steel, rather than he "was" honed like steel. Anytime you speculate or characterize other than by direct observation or by quoting someone else's direct observation, you should use a qualifier.

Mannerisms. Mannerisms are habits. The things people do or say without thinking. Mannerisms can describe behavior—how people act in different situations. Did she warmly embrace people or was she cool towards them? Was his gait was more a march or a stroll? Was he more likely to pet a dog or be annoyed by it?

Describing the effect of a mannerism paints a more vivid picture than making a statement about a mannerism. For example: "He rarely relaxed without a dog in his lap," is more revealing than "He loved dogs."

Mannerisms can describe speech or speech patterns. Did she sign each letter "fondly yours" or "love you always"? Did he start his stories the same way? Did he use colloquialisms? Were they common to the area or from another place or time? Were words from another language thrown in occasionally? Did she use jargon from her profession? Did she speak quickly? Was he soft-spoken, loud and boisterous, or colorful?

I often get the question, "Can you use dialog in non-fiction?" The answer is yes, if you are relaying what you have heard, or if you are quoting from a court record, diary or letter. For example: "Grandma never called them 'the boys' the way we did. She always called them 'the fellas.'"

Giving the reader a bit of flavor using a person's accent or unique way of speaking is fine. A lengthy segment of "pahking cahs in Hahvad yahd," however, is difficult to read (and can be annoying).

Mannerisms can also describe gestures. Did he often push his glasses up on his nose? Did she twist her hair when she was nervous? Did he use his hands when he spoke? Mannerisms can include personality quirks, eccentricities, temperament, bad habits, vices, or sense of humor.

Including mannerisms, creates a sense of the person. Using too many mannerisms, however, is a pitfall. It can make the person seem unnatural, unreal or unbelievable.

Attributes. Some attributes are harder to categorize but may influence the way a person is characterized. The following are some attributes to consider: religion, years of schooling, family background, status, income, occupation, skills, abilities, talents, military service, hobbies, interests, sports, or pastimes. Any of these attributes could also affect mannerisms, thoughts or his or her effect on others.

Thoughts. Another way to characterize someone indirectly is by their thoughts or an expression of their opinion (attitudes). One thing you *cannot* do, is to get inside a person's head as if you know what he or she was thinking. For example: "He drove his work crews because he *knew* the railroad had to make it across the pass before winter."

Rather than telling what a character thinks to explain his action, it is better to let the reader experience the story element dramatically at the same time the character experiences it. For example: "He drove his work crews hard in September of 1867. As the days grew shorter, the possibility of snow at high altitudes was ever present. The year before, John Williston lost forty men in a blizzard that lasted for eighteen days before they could descend off the mountain. Sam Fulton's crew laid thirty-three miles of track and left the 8,000 foot pass behind as they moved through the low valley in November."

It is easy to assume what someone must have been thinking when events were taking place. If you have direct evidence, then quote it. If you do not, tell the story in a way that does not assume thoughts not in evidence (so to speak).

Other issues that fall into knowing someone's thoughts include prejudices, gripes, political opinions, goals, and fears.

Effect on Others. What effect does the person have on other people? How do others feel about him or react to her? Here again, you cannot get into the heads of a person's friends and associates either, but there may be evidence of relationships that you can write about. For example: "The newspaper ran a half-page article about his funeral. Every member of his Masonic lodge was in attendance. Even a few members who had left the area, returned to take part. The cemetery sexton said he had never seen so many people in the cemetery at a single gathering in the thirty years he had worked there."

Storytelling Techniques

The following storytelling techniques also can be used with non-fiction subjects to help you write factual information in a compelling way.

Hooks. Hooks are used in advertising to gain the reader's attention and make the reader want to know more. They are used the same way in narratives, often as a way to begin a scene. "The cannon rests quietly today at the corner of the courthouse, but to the men of Sullivan County, it was 'the meatgrinder.'"

Les Edgerton's book, *Hooked: Write Fiction that Grabs Readers at Page One and Never Lets Them Go*, is a primer on starting a story with a bang.

Foreshadowing. Foreshadowing alludes to action that will happen later in the book. It builds anticipation, dramatic tension or suspense.

In the Prologue of his book, *Only a Few Bones: A True Account of the Rolling Ford Tragedy and Its Aftermath*, John Colletta sets up the events that will take place in the book, but ends with a good example of foreshadowing:

> The packet Joe intended to board this morning to return to Vicksburg never showed. So he is spending one more night in the Ring & Co. store.
>
> His last.

Without the other setup, those three lines not only would have been foreshadowing, but a cliffhanger.

Flashbacks. Flashbacks are the most common way to introduce elements of the past that affect a story in the present. They can also be annoying if overused. A good flashback will move the reader seamlessly from the story's present using a catalyst to trigger a release of information about the past.

For example: "As an old man, John Friedman was a wonder. He had been mayor, clerk of the court, and the first to volunteer when a posse was needed, which was remarkable given the events of his sixteenth year. He was an eager young man, then. Eager to prove himself, so he lied about his age to join the local regiment. It was in battle that he lost his left arm. What he never lost, was his keen eyesight. Even as an old man, he could hit a rabbit on the move with a revolver and could stop local ruffians on the run just by threatening to shoot."

An inartful use of a flashback will leave readers wondering about what is happening when. Watch the tenses carefully. If you are already telling a story in the past, and you jump even further back for a flashback, returning to the story's present (in the actual past) can be problematic.

Transitions. Readers today are sophisticated media consumers, so transitions in your book can mimic those found in other entertainment.

The jump cut is the most common transition used in books today. Put a little white space on the page to indicate that something has changed and go on to the next subject. Readers do not need the big "back at the ranch" sign to let them know the something has changed.

On occasion, you may want to use a transition to introduce a time change, such as "It took two full seasons to clear enough land to begin planting."

Another way to transition from one topic to the next is to use a phrase taken from the last paragraph to begin the next paragraph. For example:

"His wife often expressed frustration with his *slow and methodical* pace.

Slow and methodical, however, was what made his reputation. His craftsmanship was second to none."

Use transitions to lead the reader from one subject or scene to the next while minimizing any confusion.

Pace. One of the most common mistakes is letting the narrative slow to a pace that the reader skips ahead to see what is next. To quicken the pace, examine the manuscript for anything unnecessary—setup descriptions, empty scenes, overlong explanation, and so on. Shorter chapters and shorter sentences will quicken the pace.

To slow the pace down, use longer sentences and chapters, spend more time setting a mood, or give a more thorough explanation.

Anecdotes. Anecdotes are short stories. They are a way to reminisce, make readers laugh, give a caution against doing something unwise, to persuade or inspire.

It is relatively easy to tell short story snippets about people you know or have known. It is more difficult with a historical figure or someone you have never met. The best anecdotes are those that illustrate something about the person.

The following is an example of an anecdote from David Bruce's eBook, *Mark Twain Anecdotes and Quotes*: "When Samuel Langhorne Clemens was a schoolboy, he was very good at spelling, and usually won the Friday afternoon spelling bee in his class. However, one Friday, he deliberately misspelled a word so a young girl he liked would win."

Analogy. An analogy is a comparison used to explain an object or an idea giving readers a way to use something familiar to gain insight into something unfamiliar. Analogies can be simple, such as, "There is a resemblance between the boy and his father." They can also be more complex, such as: "A doctor searching for a difficult diagnosis is like a detective searching for clues in an unsolved crime."

Similes and metaphors are specific methods used to create analogies.

A simile compares one object to another quite different from it. For example: "Standing before the class explaining his science project he was *as brave as a lion*," or "The robbery suspect was *squirming like a fish out of water*." Similes often employ the words "like" or "as" to make the comparison.

A metaphor makes a direct comparison between objects that are different from each other but share similar characteristics. For example: "After we sampled the pie, Mother was *boiling mad*," or "After we made it past the kitchen door, it was *clear sailing* ... at least until Mother caught up with us."

Analogies, similes, and metaphors can add color to a story or to an explanation of facts. Be careful not to use them too often or to reach for an easy cliché because it is familiar.

Imagination

If you want to write in an engaging way, a little imagination goes a long way. That is not to say that I am encouraging you to make up the facts. I am not. But if you are writing about a subject that has been written about before, find a different way to present it. Use your words to help readers develop a detailed picture in their heads, to believe that they are there in the moment, or to feel something for your subject.

Effective, engaging—even creative—non-fiction techniques will strengthen your relationship with the reader and help to boost interest in the subject and what you have to say about it.

❧❧

Working with a Ghostwriter

A ghostwriter will take your ideas and turn them into a book. An astounding fifty percent of books in the marketplace today are written by talented ghostwriters, mostly for people who have great ideas but neither the time nor the skills to produce a well-written book (article, speech, movie script or screenplay).

The typical process includes an interview with you to understand your ideas and the scope of your planned book. The ghostwriter will take a look at your research, and may conduct additional research, mostly to help him or her better understand the events and the time period. The ghostwriter will then produce the manuscript in the format you agree upon. In most cases, book manuscripts are delivered complete, fully edited, and ready for typesetting. Your name will appear as the author, the ghostwriter's name will not appear, even as a co-author. The ghostwriter will be paid a fee, and if the book is sold, the ghostwriter will expect no royalties or further compensation.

It is best, of course, to use a ghostwriter who specializes in non-fiction. You will find an abundance of ghostwriters through the Association of Ghostwriters (associationofghostwriters.org) and their individual websites. If you cannot find someone with experience in your subject, look for a ghostwriter with strong research skills who has written in many different subject areas.

Portfolio

Ask to see books the ghostwriter has written. Public portfolios can be problematic for ghostwriters who work for people who would rather the world not know they used a ghostwriter. Most ghostwriters also write under their own names. Choosing a ghostwriter who is familiar with the publishing process because they have been through it, is a good idea.

Cost

Costs vary widely from one ghostwriter to the next. Most give an estimate based upon the scope of the project. If you have a limited budget, let the ghostwriter know before he or she gives you an estimate. Be prepared for how much a ghostwritten book may cost. Professional ghostwriters charge professional fees for professional work. Be wary of ghostwriters who cannot possibly make a living by what they are charging. You do not want to hire someone who is perpetually overbooked, or who subcontracts out the writing to a cheap site overseas.

Expectations

The interviews should give you a sense of whether you and the ghostwriters have the same expectations for the book. If expectations differ greatly, find a different ghostwriter. At the end of the initial set of interviews, the ghostwriter should understand how you want the book written, how you wish your specialty to be perceived, and who your audience is.

Communication

After an initial set of interviews to lay out the project, the ghostwriter may need to check in with you from time to time to get your opinion. Rarely will that exceed more than an hour a week since most ghostwriters are accomplished project managers who can keep a project moving forward on schedule.

Approvals

You may want to see chapters as completed to gain a sense of how the project is proceeding. Keep in mind that the chapters you will be seeing may still be in their rough form. You will not want to put a final stamp of approval on the work until after the manuscript has been fully edited.

A full-length book can take as long as six months, and completion deadlines will reflect this. Payment deadlines vary from ghostwriter to ghostwriter, but often include half down, a quarter at a determined point in the project, and the final quarter upon completion.

Services Included

Most ghostwriters include a certain number of revisions in the price of the project to allow for you to request changes. Professional editing is often included within the contract, as well. Most ghostwriters have editors they work with often, and will contract for that service on their own.

Write a Formal Proposal or Contract

Most ghostwriters have a contract format they regularly use. If he or she does not, write a formal proposal or contract that includes a complete project description, all services and fees, deadlines, how you will communicate, and how the final product will be delivered to you.

❧❦

Learning the mechanics and techniques of creative non-fiction requires patience and practice. If you are willing to try out the techniques, they will take your narrative from flatline to fantastic, your characters from uninteresting to fascinating, and help you write a book that other interested researchers will actually read.

Chapter 13

Creating Your Own Style Guide

Styles vary from newspaper to newspaper, magazine to magazine, and publisher to publisher. There is no one, all-encompassing style guide. There are a few stylistic conventions you may want to conform to because they are what readers will expect, and, usually, because the style helps reading comprehension. The final decisions, however, are up to you.

The purpose of creating your own style guide is to save time while you are writing the first draft and later when you edit. Create a file or a hand-written list that you can keep handy as you write to record each style decision you make as you make it. That way, you can adhere to your style guide as the book progresses.

Industry Style Guides

The two most used style guides are William Strunk & E.B. White's, *The Elements of Style* (or William Strunk Jr.'s *The Elements of Style, 2014*) and *The Chicago Manual of Style, 16th Edition*. There are dozens of other style guides available, most of which are designed for students, business writing, technical writing or other specific purposes.

Evidence Explained by Elizabeth Shown Mills is a source citation guide not a style guide for the body of the manuscript. You may choose to use her style guide for your footnotes or endnotes, or not.

If you have no experience with formatting a manuscript, you may want to jump ahead and read the four chapters on typesetting to get an idea of what conventions to follow during the production stage before you create styles that conflict with what will make the book look its best and read easiest.

Abbreviations and Acronyms

Use abbreviations to avoid incessant repetition of long expressions. If you abbreviate, be consistent and provide the reader with a key to the abbreviations in the front matter.

Common abbreviations in a genealogy are: born (b.), christened (chr.), married (m.), divorced (div.), died (d.) and buried (bd.). These abbreviations are fine where you are giving the details of a person's life in a short paragraph. Depending upon what your subject is, you may wish to use these abbreviations. In the narrative or explanatory text, however, it may be better to spell out the words. You will not be saving a tremendous amount of typing or space by not doing so, and abbreviations may seem odd or worse, may cause confusion.

Acronyms, on the other hand, are expected. NASA is a good example. Few people will misidentify NASA as something other than the National Aeronautic and Space Administration. For most acronyms there is no need for punctuation between the letters—so NASA, not N.A.S.A. As with abbreviations, if you create acronyms that are not familiar to the reader, use the full name in the text first, followed by the acronym in parentheses. In some cases, you may want to use the full name a few times so that the reader becomes familiar with the name before switching to an acronym. For example: Rocky Mountain & Overland Stagecoach Company (RM&OS Co.) Include the acronym in your list of abbreviations and acronyms in the front matter.

Genealogical Charts

Whether or not you use genealogical charts, is entirely dependent upon your subject matter. For the most part, I consider genealogical charts as images rather than text, but I include them here because they can help readers become familiar with the relationships between people at a glance.

Genealogical charts do not have to be uniform throughout the book, but should be consistent enough in appearance and content that the reader can find roughly the same information in each. In other words, do not use a four-generation pedigree chart on one page, and a ten-generation linear chart on the next.

Numbering Systems

Numbering systems are necessary for a genealogy to help readers understand relationships. In a how-to or instructional guide, use them if the explanation warrants a clear understanding of the relationships between individuals.

Use the Ahnentafel numbering system to go backward in time (ancestors) and the register-style numbering system to come forward in time (descendants). The modified register-style used by the National Genealogical Society Quarterly is also acceptable.

Most genealogical software will generate descendants or ancestors lists for you. If you are not using genealogical software, consult *Genealogical Writing in the 21st Century: A Guide to Register Style and More* by Henry B. Hoff, or *Dollarhide Numbering for Genealogists—An Authorized Guide for the Serious User* by Brian R. Smith.

Place Names

Place names may or may not be an issue in your specialty. If they are, keep in mind the readers who may not be as familiar with the place as you are. In a genealogy, for example, readers would expect to see place names spelled out in their entirety, such as Stanley Township, Lyon County, Minnesota, United States. In a book about finding original source materials in a single county, you may not need to spell the full names out.

If you use simple place names in a narrative, however—for clarity—include full details of each place in footnotes or endnotes, or in an appendix in the back matter. Include city (or township), county, state and country *as they existed* at the time you are describing in the narrative.

If all locations are within the same country, however, you may indicate that fact somewhere at the beginning of the appendix or place names list, so that you do not have to repeat United States (or other country names) in each listing.

Spell checking place names can be challenging, but necessary. If in doubt, keep a geographical atlas handy while you are writing or get the place name from a good online map site, such as Google Maps or Bing Maps.

Most publishers use the Anglicized names of non-U.S. places when books are written in English because Anglicized names may be more familiar to the reader. How you wish to handle place names, both in the narrative and a place names list, is up to you. However, if a place name would be difficult for an English-speaker to recognize in the native language, give reference to both the local version and the Anglicized version. There are some locations (many in Eastern Europe) that have changed hands and languages a number of times for which you may want to give the reader an idea of the time period a place held one name, and when the name changed.

Names

The following are a few considerations if you must include names in your how-to or instructional guide:

Spellings

Surnames, in particular, have been known to change over time, or even within close families depending upon individual preference. Sometimes, a name change requires explanation either within the narrative or in a footnote or endnote. If you use a common or single spelling, even though documentary evidence suggests alternatives, explain that somewhere.

Name Changes

When people changed their names entirely, more often than not, an explanation within the narrative will be necessary. A cross reference in the index and any other list of names would be helpful, as well.

Nicknames

It is fine to use a person's nickname in the narrative if a nickname was the only name that person ever used. And, it is fine to use a formal name as well as a nickname if friends used nicknames, but parents and other relatives used another, as long as you make it clear. Include the nickname in the index and other lists of names, as well.

Women's Names

In the narrative, a woman should be referred to by the name she would have used at the time she appears in the story. In the index and other lists of names, include both maiden and married names. If a maiden name is unknown, you may want to use a symbol such as "(—)" to inform the reader. The following are examples of ways to list women's names:

> Mary Jane Robertson (nee Smith)
> Mary Jane (Smith) Robertson
> Mary Jane Smith Robertson

Prefixes or Titles

There may be occasions within the narrative when you want to use Mr., Mrs., or Miss; or a title such as Reverend (Rev.) or Doctor (Dr.) as a prefix to a person's name. Prefixes are helpful to the reader when gender is not obvious from the name. Miss Leslie Gore would have a clearer meaning than simply Leslie Gore without other context. Use titles only after the individual earned the title, thus a high-school aged Martin Luther King would not hold the title of Reverend.

If you abbreviate, be consistent. The abbreviations for mister and missus are well-enough known that they need not be included in your list of abbreviations. Reverend (Rev.) and Doctor (Dr.) are well understood, as are most military ranks. If you have any doubts, include the abbreviation in your list.

Suffixes

Suffixes within the narrative can help distinguish one person from the other. Common suffixes are Sr., Jr., a roman numeral (such as III or IV), Esq., MD or M.D. (doctor), PhD or Ph.D. and DDS or D.D.S. (dentist). Some style guides use punctuation in suffixes, others do not.

Business Names

Business names, in general, should be listed however the business uses its own name. So, if the firm of Blanding & Fell, Inc., uses the abbreviation for incorporation after its name, so should you. If, at some point, you choose to abbreviate an unfamiliar business name, use the full name enough times in the narrative for readers to become familiar with it. In academic writing, it is acceptable to use the name once followed by the abbreviation in parentheses and never use the formal name again throughout the work. Readers may be frustrated, however, at having to remember an unfamiliar business name by its abbreviation.

Dates

The genealogical convention for dates is to use the day (expressed in numbers) followed by the month (spelled out or abbreviated) followed by a four-digit year, such as 24 March 1900 or 24 Mar 1900. The reason for this is clarity. There is no mistaking whether someone is using the American-style Month/Day/Year or the European-style Day/Month/Year. Looking at 9/3/26 leaves readers wondering whether that date is the 9th of March or the 3rd of September and in the 26th year, but of what century?

In narratives, the most common date style is month (spelled out or abbreviated), day (expressed in numbers), followed by a comma, and a four-digit year, such as March 24, 1900, or Mar 24, 1900. Written dates may read better if they are given the way they would be spoken, such as March 24th, 1900.

If you include dates where a change from the Julian Calendar to the Gregorian Calendar will cause confusion, show original dates followed by new dates in brackets or some other way to set them off (e.g. September 2, 1752 [September 14, 1752]).

Numbers

There are long-established rules for numbers that do not occur within dates. These rules are not hard and fast, although most publishers stick to the rules. Spell out numbers one through ten. You may use roman numerals for numbers 11 and greater. Similarly, centuries earlier than the tenth are spelled out (e.g. eighth century), but after the tenth, you may choose between spelled out or numerals (e.g. nineteenth century or 19th century) as long as you are consistent.

If two numbers appear in the same sentence referring to the same subject, follow the same rule. For example: "The glacier advances approximately one and a half inches per month or eighteen inches per year." And not, "The glacier advances approximately one and a half inches per month, or 18 inches per year."

When numbers occur next to each other, use a style that makes them easiest to read. For example: "He hauled 106 fifteen-foot boards" rather than "He hauled 106 15' boards."

When numbers begin a sentence, either spell them out or re-word the sentence to place the number later in the sentence. This is especially true if the number is large. For example: "Twenty-thousand four hundred and fifty-one people voted in the territorial election," would read better as, "In the territorial election, 20,451 people voted."

Captions

Every image should carry a caption identifying who or what is in the image, who owns the image and any permissions granted to use the image. The exception to this is if all of the images come from a single collection. In that case, use the caption to identify the subject of the image, but only the first image in the book need include name of the collection and any permissions granted. Another option is to create a list of permissions or credits and place those in the back matter. The captions, however, should stay with the photograph.

In Quotes or Italics?

Conventional style guides put the titles of articles, short stories and poems in quotes, but the titles of books, plays, magazines, newspapers, films, television programs, major musical compositions, and epic poems in italics. Use italics for foreign words or phrases, and if unfamiliar to your readers, explain them in a glossary. Use italics for the names of ships, aircraft, and space vehicles, as well.

Footnotes or Endnotes

Make a decision about how you will handle the placement of source citations, in footnotes or endnotes, before you begin writing. Most word processing software makes it easy to create either. The important consideration is what you feel will be easiest for your readers.

A suggestion: although footnotes provide instant access to a citation or supplemental information, if your footnotes could squeeze the main text down to less than half the real estate on the page, use endnotes. Most readers are more interested in what happens next than background information or explanation, and will ignore the footnotes anyway.

※

Style guides have evolved over time, but their purpose is to help readers understand the text. For the most part, following established style guides is in your book's best interest, although there is room for your personal preferences.

Chapter 14

Writing a First Draft

The process of writing a first draft is different for each writer. Some prefer to get the entire book down on paper before going back to edit. Others tackle one section at a time until it shapes up. Proceed in whatever way makes the most sense to you. However, avoid fiddling and fussing with a single section so much that the thought of finishing the book becomes overwhelming.

Set Up Your Manuscript Files

Before you do anything else, set up your book in chapters so that your entire manuscript is not in one enormous file. It will be easier to work with smaller files. If you want feedback from others, you can send a small file at a time, and when you get ready to lay the book out in its final form, you will have all of the parts assembled in a way that makes creating the book easy.

To set up my manuscript files, I use a file-naming convention that lets the computer organize the files for me. I divide the book into front matter (FM), parts (P), chapters (CH) and back matter (BM).

The numbers preceding the file names are split up into front matter, body, and back matter. The front matter files all begin with 00_. Because there are parts in addition to chapters, Part 1 and the chapters within that part are given a file starting number of 10_. Part 2 starts with 20_, and so on. The back matter files start with 60_ because there are only five parts preceding the back matter.

An abbreviated file names list for this book would look like:

001FM_Title Page/Copyrights
002FM_Dedication
...

101P01_Getting Started
102CH1_Who Needs This Book?
...
201P02_Before You Write
202CH6_Identifying Your Target Market
...
301P03_Writing
302CH12_Engaging While Explaining
...
401P04_Production
402CH16_Creating a Page Layout
...
501P05_Marekting
502CH23_Creating a Marketing Plan
...
601BM_Conclusion
602BM_About the Author
...

Wait to Add Images

If you add images to the manuscript files, they can become quite large, especially if you are adding the images in the correct size and resolution for printing. To save time, wait to add images until you are finished editing. If you need to give yourself a reminder of what image goes where, put the image name in brackets next to the appropriate text (e.g. [auto_ca1903.jpg]).

Learn a Few Word Processing Features

A few features in word processing programs can make your writing life easier if you take the time to learn them. Most word processing software has customizable features. Use the help guide in your word processing software to determine how to enable the following functions.

Track Changes

Enabling the Track Changes feature will allow you to show your manuscript to an editor, who can type their suggested changes directly into the document. You then have the option of accepting the changes you want and ignoring the ones you do not without any re-typing.

Customize AutoCorrect

If you find it annoying to type the same information repeatedly, you can set up a command that will automatically fill in the blank as you start typing. For example, if you must repeat the expression, "Clifton Forge, Alleghany County, Virginia," you could set up an AutoCorrect command to replace "Clift" with the full name of the city, county and state.

Customize AutoText

Most word processing programs allow you to build a gallery of frequently typed text or frequently inserted images (such as a logo or an icon), so that a simple combination of a function key and a letter will automatically add the text or image to your document.

Build a Custom Dictionary

If you use foreign words or have names that incorrectly trigger AutoCorrect or the squiggly red line of Spell Check, add them to the dictionary as you use them to save time spell checking later. I have managed to teach Microsoft Word to respect the iTunes company name even when the little "i" begins a sentence.

Use the Synonym Finder

If you are searching for a word and cannot come up with the perfect expression to convey your meaning, type a word with a similar meaning, then right-click on the word to activate the synonym finder for suggestions.

Find/Replace

Inevitably, I find mistakes in my manuscripts that could use a good, global Find and Replace, such as double spaces where only one was needed, the persistent misspelling of a name, or an incorrect use of a font or a feature. Each of these can be found and replaced using the Find/Replace feature in your software. In fact, you can replace text with other text, an icon or an image by using the characters "^c" in the replace field. This function grabs whatever you copied into the clipboard and places it into the manuscript.

Preliminary Fact Checking

For most professional book projects, fact checking is a part of the editing. You can save yourself time and frustration, however, if you take a critical look over your outline before you create a detailed outline for the entire book (see below).

The best reason to fact check before you create a detailed outline is perspective. A detailed outline forces you to take a closeup look at information. To catch major errors, look at the bigger, broader picture.

Once you begin writing, if you have doubts about any detail, stop and check before you continue. It is much easier to correct a few details in your outline, than it is to rewrite.

Create a Detailed Outline

Most writers benefit from a detailed outline. It will help you remember details from your research and keep you from wandering off onto tangents that do not fit the book as a whole. Also, it will give you an easy way to skip ahead a bit if you get stuck.

If your preliminary outline has enough detail for you to begin writing, then great, get started. If not, add whatever you need to the outline to write each section in an easy-to-follow way.

If You Get Stuck, Get Help

Undertaking a how-to or instructional guide is an incredible task, even for experienced or professional writers who have an abundance of people with similar experience to ask for help if the writing bogs down. For those with less experience, it may take a good coach marking up a chapter or two before you can see your own errors or mis-communications clearly. If you become stuck or frustrated, banish any thoughts of abandoning the project and get help.

Attend a Writing Class

Most communities have extension learning courses where adults can take classes. Many local governments, senior services, universities, colleges and community colleges offer extension classes. If you can find a class on writing non-fiction, fantastic. More likely, you will find writing courses on specific topics such as travel or business writing, which also demands clear, logical presentation, so a course in business writing may be helpful.

Hire a Writing Coach

While you are searching through the extension learning catalogs for your area, look at who are teaching the courses. You may be able to find a writing coach by contacting an instructor. Look at the faculty of your local schools, as well. You may find an excellent writing coach in the local high school English department.

Join a Writer's Group

Most writer's groups are aimed at fiction writers. That does not mean you cannot get good, constructive criticism from a fiction-based writer's group, but if you can find other writers who are working on how-to or instructional guides where clean, concise communication is the objective, you are more likely to get the kind of help that will be the most beneficial to you.

Most writer's groups will allow prospective members to attend a few meetings without contributing any writing to observe how the group works. Do so. A meeting or two will give you a feel for how constructive the criticism is and whether the group will be able to give you good advice.

I have a Facebook group called Genealogical Writers and Publishers (www.facebook.com/groups/187826861370278/). Come on in. Ask your questions. Perhaps someone in the group will have a great idea for you.

I have mentioned previously that showing your work to friends or family has potential pitfalls, and I will reiterate that sentiment here. Friends and family members who are not writers tend to fall into two groups—those who do not want to hurt your feelings, and those who do. I must warn you that some people who attend writing classes, coach writers and join writer's groups fall into the same categories.

You need neither obsequious nor domineering critics. If you encounter them, find another way to get help. What you need are honest critics with good intentions, and enough humility to let the good critics guide your writing without diminishing your enthusiasm for the project. Frankly, if you can listen to good criticism of your work and boldly return to the computer the next day to make necessary changes, I have no doubt you will finish your book.

✷

The only thing left to do is to start writing.

Chapter 15

Editing Your Manuscript

Professional editing benefits most books. Unfortunately, professional editing is expensive. If you are going to invest in editing—even if you trade editing projects with another how-to writer—edit the manuscript yourself first, to catch any obvious errors and to make the manuscript the best it can be before you turn it over.

Professional editing addresses a manuscript first from the big, broad strokes (the themes, context, and organization) before looking at the finer details (spelling, punctuation, fact checking and typographical errors). While you edit your own work, you should do the same.

Context Editing

When a professional editor takes on a manuscript for the first time, the initial read through should reveal whether the book feels like a single entity or whether there are loose ends that need to be clipped or re-worked.

Does the manuscript reflect your focus for the project? Have you maintained the scope and audience you intended? Or have you strayed into tangents? Straying is easy, especially if the additional information is interesting. Bringing the focus back to the original intent, however, may tighten up the book and make it feel more coherent overall.

Did you focus too narrowly? Did you intend to write to write for other experts and instead wrote for beginners? If that is the case, your focus changed while writing. If the book feels complete as is, fine as long as you adjust your description of the book to let the audience know who the book will help most.

Examine your literary crutches. Have you overused any techniques, such as bullet points? It is not uncommon for writers to develop a method of introducing elements into an explanation in a way that is easiest at first, but becomes a habit over time. When the technique serves the material well, it is fine. Giving a critical eye to your own habits is hard but will improve your explanations and your book.

Is your meaning clear? Determining whether readers will understand what you wrote, is the part of context editing that may be difficult for you to address yourself. You have the benefit of much more knowledge than the reader because of the entire body of your research. Readers cannot know what you *meant* to write. They have only the words on the page to make sense of the information.

Is the book organized logically? Ask yourself whether there is anything about the way the information is organized or told that will confuse readers? This is another area you may have difficulty judging. As you read, you can fill in holes with independent knowledge. It may not be as obvious to you that an element is missing as it would be to a reader.

If you are unsure, put the manuscript aside and read it again later. Inconsistencies may become more apparent with a little distance.

When context editing, set the font to a size that is comfortable for you to read, and use margins of an inch or more so that you have room to write notes while you read. Take your manuscript file to the local copy shop and have it printed on both sides of each page, and spiral bound. Even though the book will not be formatted or bound as it will be for final production, it will give you a sense of how the book reads.

If the manuscript requires changes, make them before you move to the next stage of editing.

Content Editing

Content editing is about making certain you wrote what you meant. Author and editor William Zinsser describes it as, "stripping down every sentence to its cleanest components." I like to describe it as making sure every sentence conveys your meaning and sounds like you wrote it.

I do not think a how-to or instructional guide must be written with such strict adherence to literary and grammatical rules that it comes out sounding like Leo Tolstoy wrote it. However, deleting the clutter, making meaning clear, assuring subjects and verbs agree, keeping to the active not passive voice when appropriate, and using clear, concise explanations will make your book better.

The content editing stage is also where you evaluate whether you have given some subjects too much attention (overkill). If you find long explanations, break them up. Turn essential elements into bullet points.

There are some situations that are so obvious they need no explanation. If you have explained what should be common knowledge or common sense, eliminate it. Admittedly, cutting good writing is difficult. Deleting words or phrases you have struggled to put down on the page can be painful. However, if a slimmer, sleeker version serves the explanation better, cut away.

If, on the other hand, you find areas that are dull or confusing, re-write them to give them more impact. The goal, remember, is not just to write. It is to explain the subject in a way that makes readers turn the pages. "Rewriting isn't bitter medicine, it's professional awareness," writes Kathleen Krull in her book, *12 Keys to Writing Books that Sell*. While you may not be a professional writer, I am sure you want your book to be as well-written and eagerly read as possible.

Look for redundancies. Do you use the same word again and again in the same paragraph? Are there repetitious elements? Have you explained the same issue more than once? It happens, and not infrequently over a long manuscript. Content editing is a chance to eliminate the excess.

Look for contradictions. In a how-to, it is not unusual to have contradictions because there may be more than one way to accomplish a task or achieve the same goal. Look for those areas and make two sets of instructions rather than muddling one with exception after exception.

When you are ready to edit for content, print your manuscript. Errors and contradictions are more obvious on paper than on the computer screen. Double space your manuscript so that it will be easy to make corrections between the lines. Print it single-sided on three-hole-punch paper, so you can remove a small section at a time from a binder, to edit. Make any changes necessary before moving on to copy editing.

Copy Editing

I promised no death by grammar, but the copy editing stage is when you *should* closely examine your words.

Have you mixed your metaphors, or used the active voice when a passive construction would be clearer? Have you let commas or exclamation points run amok? Have you used parallel construction in compound sentences and bulleted lists? Have any malapropisms slipped in? Do subjects and verbs agree, and have you used pronouns properly without muddling the meaning?

Have you followed your style sheet? Do dates conform? Are names spelled the way you intended throughout the book? Are abbreviations and acronyms consistent? Are sources cited appropriately?

Copy editing is what author Guy Kawasaki, in his book *APE: Author, Publisher, Entrepreneur—How to Publish a Book,* describes as "turning an amateurish book into a polished, professional one."

One of my favorite resources is *The Copyeditor's Handbook: A Guide for Book Publishing and Corporate Communications* by Amy Einsohn. She gives easy-to-read explanations for the most common grammatical errors and problems. Before you begin copy editing, you may want to consult this book.

The following software will check grammar, word use and suggest changes:

- Grammarly (www.grammarly.com)
- Hemingway App (www.hemingwayapp.com)
- StyleWriter (www.stylewriter-usa.com)

While context and content editing take time, for me, copy editing is a chore. In fact, my house is never cleaner than during the copy editing stage because even cleaning out the garage can look like a lark, by comparison.

Steel yourself. Print out the manuscript double spaced, single sided on three-hole-punched paper so you can pull out a small section at a time from a binder. Set up a comfortable chair and table on which to spread out your style guide, a good dictionary, and a copy editing reference, or your laptop if you prefer Internet-based guides. I give you permission to stay in your jammies, drink as much coffee as you require, and consume an entire box of chocolates if need be.

Fact Checking

If you misstate facts, someone will notice and take issue with it. Errors not only cast doubt on other facts within the book, they diminish your relationship with your readers, especially in the case where you are writing about your own expertise. Not every reader will notice every error, mind you, but if you can catch the errors before readers have a chance to, why not?

Some writers will fact check while copy editing. I cannot. I prefer to have the language in tip top shape before I crawl through every date, place and event in the book for accuracy. I will correct errors as I catch them, however, in whatever stage of editing it happens.

The most common errors that sneak into historical and genealogical subjects are:

Wrong Dates

In particular, look for places where the century was mis-typed. A person cannot die in 1919 and be born in 1956. Not many people live past one hundred, let alone more than one hundred and ten. Watch for dates that make a lifespan highly improbable.

Wrong Places

Arkansas is not abbreviated as AK. Abbreviations tend to be misused much more often than actual place names. However, look for places where the same city is listed in different counties, or the same counties are listed in different states. A change of boundaries can lead to the circumstance above, but make sure there is an explanation so that the reader does not assume you made an error.

Improbable Events

Look for events that were unlikely to have happened. Not many soldiers enlisted at the age of nine. If it happened and you have documentary evidence of it, fantastic. Look for women having children before or after their child-bearing years, and children attributed to women who have already died or not yet married their husbands. These children are most probably the result of a different marriage.

John Colletta tells the story of the letter he received from an ornithologist who read Colletta's book, *Only a Few Bones: A True Account of the Rolling Fork Tragedy and Its Aftermath*. The ornithologist took issue with the description of starlings in the book, explaining that starlings were not introduced into the area until later. An incorrect fact about something as easy to gloss over as the presence of a specific species of bird, damaged the credibility of the book for that reader.

Graphic Elements

I usually wait until I have a manuscript in its best shape before I add images. Some writers prefer to see the images with the text as they write, and I appreciate that. If you have done so, great. If you have not, whether you add them now before a final proofread or as a part of your final draft, is up to you.

During the discussion of scanning in Chapter 8: Scanning and Optical Character Recognition, I made a suggestion that you scan each image at a size and resolution big enough for print production. One thing that is hard to determine at this stage, however, is the exact size you will need based upon the layout you will choose for the final book. Chapter 16: Creating a Page Layout will cover this.

Another consideration is whether you will create an eBook version because the size and resolution, as well as where the images are placed within an eBook, are different than for a print edition.

The best time-saving advice I can give you is to leave the images out until the manuscript is as close to perfect as it is ever going to be. That way, you can make a copy of the manuscript to be used for an eBook version and another for the print edition because the images will be placed into the manuscript in different ways. In addition, I usually leave one copy of the completed manuscript alone as a backup, and work from copies to create final eBook and print editions.

Once images are added in their appropriate size, resolution and placement for as many editions are you are planning, you can proofread the captions, copyrights and permissions that go along with the images.

Proofreading

I am sure you must be thinking, "I have just edited a half a dozen times, and now I have to proofread?" Well, yes. Every time you make changes to the manuscript, you introduce the possibility that an error crept in.

While spell check and grammar editors are helpful tools, there is nothing like a fresh set of eyes to catch the errors that software-based tools cannot. Your word processor will not alert you if you typed lack, when you meant lake.

Proofreading is a task that you could hand over to a paid professional or someone who is well-read. Make your instructions clear, however that you are asking for proofreading, not editorial advice.

Many proofreaders read each page starting at the bottom so that they are looking at snippets of sentences rather than whole passages. Misspellings are easier to spot this way. The misuse of words is easier to spot, however when reading in context.

If you hand over a printed copy to proof, ask your proofreader to use a red pen, common proofreader's marks, and to place a small "x" in the margin wherever a change has been made. You will find a nice chart of proofreader's marks on the Merriam-Webster website (www.merriam-webster.com/mw/table/proof-rea.htm). A more efficient method, however, is to use the review features of your word processor (e.g. Track Changes in Word) so that your proofreader can type directly into a copy of the manuscript file, and so you can accept or reject any changes with the click of a mouse.

Typescript Editing

The next stage in the publishing process is production, where you will typeset (format) the manuscript. It is not unusual for errors to creep in during the typesetting process. Typescript editing is one final chance to make changes. It occurs after the manuscript has been typeset or laid out as an eBook, and is described more fully in Chapter 22: Preparing the Final Files.

Making changes to the typescript can be problematic. It is frustrating to have to re-work perfect-looking pages to correct a misused word or phrase, and if a professional typesets your manuscript, changes can be expensive.

∝∝

Every manuscript can use a good edit. There are many people who can catch typos for you, fewer who can fact check, and even fewer who can conduct a professional edit while giving constructive advice. Professional editors are good at what they do, and charge accordingly. If your book is likely to appeal to the general public and therefore generate thousands of sales, you may wish to invest in professional editing before you release the book.

Working with an Editor

Editors help authors express what they mean. Editors know when to stick to the rules and when to break them. They look for consistency and fix muddled meaning. Most books benefit from professional editing, but a good editor can be expensive. Editors offer a range of services similar to the styles of editing described above. The more comprehensive the edit, the greater the cost.

Cost

Most editors charge either by the page or by the hour. The more experienced the editor, the more the hourly rate makes sense. Ask for an estimate based upon the number of pages in the final manuscript on standard paper with normal margins, double-spaced. An editor usually will want to see the table of contents and at least a chapter or two prior to giving you an estimate.

Portfolio

Most editors will be able to point you to commercially available work they have edited, and will have chapters or article-length pieces ready to show you.

Expectations

It is important for both you and the editor to make expectations clear in the beginning. Ask for what the book needs. The job and the cost of proofreading are different than content or context editing. Some editors do not proofread. They specialize in the bigger picture and will leave the proofreading or fact checking to others.

If you are asking for a more comprehensive edit, most editors will offer to edit a chapter to give you an idea of the editor's style before you give the go-ahead.

Personal Style

Good editors will tell you what you *need* to hear rather than what you *want* to hear about your work. That part of the job is not easy. Your editor should offer criticism in a way that will inspire you to make changes for the good of the book. He or she will never belittle or undermine your confidence. If you run into an editor who consistently rubs you the wrong way, find another editor.

Professional Style

The most common conflict between authors and editors is stylistic. No editor and author will write exactly the same way. Editors do not have the final say in what stays or goes in your manuscript, you do. Most editors will not suggest changes that alter your writing style without good reason. A good editor, when confronting stylistic problems, will stop the editing process and consult you before proceeding. There may be instances where your style conflicts enough with the editor's that choosing a different editor is best. A good editor will recognize this and tell you.

Be open to suggestion, however. Editors edit. They are going to make changes. Read the changes with an open mind, and if need be, leave it alone for a few days, and come back for a fresh look. A good editor wants you to be successful. He or she is making suggestions in the best interest of the manuscript.

Give the editor your best work. Run the spelling and grammar check. Use proper capitalization and punctuation. Give the book a good once-over before you give it to your editor.

Communication

Communication is a two-way street. If you hear feedback that does not make sense or hurts your feelings, say so. Misunderstandings have ruined many an author-editor relationship. If you have a question, ask. If you do not like the direction things are going, say so. Keep frustration between you and your editor private. Leave it out of your Twitter feed and off of your Facebook page. Spouting off in public will not end well.

Follow the Instructions

Most editors have a process. Give the manuscript to your editor in the form they prefer and follow the instructions for accepting or rejecting changes. The goal is to get the manuscript back to you in the fewest number of complete edits to keep costs down. If you make changes during the initial edit, for example, each section you change must be re-edited as a part of the whole. Anything that slows down the process, raises the cost.

Deadlines

Both you and your editor have schedules and deadlines to meet. Be realistic when setting deadlines to make certain you can both meet them. Giving an editor a month with your manuscript is a starting point. And, your book may be competing with others for time in the editor's schedule.

Write a Formal Proposal or Contract

Once you have a cost estimate from the editor, write an additional proposal making your expectations clear about the work to be done as well as deadlines for submissions, returns, and payment. Expect to pay half down, and half upon completion. Include how you will send the manuscript, receive changes, and communicate with the editor. Include all charges and fees, as well as a do-not-exceed clause if you want the editor to stick within a defined budget.

A Less-Costly Alternative

Some authors crowdsource the editing. They put the manuscript up online, ask readers for feedback and require that no one distribute the book. I like this idea for a non-fiction or a how-to book, but crowdsourcing may work best in the early stages of planning while you are still gathering ideas. Beware, also, the potential pitfalls. You may get stellar advice, or you may get drivel—and the drivel is often mean-spirited.

∾∾∾

I often feel triumphant when finishing a manuscript. Unfortunately, triumph fades when the shadow of editing looms. Be kind to yourself in the first round of editing. Read the book through and put it away for a few days. Then, return to editing with a critical eye and a red pen to benefit the book.

SECTION 4

The goal in this section is for you to learn how to produce a book that looks as good and reads as easily as any book produced by a traditional publisher.

There is not enough space in this book to give instructions for formatting using each of the major word processing or page layout programs. The terminology used in this section, however, should give you what you need to use the help features in your software to accomplish each task.

Most of this Section is devoted to print production because most how-tos or instructional guides are printed. If you are interested in producing an electronic or online version of your book, there is information about those formats in Chapter 22: Preparing the Final Files, or a more comprehensive look at the process is available in *Set Yourself Up to Self-Publish: A Genealogist's Guide*.

Baby Steps

If you are not familiar with your software and you are not interested in learning how to lay out the interior of your book, there are templates you can download from the Internet, or you can engage the services of a typesetter or book packager (more on this in Chapter 17). These services will also help you ready your images for print at the right size and resolution.

Many of the print-on-demand printers offer templates or there are templates for sale at sites such as Joel Friedlander's Book Design Templates (www.bookdesigntemplates.com). Even if you employ a template, it is still up to you to make sure the final product looks as good as it should.

Next Steps

A template is not right for every book, and you may want more flexibility to make your book look just right. If you can master the page layout basics (Chapter 16), choose appropriate fonts, set up paragraphs correctly, and avoid widows and orphans (Chapter 17), you will be well on your way to a professional-looking book layout.

Giant Leaps

If you want your book to be the best it can be, to pass muster with even the pickiest of critics, then you must learn the remaining rules for page layouts and typesetting (Chapters 16–20). And if you have gone this far, you may as well learn how to create a stunning book cover (Chapter 21), and to prepare the final files for the printer (Chapter 22).

Note: In this section you will see examples that are filled with text beginning, "Lorem ipsum." Latin text is used as filler so that you can see how different layouts would look.

Chapter 16

Creating a Page Layout

The most important element in laying out a page for print is to make the page easy to read. A poorly or unusually designed book may make your readers skeptical of the quality of the information. Too much work goes into researching your subject and writing a book to have that effort spoiled by poor design, when good design is so easy to accomplish.

The best way to create a good page layout design is to follow the long-established rules of readability. Desktop publishing offers many options for innovative ways to create columns, employ fonts, and place illustrations—too many perhaps. Leave the wild innovating to the graphic designers on magazine staffs. The tried and true rules for book design are still the best.

Page Size

How much real estate you have to work with depends upon the trim size of the page. The trim size is the finished size of the book. Choosing a trim size pits look against cost, and usability. A 12" x 12" coffee table book is fabulous to look at, but a 6" x 9" book is much easier to sit and read.

An offset printer can create books in just about any size, but you must order a minimum number of books to make the price per book worth it. If the cost of setup for a run of specially sized books is $500 and the print-per-book charge is $20, if you only order 10 books, the cost per book would be $70 ($50 + $20).

You will save money if you choose one of the common page sizes offered by print-on-demand printers. Most print-on-demand printers do not charge a fee for setup, they only charge to produce each book—and they can produce books one at a time. The most common page sizes for print-on-demand printers are (in inches) 6 x 9, 7 x 10 and 8.5 x 11.

No matter what page size you choose, the rules for good layout are essentially the same. The one small exception is that the larger the page, the larger proportionally the elements such as fonts, white space and images should be.

Page Count

Book interiors must be multiples of two (front and back of a single sheet). If you use an offset printer, they may require page counts in signatures (multiples) of 4, 8, 16, 32, 48, 64 or even 80. Offset printers print use paper on rolls many feet wide, and when the paper is folded and cut, it will form a signature of one of the multiples of four (4).

Signatures can be an issue if, for example, you have written a one hundred-page book, but the printer's signature requirement is eighty pages. In that case, you would have to reduce your book by twenty pages, or increase it by sixty pages in order to meet the signature requirement. Otherwise, you would have sixty blank pages at the end of your one hundred-page book.

Luckily, print-on-demand printers use simple two-page signatures—front and back.

Blank Pages

By publishing tradition, chapters and most front matter and back matter elements, should begin on a right-hand page. You may have blank pages if a chapter runs an odd number of pages because the last page will be blank so that the next element will begin on a right-hand page.

If you have blank pages, they should be completely blank—no headers and no page numbers.

White Space

The biggest misconception about laying out a book is that you must economize the space by cramming as much as you can onto a single page. Please do not. The reader needs a break from solid text either from the margins around the edges, the space between columns, paragraphs, words, and letters, or all of the above.

Altering the spacing between the letters (tracking) and the space between the lines of text (leading) can make the page look more or less dense. If you want to make the page look a little less dense or dark, use a book font such as Bookman because it is wider and more open, rather than a newspaper font such as Times which is thin and meant to be read in narrow newspaper columns. By increasing the space between the lines of text (leading) or between the paragraphs, the page will look less dense. In the example, the page on the left looks dense. The one on the right is much more open.

While giving the page white space, you must also follow the rules governing proximity. Proximity means that objects that belong together should be closer

Lorem ipsum dolor sit amet, consectetur adipisicing elit, sed do eiusmod tempor incididunt ut labore et dolore magna aliqua. Ut enim ad minim veniam, quis nostrud exercitation ullamco laboris nisi ut aliquip ex ea commodo consequat. Duis aute irure dolor in reprehenderit in voluptate velit esse cillum dolore eu fugiat nulla pariatur. Excepteur sint occaecat cupidatat non proident, sunt in culpa qui officia deserunt mollit anim id est laborum.

Lorem ipsum dolor sit amet, consectetur adipisicing elit, sed do eiusmod tempor incididunt ut labore et dolore magna aliqua. Ut enim ad minim veniam, quis nostrud exercitation ullamco laboris nisi ut aliquip ex ea commodo consequat. Duis aute irure dolor in reprehenderit in voluptate velit esse cillum dolore eu fugiat nulla pariatur. Excepteur sint occaecat cupidatat non proident, sunt in culpa qui officia deserunt mollit anim id est laborum.

Lorem ipsum dolor sit amet, consectetur adipisicing elit, sed do eiusmod tempor incididunt ut labore et dolore magna aliqua. Ut enim ad minim veniam, quis nostrud exercitation ullamco laboris nisi ut aliquip ex ea commodo consequat. Duis aute irure dolor in reprehenderit in voluptate velit esse cillum dolore eu fugiat nulla pariatur. Excepteur sint occaecat cupidatat non proident, sunt in culpa qui officia deserunt mollit anim id est laborum.

Lorem ipsum dolor sit amet, consectetur adipisicing elit, sed do eiusmod tempor incididunt ut labore et dolore magna aliqua. Ut enim ad minim veniam, quis nostrud exercitation ullamco laboris nisi ut aliquip ex ea commodo consequat. Duis aute irure dolor in reprehenderit in voluptate velit esse cillum dolore eu fugiat nulla pariatur. Excepteur sint occaecat cupidatat non proident, sunt in culpa qui officia deserunt mollit anim id est laborum.

Lorem ipsum dolor sit amet, consectetur adipisicing elit, sed do eiusmod tempor incididunt ut labore et dolore magna aliqua. Ut

Lorem ipsum dolor sit amet, consectetur adipisicing elit, sed do eiusmod tempor incididunt ut labore et dolore magna aliqua. Ut enim ad minim veniam, quis nostrud exercitation ullamco laboris nisi ut aliquip ex ea commodo consequat. Duis aute irure dolor in reprehenderit in voluptate velit esse cillum dolore eu fugiat nulla pariatur. Excepteur sint occaecat cupidatat non proident, sunt in culpa qui officia deserunt mollit anim id est laborum.

Lorem ipsum dolor sit amet, consectetur adipisicing elit, sed do eiusmod tempor incididunt ut labore et dolore magna aliqua. Ut enim ad minim veniam, quis nostrud exercitation ullamco laboris nisi ut aliquip ex ea commodo consequat. Duis aute irure dolor in reprehenderit in voluptate velit esse cillum dolore eu fugiat nulla pariatur. Excepteur sint occaecat cupidatat non proident, sunt in culpa qui officia deserunt mollit anim id est laborum.

Lorem ipsum dolor sit amet, consectetur adipisicing elit, sed do eiusmod tempor incididunt ut labore et dolore magna aliqua. Ut enim ad minim veniam, quis nostrud exercitation ullamco laboris nisi ut aliquip ex ea commodo consequat. Duis aute irure dolor in reprehenderit in voluptate velit esse cillum dolore eu fugiat nulla pariatur. Excepteur sint occaecat cupidatat non proident, sunt in culpa qui officia deserunt mollit anim id est laborum.

Lorem ipsum dolor sit amet, consectetur adipisicing elit, sed do eiusmod tempor incididunt ut labore et dolore magna aliqua. Ut enim ad minim veniam, quis nostrud exercitation ullamco laboris nisi ut aliquip ex ea commodo consequat. Duis aute irure dolor in reprehenderit in voluptate velit esse cillum dolore eu fugiat nulla

Dense page (left); Less dense (right).

to each other. A caption for a photograph, for example, should be closer to the bottom of the photograph than the next line of text.

Even spacing, between paragraphs or between subheads and paragraphs, is a red flag that the person who designed the layout has little experience. It is easiest in a word processing program to use double returns to separate paragraphs, or to put extra space between a paragraph and the next headline or subhead. Easiest, yes. Most attractive, no. Use styles to create additional space either above or below paragraphs, headlines or subheads without using an extra return. A headline or a subhead should be closer to the text below it than the paragraph above it. In the example on the next page, the type on the left has even spacing. The type on the right has correct spacing.

Page Spreads

Books are laid out in spreads (pages side by side), not individual pages. When a reader opens a book, they see page spreads as a single visual unit. Because of the binding in the center, right and left pages are laid out differently. The rules for what goes on each side of the page spread follows shortly.

Lorem ipsum dolor sit amet, consectetur adipisicing elit, sed do eiusmod tempor incididunt ut labore et dolore magna aliqua. Ut enim ad minim veniam, quis nostrud exercitation ullamco laboris nisi ut aliquip ex ea commodo consequat. Duis aute irure dolor in reprehenderit in voluptate velit esse cillum dolore eu fugiat nulla pariatur. Excepteur sint occaecat cupidatat non proident, sunt in culpa qui officia deserunt mollit anim id est laborum.

Headline Headline Headline

Lorem ipsum dolor sit amet, consectetur adipisicing elit, sed do eiusmod tempor incididunt ut labore et dolore magna aliqua. Ut enim ad minim veniam, quis nostrud exercitation ullamco laboris nisi ut aliquip ex ea commodo consequat. Duis aute irure dolor in reprehenderit in voluptate velit esse cillum dolore eu fugiat nulla pariatur. Excepteur sint occaecat cupidatat non proident, sunt in culpa qui officia deserunt mollit anim id est laborum.

Headline Headline Headline

Lorem ipsum dolor sit amet, consectetur adipisicing elit, sed do eiusmod tempor incididunt ut labore et dolore magna aliqua. Ut enim ad minim veniam, quis nostrud exercitation ullamco laboris nisi ut aliquip ex ea commodo consequat. Duis aute irure dolor in reprehenderit in voluptate velit esse cillum dolore eu fugiat nulla pariatur. Excepteur sint occaecat cupidatat non proident, sunt in culpa qui officia deserunt mollit anim id est laborum.
Lorem ipsum dolor sit amet, consectetur adipisicing elit, sed do eiusmod tempor incididunt ut labore et dolore magna aliqua. Ut enim ad minim veniam, quis nostrud exercitation ullamco laboris

Lorem ipsum dolor sit amet, consectetur adipisicing elit, sed do eiusmod tempor incididunt ut labore et dolore magna aliqua. Ut enim ad minim veniam, quis nostrud exercitation ullamco laboris nisi ut aliquip ex ea commodo consequat. Duis aute irure dolor in reprehenderit in voluptate velit esse cillum dolore eu fugiat nulla pariatur. Excepteur sint occaecat cupidatat non proident, sunt in culpa qui officia deserunt mollit anim id est laborum.

Headline Headline Headline

Lorem ipsum dolor sit amet, consectetur adipisicing elit, sed do eiusmod tempor incididunt ut labore et dolore magna aliqua. Ut enim ad minim veniam, quis nostrud exercitation ullamco laboris nisi ut aliquip ex ea commodo consequat. Duis aute irure dolor in reprehenderit in voluptate velit esse cillum dolore eu fugiat nulla pariatur. Excepteur sint occaecat cupidatat non proident, sunt in culpa qui officia deserunt mollit anim id est laborum.

Headline Headline Headline

Lorem ipsum dolor sit amet, consectetur adipisicing elit, sed do eiusmod tempor incididunt ut labore et dolore magna aliqua. Ut enim ad minim veniam, quis nostrud exercitation ullamco laboris nisi ut aliquip ex ea commodo consequat. Duis aute irure dolor in reprehenderit in voluptate velit esse cillum dolore eu fugiat nulla pariatur. Excepteur sint occaecat cupidatat non proident, sunt in culpa qui officia deserunt mollit anim id est laborum.
Lorem ipsum dolor sit amet, consectetur adipisicing elit, sed do eiusmod tempor incididunt ut labore et dolore magna aliqua. Ut enim ad minim veniam, quis nostrud exercitation ullamco laboris nisi ut aliquip ex ea commodo consequat. Duis aute irure dolor in reprehenderit in voluptate velit esse cillum dolore eu fugiat nulla

Even spacing (left); Correct proximity (right).

Grids

A basic grid pattern imposes order on the layout. Grids align objects and space them properly which is pleasing to the eye. Used throughout, grids employ repetition to help the reader move through the book easily.

Grids help with consistency. For the most part, columns should be the same width and used to help the text fit within the grid. Images should be sized to fit the grid and maintain uniform distance from the text. Grids are determined by margins, columns, and the size of the page. The smaller the page, the fewer columns you can use comfortably before they become too narrow. The larger the page, the more columns you need to keep line lengths short enough to read easily.

In the example, you can see a 3x4 grid on the left-hand page, and a 3x3 grid on the right. Another possibility for smaller pages is a 2x2 grid.

Text can flow across two grid columns as seen on the left-hand page in the example labeled "Filled-in grid," or, an image could fill two grid columns as seen on the right-hand page example. A grid should not limit flexibility, rather, it should bring predictability to the page.

Lines, also called rules or strokes, should be of the same weight whenever they are used, with rare exceptions for emphasis (see Pull Quotes below).

3x4 grid (left); 3x3 grid (right).

2x2 grid (left); 2x3 grid (right).

6   Book Title

Lorem ipsum dolor sit amet, consectetur adipisicing elit, sed do eiusmod tempor incididunt ut labore et dolore magna aliqua. Ut enim ad minim veniam, quis nostrud exercitation ullamco laboris nisi ut aliquip ex ea commodo consequat. Duis aute irure dolor in reprehenderit in voluptate velit esse cillum dolore eu fugiat nulla pariatur. Excepteur sint occaecat cupidatat non proident, sunt in culpa qui officia deserunt mollit anim id est laborum.

Lorem ipsum dolor sit amet, consectetur adipisicing elit, sed do eiusmod tempor incididunt ut labore et dolore magna aliqua. Ut enim ad minim veniam, quis nostrud exercitation ullamco laboris nisi ut aliquip ex ea commodo consequat. Duis aute irure dolor in reprehenderit in voluptate velit esse cillum dolore eu fugiat nulla pariatur. Excepteur sint occaecat cupidatat non proident, sunt in culpa qui officia deserunt mollit anim id est laborum.

Lorem ipsum dolor sit amet, consectetur adipisicing elit, sed do eiusmod tempor incididunt ut labore et dolore magna aliqua. Ut enim ad minim veniam, quis nostrud exercitation ullamco laboris nisi ut aliquip ex ea commodo consequat. Duis aute irure dolor in reprehenderit in voluptate velit esse cillum dolore eu fugiat nulla pariatur. Excepteur sint occaecat cupidatat non proident, sunt in culpa qui officia

Lorem ipsum dolor sit amet, consectetur adipisicing elit, sed do eiusmod tempor incididunt ut labore et dolore magna aliqua. Ut enim ad minim veniam, quis nostrud exercitation ullamco laboris nisi ut aliquip ex ea commodo consequat. Duis aute irure dolor in reprehenderit in voluptate velit esse cillum

Lorem ipsum dolor sit amet, consectetur adipisicing elit, sed do eiusmod tempor incididunt ut labore et dolore magna aliqua. Ut enim ad minim veniam, quis nostrud

Chapter Title   7

Lorem ipsum dolor sit amet, consectetur adipisicing elit, sed do eiusmod tempor incididunt ut labore et dolore magna aliqua. Ut enim ad minim veniam, quis nostrud exercitation ullamco laboris nisi ut aliquip ex ea commodo consequat. Duis aute irure dolor in reprehenderit in voluptate velit esse cillum dolore eu fugiat nulla pariatur. Excepteur sint occaecat cupidatat non proident, sunt in culpa qui officia deserunt mollit anim id est laborum.

Lorem ipsum dolor sit amet, consectetur adipisicing elit, sed do eiusmod tempor incididunt ut labore et dolore magna aliqua. Ut enim ad minim veniam, quis nostrud exercitation ullamco laboris nisi ut aliquip ex ea commodo consequat. Duis aute irure dolor in reprehenderit in voluptate velit esse cillum dolore eu fugiat nulla pariatur. Excepteur sint occaecat

cupidatat non proident, sunt in culpa qui officia deserunt mollit anim id est laborum.

Lorem ipsum dolor sit amet, consectetur adipisicing elit, sed do eiusmod tempor incididunt ut labore et dolore magna aliqua. Ut enim ad minim veniam, quis nostrud

exercitation ullamco laboris nisi ut aliquip ex ea commodo consequat. Duis aute irure dolor in reprehenderit in voluptate velit esse cillum dolore eu fugiat nulla pariatur. Excepteur sint occaecat cupidatat non proident, sunt in culpa qui officia deserunt mol-

Lorem ipsum dolor sit amet, consectetur adipisicing elit, sed do eiusmod tempor incididunt ut labore et dolore magna aliqua. Ut enim ad minim veniam, quis nostrud

Lorem ipsum dolor sit amet, consectetur adipisicing elit, sed do eiusmod tempor incididunt ut labore et dolore magna aliqua. Ut

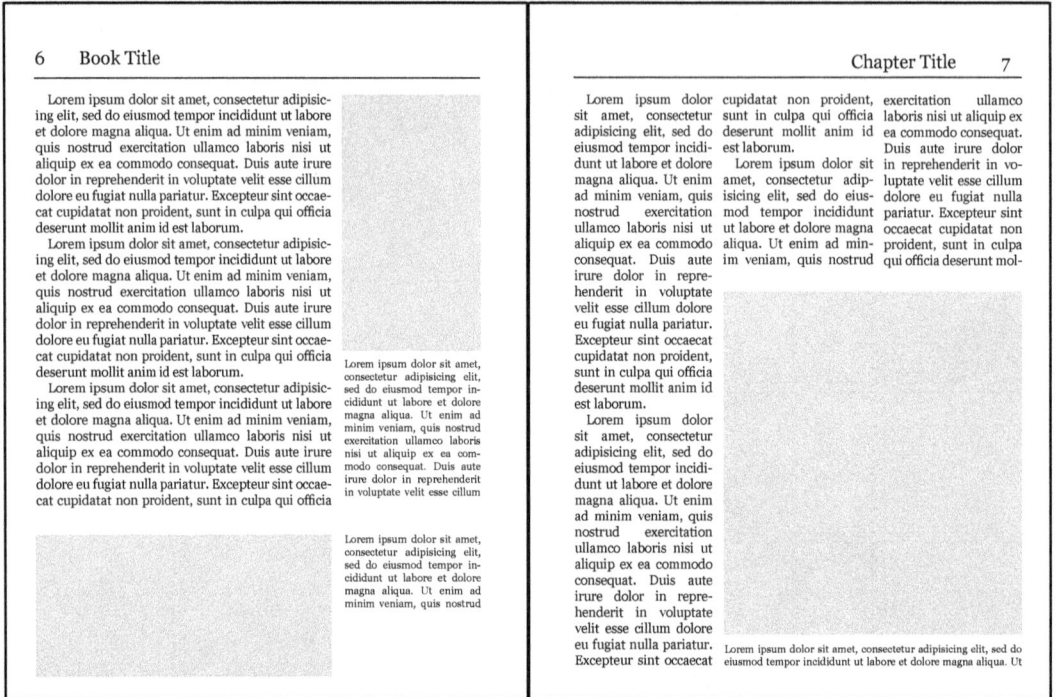

Filled-in grid.

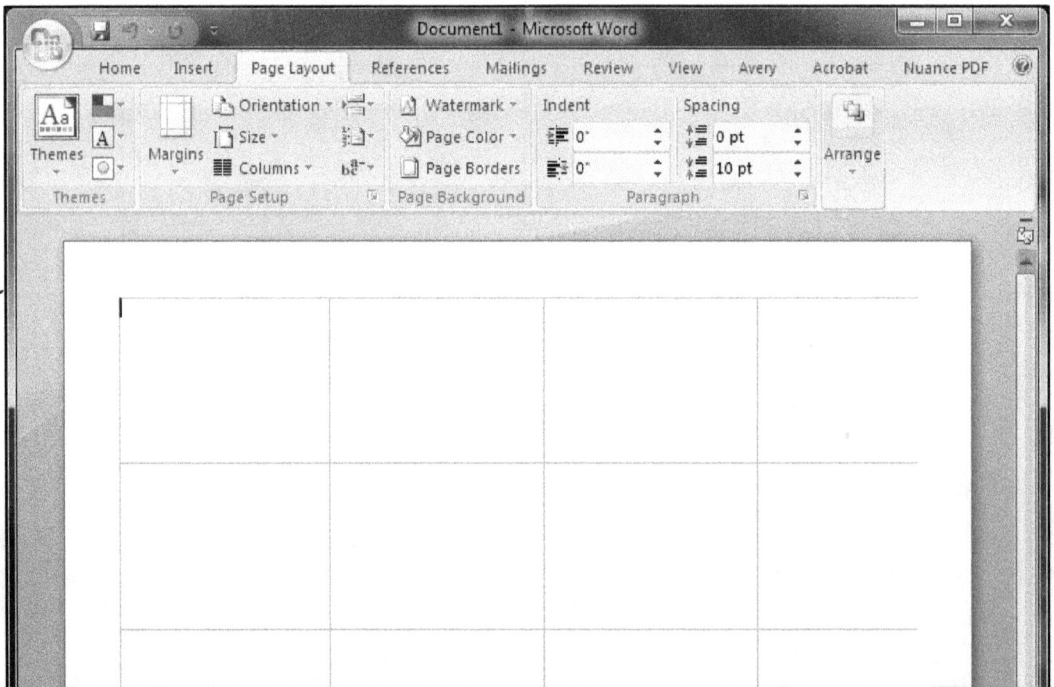

Four column grid in Word.

188

In a page layout program, you can set up margins and columns in master pages—different master pages for different uses, such as the first page in a chapter, main body pages, and a final blank page, if needed.

In a word processing program, you can establish the size of the grid squares and turn on the grid lines so that you can see them as you work. Word processing programs are not as flexible with layouts as page layout programs. You can design a good looking book using a word processing program, however, if you will learn the more advanced features of the software.

Margins

Set your margins to accommodate headers, footers, the text and images. In general, no element should violate the margins. All elements, headers, footers, page numbers, text and images must fit within the margins. Margins impose order and help create white space on the page.

When the Gutenberg bible was printed, margins were set so that facing pages were close together. That was the style of the times—to make a two-page spread look as if it were a single image.

With binding methods today, text set too close to the middle creates an optical illusion that the pages run together. Set a slightly larger margin toward the

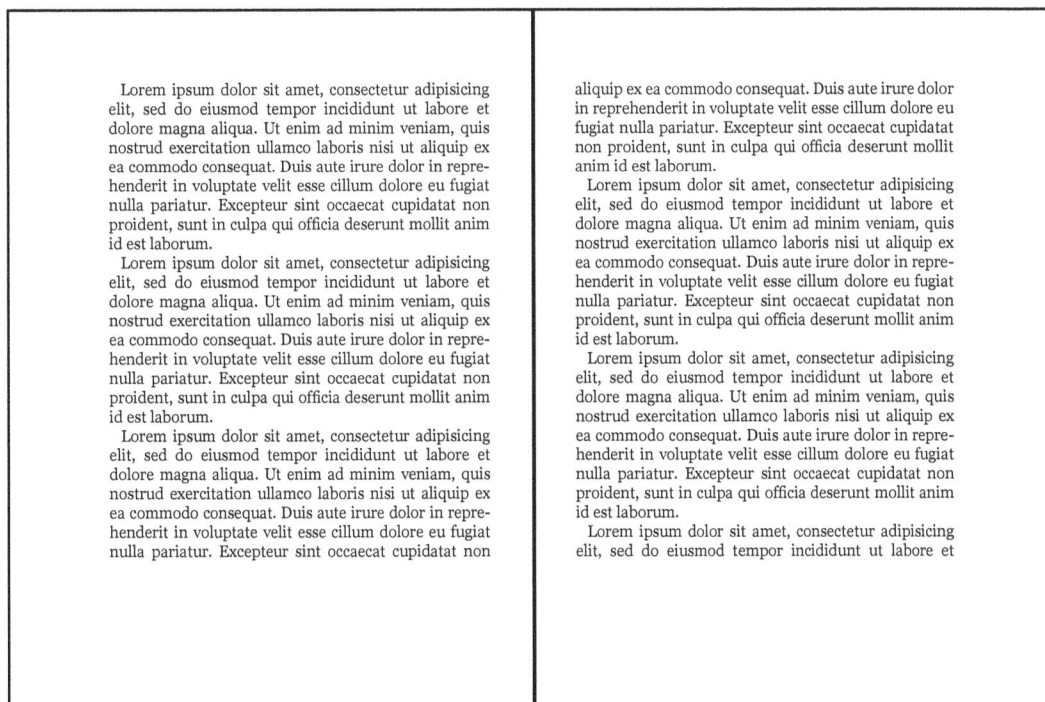

Margins in the Gutenberg bible.

Lorem ipsum dolor sit amet, consectetur adipisicing elit, sed do eiusmod tempor incididunt ut labore et dolore magna aliqua. Ut enim ad minim veniam, quis nostrud exercitation ullamco laboris nisi ut aliquip ex ea commodo consequat. Duis aute irure dolor in reprehenderit in voluptate velit esse cillum dolore eu fugiat nulla pariatur. Excepteur sint occaecat cupidatat non proident, sunt in culpa qui officia deserunt mollit anim id est laborum.

Lorem ipsum dolor sit amet, consectetur adipisicing elit, sed do eiusmod tempor incididunt ut labore et dolore magna aliqua. Ut enim ad minim veniam, quis nostrud exercitation ullamco laboris nisi ut aliquip ex ea commodo consequat. Duis aute irure dolor in reprehenderit in voluptate velit esse cillum dolore eu fugiat nulla pariatur. Excepteur sint occaecat cupidatat non proident, sunt in culpa qui officia deserunt mollit anim id est laborum.

Lorem ipsum dolor sit amet, consectetur adipisicing elit, sed do eiusmod tempor incididunt ut labore et dolore magna aliqua. Ut enim ad minim veniam, quis nostrud exercitation ullamco laboris nisi ut aliquip ex ea commodo consequat. Duis aute irure dolor in reprehenderit in voluptate velit esse cillum dolore eu fugiat nulla pariatur. Excepteur sint occaecat cupidatat non proident, sunt in culpa qui officia deserunt mollit anim id est laborum.

Lorem ipsum dolor sit amet, consectetur adipisicing elit, sed do eiusmod tempor incididunt ut labore et dolore magna aliqua. Ut enim ad minim veniam, quis nostrud exercitation ullamco laboris nisi ut aliquip ex ea commodo consequat. Duis aute irure dolor in reprehenderit in voluptate velit esse cillum dolore eu fugiat nulla pariatur. Excepteur sint occaecat cupidatat non proident, sunt in culpa qui officia

Lorem ipsum dolor sit amet, consectetur adipisicing elit, sed do eiusmod tempor incididunt ut labore et dolore magna aliqua. Ut enim ad minim veniam, quis nostrud exercitation ullamco laboris nisi ut aliquip ex ea commodo consequat. Duis aute irure dolor in reprehenderit in voluptate velit esse cillum dolore eu fugiat nulla pariatur. Excepteur sint occaecat cupidatat non proident, sunt in culpa qui officia deserunt mollit anim id est laborum.

Lorem ipsum dolor sit amet, consectetur adipisicing elit, sed do eiusmod tempor incididunt ut labore et dolore magna aliqua. Ut enim ad minim veniam, quis nostrud exercitation ullamco laboris nisi ut aliquip ex ea commodo consequat. Duis aute irure dolor in reprehenderit in voluptate velit esse cillum dolore eu fugiat nulla pariatur. Excepteur sint occaecat cupidatat non proident, sunt in culpa qui officia deserunt mollit anim id est laborum.

Lorem ipsum dolor sit amet, consectetur adipisicing elit, sed do eiusmod tempor incididunt ut labore et dolore magna aliqua. Ut enim ad minim veniam, quis nostrud exercitation ullamco laboris nisi ut aliquip ex ea commodo consequat. Duis aute irure dolor in reprehenderit in voluptate velit esse cillum dolore eu fugiat nulla pariatur. Excepteur sint occaecat cupidatat non proident, sunt in culpa qui officia deserunt mollit anim id est laborum.

Lorem ipsum dolor sit amet, consectetur adipisicing elit, sed do eiusmod tempor incididunt ut labore et dolore magna aliqua. Ut enim ad minim veniam, quis nostrud exercitation ullamco laboris nisi ut aliquip ex ea commodo consequat. Duis aute irure dolor in reprehenderit in voluptate velit esse cillum dolore eu fugiat nulla pariatur. Excepteur sint occaecat cupidatat non proident, sunt in culpa qui officia

Top margin allowing for the book title, chapter title and page number.

spine than on the outside. The smallest margin you should consider is a one-half inch (.5") margin, and the larger the page size, the larger the margins should be.

Typical margin settings for a 6" x 9" book are: top—1"; inside—.75"; outside—.625" and bottom—.625." On an 8.5" x 11" book, typical margins are: top—1.25" to 1.5"; inside—1"; outside—.75"; and bottom—.75." The most common error is creating margins that are too narrow and of equal size.

Most books have running headers with the book's title on the left-hand page, and the chapter title on the right-hand page. Headers may also include the page numbers. If the header includes the page number, do not repeat page numbers in the footer.

In a page layout program, set up your master pages so that the top margin allows the book title or chapter title to rest above the text. In a word processor, choose one of the pre-installed headers for left and right pages and enter the appropriate text.

Page Numbers

Place page numbers in either the header or footer. Typically they are placed at the outside edge or in the center of the page, but not at the spine edge. It is difficult to locate page numbers while flipping through the book if they are near the spine.

Page numbers in the front matter (title page, table of contents, and so on) are given in lowercase Roman numerals, so the first half-title page would be page

i. Page numbers beginning with the introduction are given in Arabic numerals, so the first page of the introduction would be page 1, although some publishers continue page numbering from the front matter.

Columns

Columns are the easiest way to control line length. Text stretching too far across the page is difficult for the reader to follow. Pages six inches wide or narrower can be set in a single column, but larger books need two or more columns.

Columns have two components—distance between (gutter) and width (line length). Try to keep line lengths from 60 to 70 characters. Columns do not have to be equal in width, but most often they look best when they are. In both page layout programs and word processors, you can adjust the number of columns, the line length, and the distance between the columns. A distance of one-quarter of an inch (.25") is a good starting place. Too much distance between columns looks awkward, and too little distance between columns makes the text difficult to read, as you can see in the example.

Images

Adding images to a page can present layout challenges, especially if the image does not fit neatly into the grid. Your book will look best if they do, however, so you may need to re-scan at a larger size or crop images down to fit.

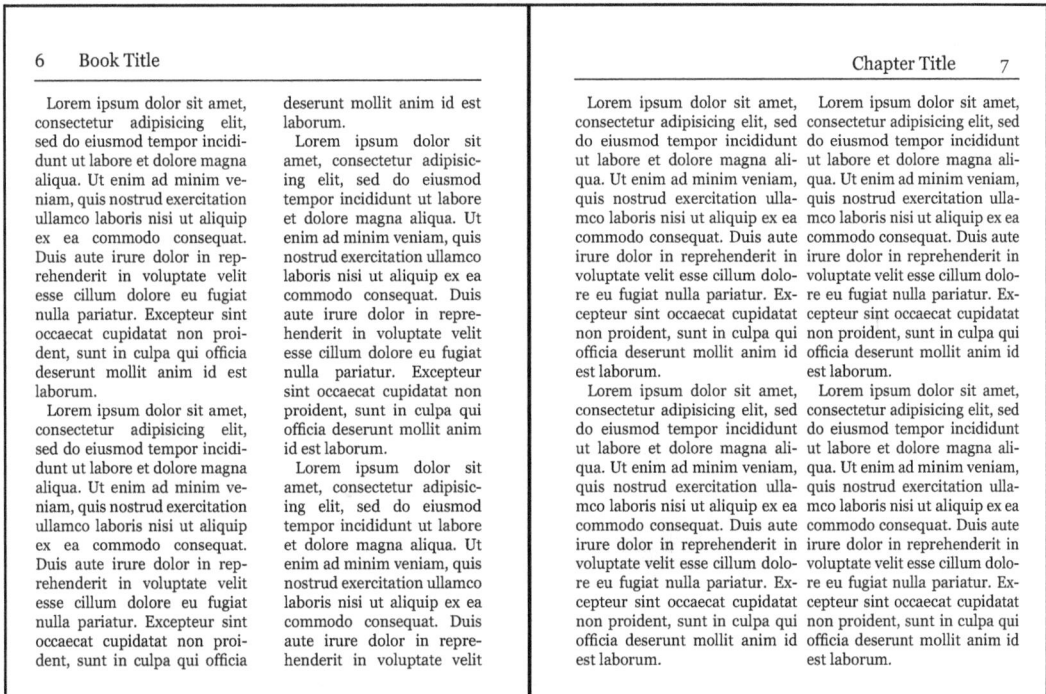

6   Book Title

Lorem ipsum dolor sit amet, consectetur adipisicing elit, sed do eiusmod tempor incididunt ut labore et dolore magna aliqua. Ut enim ad minim veniam, quis nostrud exercitation ullamco laboris nisi ut aliquip ex ea commodo consequat. Duis aute irure dolor in reprehenderit in voluptate velit esse cillum dolore eu fugiat nulla pariatur. Excepteur sint occaecat cupidatat non proident, sunt in culpa qui officia deserunt mollit anim id est laborum.

Lorem ipsum dolor sit amet, consectetur adipisicing elit, sed do eiusmod tempor incididunt ut labore et dolore magna aliqua. Ut enim ad minim veniam, quis nostrud exercitation ullamco laboris nisi ut aliquip ex ea commodo consequat. Duis aute irure dolor in reprehenderit in voluptate velit esse cillum dolore eu fugiat nulla pariatur. Excepteur sint occaecat cupidatat non proident, sunt in culpa qui officia

deserunt mollit anim id est laborum.

Lorem ipsum dolor sit amet, consectetur adipisicing elit, sed do eiusmod tempor incididunt ut labore et dolore magna aliqua. Ut enim ad minim veniam, quis nostrud exercitation ullamco laboris nisi ut aliquip ex ea commodo consequat. Duis aute irure dolor in reprehenderit in voluptate velit esse cillum dolore eu fugiat nulla pariatur. Excepteur sint occaecat cupidatat non proident, sunt in culpa qui officia deserunt mollit anim id est laborum.

Lorem ipsum dolor sit amet, consectetur adipisicing elit, sed do eiusmod tempor incididunt ut labore et dolore magna aliqua. Ut enim ad minim veniam, quis nostrud exercitation ullamco laboris nisi ut aliquip ex ea commodo consequat. Duis aute irure dolor in reprehenderit in voluptate velit

Chapter Title   7

Lorem ipsum dolor sit amet, consectetur adipisicing elit, sed do eiusmod tempor incididunt ut labore et dolore magna aliqua. Ut enim ad minim veniam, quis nostrud exercitation ullamco laboris nisi ut aliquip ex ea commodo consequat. Duis aute irure dolor in reprehenderit in voluptate velit esse cillum dolore eu fugiat nulla pariatur. Excepteur sint occaecat cupidatat non proident, sunt in culpa qui officia deserunt mollit anim id est laborum.

Lorem ipsum dolor sit amet, consectetur adipisicing elit, sed do eiusmod tempor incididunt ut labore et dolore magna aliqua. Ut enim ad minim veniam, quis nostrud exercitation ullamco laboris nisi ut aliquip ex ea commodo consequat. Duis aute irure dolor in reprehenderit in voluptate velit esse cillum dolore eu fugiat nulla pariatur. Excepteur sint occaecat cupidatat non proident, sunt in culpa qui officia deserunt mollit anim id est laborum.

Lorem ipsum dolor sit amet, consectetur adipisicing elit, sed do eiusmod tempor incididunt ut labore et dolore magna aliqua. Ut enim ad minim veniam, quis nostrud exercitation ullamco laboris nisi ut aliquip ex ea commodo consequat. Duis aute irure dolor in reprehenderit in voluptate velit esse cillum dolore eu fugiat nulla pariatur. Excepteur sint occaecat cupidatat non proident, sunt in culpa qui officia deserunt mollit anim id est laborum.

Columns incorrectly spaced; too far (left); too close (right).

PUBLISH YOUR SPECIALTY

6   Book Title

Lorem ipsum dolor sit amet, consectetur adipisicing elit, sed do eiusmod tempor incididunt ut labore et dolore magna aliqua. Ut enim ad minim veniam, quis nostrud exercitation ullamco laboris nisi ut aliquip ex ea commodo consequat. Duis aute irure dolor in reprehenderit in voluptate velit esse cillum dolore eu fugiat nulla pariatur. Excepteur sint occaecat cupidatat non proident, sunt in culpa qui officia deserunt mollit anim id est laborum.

Lorem ipsum dolor sit amet, consectetur adipisicing elit, sed do eiusmod tempor incididunt ut labore et dolore magna aliqua. Ut enim ad minim veniam, quis nostrud exercitation ullamco laboris nisi ut aliquip ex ea commodo consequat. Duis aute irure dolor in reprehenderit in voluptate velit esse cillum dolore eu fugiat nulla pariatur. Excepteur sint occaecat cupidatat non proident, sunt in culpa qui officia deserunt mollit anim id est laborum.

Lorem ipsum dolor sit amet, consectetur adipisicing elit, sed do eiusmod tempor incididunt ut labore et dolore magna aliqua. Ut enim ad minim veniam,

Chapter Title   7

Lorem ipsum dolor sit amet, consectetur adipisicing elit, sed do eiusmod tempor incididunt ut labore et dolore magna aliqua. Ut enim ad minim veniam, quis nostrud exercitation ullamco laboris nisi ut aliquip ex ea commodo consequat. Duis aute irure dolor in reprehenderit in voluptate velit esse cillum dolore eu fugiat nulla pariatur. Excepteur sint occaecat cupidatat non proident, sunt in culpa qui officia deserunt mollit anim id est laborum.

Lorem ipsum dolor sit amet, consectetur adipisicing elit, sed do eiusmod tempor incididunt ut labore et dolore magna aliqua. Ut enim ad minim veniam, quis nostrud exercitation ullamco laboris nisi ut aliquip ex ea commodo consequat. Duis aute irure dolor in reprehenderit in voluptate velit esse cillum dolore eu fugiat nulla pariatur. Excepteur sint occaecat

cupidatat non proident, sunt in culpa qui officia deserunt mollit anim id est laborum.

officia deserunt mollit anim id est laborum.

Lorem ipsum dolor sit amet, consectetur adipisicing elit, sed do eiusmod tempor incididunt ut labore et dolore magna aliqua. Ut enim ad minim veniam, quis nostrud exercitation ullamco laboris nisi ut

Lorem ipsum dolor sit amet, consectetur adipisicing elit, sed do eiusmod tempor incididunt ut labore et dolore magna aliqua. Ut

Grid filled incorrectly.

6   Book Title

Lorem ipsum dolor sit amet, consectetur adipisicing elit, sed do eiusmod tempor incididunt ut labore et dolore magna aliqua. Ut enim ad minim veniam, quis nostrud exercitation ullamco laboris nisi ut aliquip ex ea commodo consequat. Duis aute irure dolor in reprehenderit in voluptate velit esse cillum dolore eu fugiat nulla pariatur. Excepteur sint occaecat cupidatat non proident, sunt in culpa qui officia deserunt mollit anim id est laborum.

Lorem ipsum dolor sit amet, consectetur adipisicing elit, sed do eiusmod tempor incididunt ut labore et dolore magna aliqua. Ut enim ad minim veniam, quis nostrud exercitation ullamco laboris nisi ut aliquip ex ea commodo consequat. Duis aute irure dolor in reprehenderit in voluptate velit esse cillum dolore eu fugiat nulla pariatur. Excepteur sint occaecat cupidatat non proident, sunt in culpa qui officia deserunt mollit anim id est laborum.

Lorem ipsum dolor sit amet, consectetur adipisicing elit, sed do eiusmod tempor incididunt ut labore et dolore magna aliqua. Ut enim ad minim veniam, quis nostrud exercitation ullamco laboris nisi ut aliquip ex ea commodo consequat. Duis aute irure dolor in reprehenderit in voluptate velit esse cillum dolore eu fugiat nulla pariatur. Excepteur sint occaecat cupidatat non proident, sunt in culpa qui officia

Lorem ipsum dolor sit amet, consectetur adipisicing elit, sed do eiusmod tempor incididunt ut labore et dolore magna aliqua. Ut enim ad minim veniam, quis nostrud exercitation ullamco laboris nisi ut aliquip ex ea commodo consequat. Duis aute irure dolor in reprehenderit in voluptate velit esse cillum

Lorem ipsum dolor sit amet, consectetur adipisicing elit, sed do eiusmod tempor incididunt ut labore et dolore magna aliqua. Ut enim ad minim veniam, quis nostrud

Chapter Title   7

Lorem ipsum dolor sit amet, consectetur adipisicing elit, sed do eiusmod tempor incididunt ut labore et dolore magna aliqua. Ut enim ad minim veniam, quis nostrud exercitation ullamco laboris nisi ut aliquip ex ea commodo consequat. Duis aute irure dolor in reprehenderit in voluptate velit esse cillum dolore eu fugiat nulla pariatur. Excepteur sint occaecat cupidatat non proident, sunt in culpa qui officia deserunt mollit anim id est laborum.

Lorem ipsum dolor sit amet, consectetur adipisicing elit, sed do eiusmod tempor incididunt ut labore et dolore magna aliqua. Ut enim ad minim veniam, quis nostrud exercitation ullamco laboris nisi ut aliquip ex ea commodo consequat. Duis aute irure dolor in reprehenderit in voluptate velit esse cillum dolore eu fugiat nulla pariatur. Excepteur sint occaecat

exercitation ullamco laboris nisi ut aliquip ex ea commodo consequat. Duis aute irure dolor in reprehenderit in voluptate velit esse cillum dolore eu fugiat nulla pariatur. Excepteur sint occaecat cupidatat non proident, sunt in culpa qui officia deserunt mol-

Lorem ipsum dolor sit amet, consectetur adipisicing elit, sed do eiusmod tempor incididunt ut labore et dolore magna aliqua. Ut enim ad minim veniam, quis nostrud

Grid filled correctly.

192

Avoid placing images so that their edges end in the middle of grid squares causing narrow columns of text to form beside the image. Neither should images and text fill grid columns incompletely leaving awkward white space as seen on the right-hand page in the example (previous page).

Most images can stand a bit of cropping. In fact, many images are stronger after they are cropped because the subject of the image takes center stage.

Size indicates relative importance. Try to keep this in mind when choosing images. The bigger the image, the more important the reader will think it is to the story or explanation.

Images need space around them. In most cases, the space between the columns serves as a good rule for the space to leave around your images. If the space between your columns is one-quarter of one inch (.25"), use the text wrap feature to give the image space on every side except the side where you want to place a caption. Captions, because they belong to the photo, should be closer (see below).

Note: Captions and credits are not the same. Captions explain who or what is in the image. Credits acknowledge who owns or has possession of the image. Captions should accompany the image on the page, aligned left beginning at the left edge of the photograph, not centered underneath. Centering captions creates visual obstacles for the reader. Credits can be given on the page with the image just after the caption, or in a list of credits at the end of the book or each chapter.

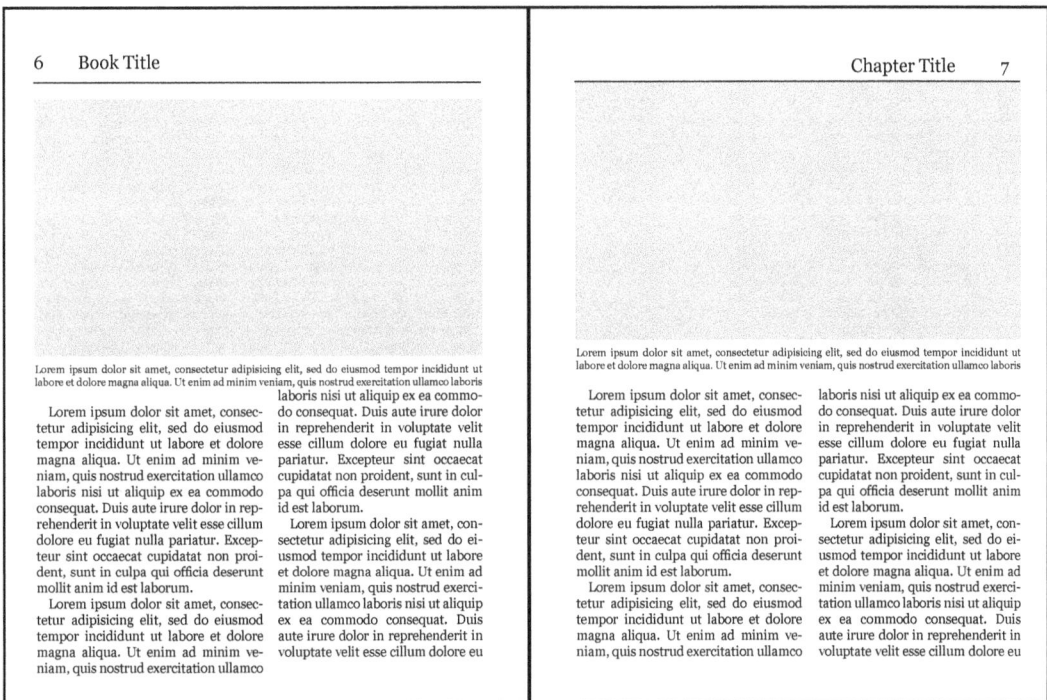

---

6   Book Title

Lorem ipsum dolor sit amet, consectetur adipisicing elit, sed do eiusmod tempor incididunt ut labore et dolore magna aliqua. Ut enim ad minim veniam, quis nostrud exercitation ullamco laboris

Lorem ipsum dolor sit amet, consectetur adipisicing elit, sed do eiusmod tempor incididunt ut labore et dolore magna aliqua. Ut enim ad minim veniam, quis nostrud exercitation ullamco laboris nisi ut aliquip ex ea commodo consequat. Duis aute irure dolor in reprehenderit in voluptate velit esse cillum dolore eu fugiat nulla pariatur. Excepteur sint occaecat cupidatat non proident, sunt in culpa qui officia deserunt mollit anim id est laborum.

Lorem ipsum dolor sit amet, consectetur adipisicing elit, sed do eiusmod tempor incididunt ut labore et dolore magna aliqua. Ut enim ad minim veniam, quis nostrud exercitation ullamco laboris nisi ut aliquip ex ea commodo consequat. Duis aute irure dolor in reprehenderit in voluptate velit esse cillum dolore eu

Chapter Title   7

Lorem ipsum dolor sit amet, consectetur adipisicing elit, sed do eiusmod tempor incididunt ut labore et dolore magna aliqua. Ut enim ad minim veniam, quis nostrud exercitation ullamco laboris

Lorem ipsum dolor sit amet, consectetur adipisicing elit, sed do eiusmod tempor incididunt ut labore et dolore magna aliqua. Ut enim ad minim veniam, quis nostrud exercitation ullamco laboris nisi ut aliquip ex ea commodo consequat. Duis aute irure dolor in reprehenderit in voluptate velit esse cillum dolore eu fugiat nulla pariatur. Excepteur sint occaecat cupidatat non proident, sunt in culpa qui officia deserunt mollit anim id est laborum.

Lorem ipsum dolor sit amet, consectetur adipisicing elit, sed do eiusmod tempor incididunt ut labore et dolore magna aliqua. Ut enim ad minim veniam, quis nostrud exercitation ullamco laboris nisi ut aliquip ex ea commodo consequat. Duis aute irure dolor in reprehenderit in voluptate velit esse cillum dolore eu

Images with captions.

---

6   Book Title

Lorem ipsum dolor sit amet, consectetur adipisicing elit, sed do eiusmod tempor incididunt ut labore et dolore magna aliqua. Ut enim ad minim veniam, quis nostrud exercitation ullamco laboris nisi ut aliquip ex ea commodo consequat. Duis aute irure dolor in reprehenderit in voluptate velit esse cillum dolore eu fugiat nulla pariatur. Excepteur sint occaecat cupidatat non proident, sunt in culpa qui officia deserunt mollit anim id est laborum.

Lorem ipsum dolor sit amet, consectetur adipisicing elit, sed do eiusmod tempor incididunt ut labore et dolore magna aliqua. Ut enim ad minim veniam, quis nostrud exercitation ullamco laboris nisi ut aliquip ex ea commodo consequat. Duis aute irure dolor in reprehenderit in voluptate velit esse cillum dolo-re eu fugiat nulla pariatur. Excepteur sint occaecat cupidatat non proident, sunt in culpa qui officia deserunt mollit anim id est laborum.

Lorem ipsum dolor sit amet, consectetur adipisicing elit, sed do eiusmod tempor incididunt ut labore et dolore magna aliqua. Ut enim ad minim veniam, quis nostrud exercitation ullamco laboris nisi ut aliquip ex ea commodo consequat. Duis aute irure dolor in reprehenderit in voluptate velit esse cil-

lum dolore eu fugiat nulla pariatur. Excepteur sint occaecat cupidatat non proident, sunt in culpa qui officia deserunt mollit anim id est laborum.

Lorem ipsum dolor sit amet, consectetur adipisicing elit, sed do ei-usmod tempor incididunt ut labore et dolore magna aliqua. Ut enim ad minim veniam, quis nostrud exercitation ullamco laboris nisi ut aliquip ex ea commodo consequat. Duis aute irure dolor in reprehenderit in voluptate velit esse cillum dolore eu fugiat nulla pariatur. Excepteur sint occaecat cupidatat non proident, sunt in culpa qui officia deserunt mollit anim id est laborum.

Lorem ipsum dolor sit amet

Lorem ipsum dolor sit amet, consectetur adipisicing elit, sed do ei-usmod tempor incididunt ut labore et dolore magna aliqua. Ut enim ad minim veniam, quis nostrud exercitation ullamco laboris nisi ut aliquip ex ea commodo consequat. Duis aute irure dolor in reprehenderit in voluptate velit esse cillum dolore eu fugiat nulla pariatur. Excepteur sint occaecat cupidatat non proident, sunt in culpa qui officia deserunt mollit anim id est laborum. Ut

---

Chapter Title   7

Lorem ipsum dolor sit amet, consectetur adipisicing elit, sed do eiusmod tempor incididunt ut labore et dolore magna aliqua. Ut enim ad minim veniam, quis nostrud exercitation ullamco laboris nisi ut aliquip ex ea commodo consequat. Duis aute irure dolor in reprehenderit in voluptate velit esse cillum dolore eu fugiat nulla pariatur. Excepteur sint occaecat cupidatat non proident, sunt in culpa qui officia deserunt mollit anim id est laborum.

Lorem ipsum dolor sit amet, consectetur adipisicing elit, sed do eiusmod tempor incididunt ut labore et dolore magna aliqua. Ut enim ad minim veniam, quis nostrud exercitation ullamco laboris nisi ut aliquip ex ea commodo consequat. Duis aute irure dolor in reprehenderit in voluptate velit esse cillum dolore eu fugiat nulla pariatur. Excep-

niam, quis nostrud exercitation ullamco laboris nisi ut aliquip ex ea commodo consequat. Duis aute irure dolor in reprehenderit in vo-luptate velit esse cillum dolore eu fugiat nulla pariatur. Excepteur sint occaecat cupidatat non proident, sunt in culpa qui officia deserunt mollit anim id est laborum.

Lorem ipsum dolor sit amet, consectetur adipisicing elit, sed do ei-usmod tempor incididunt ut labore et dolore magna aliqua. Ut enim ad minim veniam, quis nostrud exerci-tation ullamco laboris nisi ut aliquip ex ea commodo consequat. Duis aute irure dolor in reprehenderit in voluptate velit esse cillum dolore eu fugiat nulla pariatur. Excepteur sint occaecat cupidatat non proident, sunt in culpa qui officia deserunt mollit anim id est laborum.

Lorem ipsum dolor sit amet

teur sint occaecat cupidatat non proi-dent, sunt in culpa qui officia deserunt mollit anim id est laborum.

Lorem ipsum dolor sit amet, consectetur adipisicing elit, sed do eiusmod tempor incididunt ut labore et dolore magna aliqua. Ut enim ad minim ve-

Lorem ipsum dolor sit amet, consectetur adipisicing elit, sed do ei-usmod tempor incididunt ut labore et dolore magna aliqua. Ut enim ad minim veniam, quis nostrud exerci-tation ullamco laboris nisi ut aliquip ex ea commodo consequat. Duis aute irure dolor in reprehenderit in voluptate velit esse cillum dolore eu fugiat nulla pariatur. Excepteur sint occaecat cupidatat non proident, sunt in culpa qui officia deserunt mollit anim id est laborum. Ut

Pull-quotes across columns (left); Pull-quotes within a column (right).

---

6   Book Title

Lorem ipsum dolor sit amet, consectetur adipisicing elit, sed do eiusmod tempor incididunt ut labore et dolore magna aliqua. Ut enim ad minim veniam, quis nostrud exercitation ullamco laboris nisi ut aliquip ex ea commodo consequat. Duis aute irure dolor in reprehenderit in voluptate velit esse cillum dolore eu fugiat nulla pariatur. Excepteur sint occaecat cupidatat non proident, sunt in culpa qui officia deserunt mollit anim id est laborum.

Lorem ipsum dolor sit amet, consectetur adipisicing elit, sed do eiusmod tempor incididunt ut labore et dolore magna aliqua. Ut enim ad minim veniam, quis nostrud exercitation ullamco laboris nisi ut aliquip ex ea commodo consequat. Duis aute irure dolor in reprehenderit in voluptate velit esse cillum dolore eu fugiat nulla pariatur. Excepteur sint occae-cat cupidatat non proident, sunt in culpa qui officia deserunt mollit anim id est laborum.

Lorem ipsum dolor sit amet, consectetur adipisicing elit, sed do eiusmod tempor incididunt ut labore et dolore magna aliqua. Ut enim ad minim veniam, quis nostrud exercitation ullamco laboris nisi ut aliquip ex ea commodo consequat. Duis aute irure dolor in reprehenderit in voluptate velit esse cillum dolore eu fugiat nulla pariatur. Excepteur sint occae-cat cupidatat non proident, sunt in culpa qui officia deserunt mollit anim id est laborum.

Lorem ipsum dolor sit amet, consectetur adipisicing elit, sed do eiusmod tempor incididunt ut labore et dolore magna aliqua. Ut enim ad minim veniam, quis nostrud exercitation ullamco laboris nisi ut aliquip ex ea commodo consequat. Duis aute irure dolor in reprehenderit in voluptate velit esse cillum dolore eu fugiat nulla pariatur. Excepteur sint occae-cat cupidatat non proident, sunt in culpa qui officia deserunt mollit anim id est laborum.

- Lorem ipsum dolor sit amet
- Consectetur adipisicing elit
- Sed do eiusmod tempor
- Incididunt ut labore
- Magna aliqua
- Ut enim ad minim veniam
- Quis nostrud exercitation

Chapter Title   7

Lorem ipsum dolor cupidatat non proident, sit amet, consectetur adipisicing elit, sed do eiusmod tempor incidi-dunt ut labore et dolore magna aliqua. Ut enim ad minim veniam, quis nostrud exercitation ullamco laboris nisi ut aliquip ex ea commodo consequat. Duis aute irure dolor in repre-henderit in voluptate velit esse cillum dolore eu fugiat nulla pariatur. Excepteur sint occaecat cupidatat non proident, sunt in culpa qui officia deserunt mollit anim id est laborum.

Lorem ipsum dolor sit amet, consectetur adipisicing elit, sed do eiusmod tempor incidi-dunt ut labore et dolore magna aliqua. Ut enim ad minim veniam, quis nos-trud exercitation ullamco laboris nisi ut aliquip ex ea commodo consequat. Duis aute irure dolor in reprehenderit in voluptate velit esse cillum dolore Excepteur sint occaecat cupidatat non proident, sunt in culpa qui officia deserunt mollit anim id est laborum.

sunt in culpa qui officia deserunt mollit anim id Lorem ipsum dolor sit amet, consectetur adipisicing elit, sed do eiusmod tempor incidi-dunt ut labore et dolore magna aliqua. Ut enim ad minim veniam, quis nos-trud exercitation ullamco laboris nisi ut aliquip ex ea commodo consequat. Duis aute irure dolor in reprehenderit in voluptate velit esse cillum dolore

eu fugiat nulla pariatur. Excepteur sint occaecat cupidatat non proident, sunt in culpa qui officia deserunt mollit anim id est laborum.

Lorem ipsum dolor sit amet, consectetur adipisicing elit, sed do eiusmod tempor incidi-dunt ut labore et dolore magna aliqua. Ut enim ad minim veniam, quis nostrud exercitation ullamco laboris nisi ut aliquip ex ea commodo consequat. Duis aute irure dolor in repre-henderit in voluptate velit esse cillum dolore eu fugiat nulla pariatur. Excepteur sint occaecat cupidatat non proident, sunt in culpa qui officia deserunt mollit anim id est laborum. Ut

Lorem ipsum dolor sit amet, consectetur adipisicing elit, sed do eiusmod tempor incidi-dunt ut labore et dolore magna aliqua. Ut enim ad minim veniam, quis nostrud exercitation ullamco laboris nisi ut aliquip ex ea commodo

Text spread across two columns with a side bar (left); Three columns (right).

If you want to add fancy photo corners or edge effects to your images, do so in your image editing software after you have re-sized the image for its spot within the grid. Pick one or two fancy effects, and stick with them for consistency. In most how-to books, a simple line around the image as a border is best.

Advanced Page Layouts

What follows are advanced layout options often found in non-fiction books. Use them for visual interest, but only if they benefit the reader in some way.

Pull Quotes

Pull quotes are used by magazines to entice readers to stop flipping pages and start reading. They are an opportunity for a little creativity on the page. In a book, they can be used effectively, although they should be used sparingly.

Side Bars

Sidebars are another way to use your grid to add information that you may not want to include within the narrative. It may be information about a photograph that is too long for a simple caption, or something you want the reader to know alongside the narrative (see the example opposite).

❧❧

If you take the time to create a basic page layout that is easy to flow text and place images into, your book will look better than most. Look through your personal library and find a simple layout that you like. Look at books of the same physical size—it can be hard to match layouts if you do not.

Now that you have a feel for the general layout of the page, the next chapter will explore the fundamentals of typesetting.

Chapter 17

Typesetting—The Basics

Typesetting conventions have developed over the last 400 years to make books both beautiful and easy to read. If you mess with the rules of readability, reading comprehension drops dramatically.

The rest of this chapter will help you avoid leaving little clues that the book is "self-published."

The Basics

Before you can start typesetting the different parts of your book, you need a good understanding of what affects reading comprehension.

The Rules of Readability

In addition to hundreds of years of publishing tradition, modern studies have determined what affects our ability to read and comprehend type. The rules that follow are based upon the results of tradition, observation and studies.

Use serif fonts, also called typefaces. Twice as many readers are able to understand words printed in serif typefaces. Serif fonts have small extenders between letters. Sans serif typefaces are easier to read on the screen, so these fonts are fine for websites and electronic communications, but stick to serif fonts for printed books.

High contrast is best. Black type on a white page is optimal. Even dark blues and browns are more difficult to read than black. Avoid placing type on a colored background unless the background is very light. Avoid reverse outs. It is difficult for readers to digest white type on a black background for more than a one- or two-word headline.

Avoid all capitals (all caps). Not only do readers feel as if you are shouting at them, they recognize words based upon the top half of the letters. Letters in all caps lack the characteristic upper extenders and rounded forms readers use to recognize whole words at a time, so text in all caps slows reading to a crawl.

Give the letters room to breathe. Squeezing type together makes text uncomfortable, if not impossible, to read.

Use bold sparingly. Headlines and subheads in bold help the reader skim through the material, but large blocks of type in bold looks dense and is difficult to read.

> A brilliant piece of graphic design which goes unread is a waste of paper, ink, money and effort, and perhaps above all, a lost opportunity to communicate something of value.
>
> **—Colin Wheildon and Mal Warwick**
> *Type & Layout: How Typography and Design*
> *Can Get Your Message Across or Get In the Way*

Fonts

Typography does not have to be sophisticated to look good and read easily. Typefaces often come in families that include Roman (plain), italics, bold and bold italics. A few font families will also have black (heavy) or light (narrow).

Choose a serif typeface for the main body of the book. These are common serif typefaces used in books: Adobe Caslon, Adobe Garamond, Baskerville Old Face, Bookman Old Style, Goudy Old Style, Palatino, and Utopia.

Common Body Text Fonts	Common Headline Fonts		
Adobe Caslon	Franklin Gothic Book	**Gill Sans** Adobe Caslon	**Franklin Gothic Book** Goudy Old Style
Adobe Garamond	Gill Sans		
Baskerville Old Face	Hypatia Sans Pro	**Myriad Pro** Baskerville	**Tahoma** Palatino
Bookman Old Style	Myriad Pro		
Goudy Oldstyle	Tahoma	**Hypatia Sans** Bookman	
Palatino			

Common body and headline fonts (left); Font pairs (right).

You can keep the same font for headlines and subheads, but make them bolder and bigger, or you can use a sans serif typeface. If you prefer a sans serif font, choose one that creates a good contrast with your body text font. Weak contrasts do not look as good as strong contrasts.

These are common sans serif headline fonts: Franklin Gothic Book, Gill Sans, Hypathia Sans Pro, Myriad Pro, Nimbus Sans, Segoe and Tahoma.

Fonts to avoid: Times New Roman and Helvetica (both are newspaper fonts meant for narrow columns), Arial (overused), Copperplate (all caps), Courier (unless you want to look like you have used a typewriter), Papyrus (so overused it has become a cliché), Brush Script, Comic Sans, Curlz, anything that implies handwriting, and fonts supposed to make one think of the Dark Ages, the Middle Ages, the Renaissance, or the Book of Kells.

Avoid script fonts, even for something personal such as a transcription of a letter or a page from a diary. Loosely set script fonts may be fine for chapter titles but are difficult to read for more than a few words. Italics in one of the basic book fonts will distinguish itself enough to make a transcription stand out.

There are three major font file types: Open Type, TrueType and Postscript. Apple opened the world of scalable type design with its TrueType fonts. Adobe got into the game a bit later with its Type1 (Postscript) fonts. OpenType has been a collaboration of Microsoft and Adobe and looks to be winning over publishers and printers.

Some fonts require purchase in order to use them; others come pre-installed in your word processing or page layout programs already licensed for you to use. Avoid free fonts available on the Internet (mostly TrueType). Some have serious technical issues that you will not want to discover after your book is printed.

Avoid any font that will not embed into a PDF (Portable Document Format—the file type most commonly requested by printers). If you do not have a license for your fonts, they will not save correctly into a PDF. If you are unsure, type a few words in each of your chosen fonts and convert that test file into a PDF. Most word processors will save files to PDFs using a simple "save as" command. If no error messages appear, the fonts are most probably all right.

There is no need to go wild with fonts. It is rare to use more than two to three fonts in a book's interior. Stick to the commonly used book fonts. You can be a little more creative with the font on the cover.

Type Size

For the main body of the book, make the font size big enough to read easily, and appropriate to the column width. Narrower columns can handle smaller fonts.

For adults, most fonts are readable between point sizes 10 and 12. Smaller font sizes are difficult to read. Smaller type is fine for captions or footnotes, down to 7 or 8 points, depending upon the font. Larger font sizes, 14 points or larger, should be reserved for large print books made for people with impaired vision. Larger font sizes are acceptable for headlines and subheads.

Leading

The term leading comes from a time when type was set by hand and thin strips of lead divided lines horizontally to create a space above and below each line.

Standard leading is two points greater than the type height for standard text and proportionally larger with larger sized text. Your body text may be 12 points tall with 14 point leading, whereas your cover font could be 48 points tall with 58 point leading—an amount proportional to the size of the large letters.

One way to decrease the density on the page (or lengthen a manuscript) is to increase the leading. Increasing the leading too much, however, will look like double spacing which is not attractive.

Emphasis

It is always better to make the reader feel emphasis with your words rather than using typesetting tricks. Italics is the most common way to show emphasis. Italics is also used to highlight foreign words, indicate book or movie titles, and the thoughts of a character—a rare occurrence in non-fiction.

Use bold, if you must, but only for short phrases. Paragraph after paragraph of bold text looks dense and uninviting.

Keep the exclamation points under control. If everything is important, nothing is—relatively. Avoid all capitals in running text unless you want the reader to feel that you are shouting your message.

There is no need to put everyday expressions in quotes, except to indicate irony. When air quotes became a popular hand gesture, they also proliferated in printed works. Try not to litter your book with unnecessary quotes. Save them for the places where you are actually quoting another author.

Avoid underlining, except as hyperlinks. Underlining had a place when typewriters offered little else, but underlining is not used for emphasis today.

Case

In English, when to use upper case and when to use lower case is fairly straight forward. Sentence case is used in paragraphs where capital letters begin sentences. Title case is used for headlines and subheads only. In title case, most words are capitalized except prepositions (by, to, from, of, on, with, at), articles (a, an, the), and coordinating conjunctions (and, but, or, for, and nor).

Capitals are used for proper nouns, such as the names of people (George Washington), businesses (General Motors), specific places (Savannah, America, the Mississippi Delta), nationalities (German), languages (French) and religions (Methodist).

Job or honorary titles are capitalized, but only when it refers to a specific person and precedes their name. So, there are presidents elected in the United States, but President Lincoln gets a capital in his title.

Capitals, like commas, can run amok. In book publishing, fewer capitals are preferred. If in doubt, use the lowercase letter.

Letter Spacing and Kerning

Letter spacing and kerning affect the distance between letters. Letter spacing (tracking) affects the spacing between all letters. Adjusting the letter spacing can open up the look of a page and make some fonts easier to read. In most cases, however, your software will correctly determine letter spacing. On occasion, altering letter spacing can help avoid orphans (more on this shortly).

Kerning adjusts the spacing between two, side-by-side letters to make them look more natural sitting next to each other. The auto-kerning feature in most software is fine for most body text. Kerning individual pairs of letters may be important, however, to make the large letters on your cover look their best.

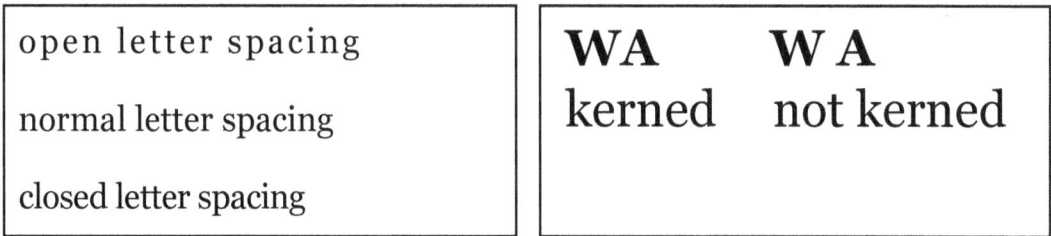

open letter spacing normal letter spacing closed letter spacing	**WA** **W A** kerned not kerned

Letter spacing (left); Kerning (right).

Titles, Headlines, and Subheads

Titles, headlines and subheads are about hierarchy—clues to what is the most important. At the top of the hierarchy (and also in the largest font size and strength) are the chapter titles. Next are the headlines that should be bigger and bolder than subheads. If needed, create sub-subheads down to a second or third level.

The lowest level could be a run-in subhead where the subhead does not sit above the paragraph, but begins the paragraph and ends in a period (see below).

For most books, headlines and subheads should be aligned flush left. Centered or right-aligned headlines and subheads can work (albeit a challenge), but only over fully justified paragraphs. Whichever style you choose, be consistent.

Keep headlines and subheads short and sweet. Avoid having them run onto a second line, if possible. Headlines and subheads do not end in punctuation, except if you are using a run-in subhead, such as:

Tuesday. On the first sunny morning in a month, ...
Wednesday. We began to harvest ...

Aesthetically, headlines and subheads are never stacked one on top of another. There is always a paragraph in between them.

Lorem ipsum dolor sit amet, consectetur adipisicing elit, sed do eiusmod tempor incididunt ut labore et dolore magna aliqua. Ut enim ad minim veniam, quis nostrud exercitation ullamco laboris nisi ut aliquip ex ea commodo consequat. Duis aute irure dolor in reprehenderit in voluptate velit esse cillum dolore eu fugiat nulla pariatur. Excepteur sint occaecat cupidatat non proident, sunt in culpa qui officia deserunt mollit anim id est laborum.

Headline Headline Headline

Lorem ipsum dolor sit amet, consectetur adipisicing elit, sed do eiusmod tempor incididunt ut labore et dolore magna aliqua. Ut enim ad minim veniam, quis nostrud exercitation ullamco laboris nisi ut aliquip ex ea commodo consequat. Duis aute irure dolor in reprehenderit in voluptate velit esse cillum dolore eu fugiat nulla pariatur. Excepteur sint occaecat cupidatat non proident, sunt in culpa qui officia deserunt mollit anim id est laborum.

Subhead Subhead Subhead Subhead

Lorem ipsum dolor sit amet, consectetur adipisicing elit, sed do eiusmod tempor incididunt ut labore et dolore magna aliqua. Ut enim ad minim veniam, quis nostrud exercitation ullamco laboris nisi ut aliquip ex ea commodo consequat. Duis aute irure dolor in reprehenderit in voluptate velit esse cillum dolore eu fugiat nulla pariatur. Excepteur sint occaecat cupidatat non proident, sunt in culpa qui officia deserunt mollit anim id est laborum.

Sub-Subhead Sub-Subhead Sub-Subhead Subhead

Lorem ipsum dolor sit amet, consectetur adipisicing elit, sed do eiusmod tempor incididunt ut labore et dolore magna aliqua. Ut enim ad minim veniam, quis nostrud exercitation ullamco laboris nisi ut aliquip ex ea commodo consequat. Duis aute irure dolor in

Lorem ipsum dolor sit amet, consectetur adipisicing elit, sed do eiusmod tempor incididunt ut labore et dolore magna aliqua. Ut enim ad minim veniam, quis nostrud exercitation ullamco laboris nisi ut aliquip ex ea commodo consequat. Duis aute irure dolor in reprehenderit in voluptate velit esse cillum dolore eu fugiat nulla pariatur. Excepteur sint occaecat cupidatat non proident, sunt in culpa qui officia deserunt mollit anim id est laborum.

Headline Headline Headline

Lorem ipsum dolor sit amet, consectetur adipisicing elit, sed do eiusmod tempor incididunt ut labore et dolore magna aliqua. Ut enim ad minim veniam, quis nostrud exercitation ullamco laboris nisi ut aliquip ex ea commodo consequat. Duis aute irure dolor in reprehenderit in voluptate velit esse cillum dolore eu fugiat nulla pariatur. Excepteur sint occaecat cupidatat non proident, sunt in culpa qui officia deserunt mollit anim id est laborum.

Subhead Subhead Subhead Subhead

Lorem ipsum dolor sit amet, consectetur adipisicing elit, sed do eiusmod tempor incididunt ut labore et dolore magna aliqua. Ut enim ad minim veniam, quis nostrud exercitation ullamco laboris nisi ut aliquip ex ea commodo consequat. Duis aute irure dolor in reprehenderit in voluptate velit esse cillum dolore eu fugiat nulla pariatur. Excepteur sint occaecat cupidatat non proident, sunt in culpa qui officia deserunt mollit anim id est laborum.

Sub-Subhead Sub-Subhead Sub-Subhead Subhead

Lorem ipsum dolor sit amet, consectetur adipisicing elit, sed do eiusmod tempor incididunt ut labore et dolore magna aliqua. Ut enim ad minim veniam, quis nostrud exercitation ullamco laboris nisi ut aliquip ex ea commodo consequat. Duis aute irure dolor in

Headlines and subheads.

Lorem ipsum dolor sit amet, consectetur adipisicing elit, sed do eiusmod tempor incididunt ut labore et dolore magna aliqua. Ut enim ad minim veniam, quis nostrud exercitation ullamco laboris nisi ut aliquip ex ea commodo consequat. Duis aute irure dolor in reprehenderit in voluptate velit esse cillum dolore eu fugiat nulla pariatur. Excepteur sint occaecat cupidatat non proident, sunt in culpa qui officia deserunt mollit anim id est laborum.

Lorem ipsum dolor sit amet, consectetur adipisicing elit, sed do eiusmod tempor incididunt ut labore et dolore magna aliqua. Ut enim ad minim veniam, quis nostrud exercitation ullamco laboris nisi ut aliquip ex ea commodo consequat. Duis aute irure dolor in reprehenderit in voluptate velit esse cillum dolore eu fugiat nulla pariatur. Ex-

cepteur sint occaecat cupidatat non proident, sunt in culpa qui officia deserunt mollit anim id est laborum.

Lorem ipsum dolor sit amet, consectetur adipisicing elit, sed do eiusmod tempor incididunt ut labore et dolore magna aliqua. Ut enim ad minim veniam, quis nostrud exercitation ullamco laboris nisi ut aliquip ex ea commodo consequat. Duis aute irure dolor in reprehenderit in voluptate velit esse cillum dolore eu fugiat nulla pariatur. Excepteur sint occaecat cupidatat non proident, sunt in culpa qui officia deserunt mollit anim id est laborum.

Lorem ipsum dolor sit amet, consectetur adipisicing elit, sed do eiusmod tempor incididunt ut labore et dolore magna aliqua. Ut enim ad minim veniam, quis nostrud exercitation

Lorem ipsum dolor sit amet, consectetur adipisicing elit, do eiusmod tempor incididunt ut labore et dolore magna aliqua. Ut enim ad minim veniam, quis nostrud exercitation ullamco laboris nisi ut aliquip ex ea commodo consequat. Duis aute irure dolor in reprehenderit in voluptate velit esse cillum dolore eu fugiat nulla pariatur. Excepteur sint occaecat cupidatat non proident, sunt in culpa qui officia deserunt mollit anim id est laborum.

Lorem ipsum dolor sit amet, consectetur adipisicing elit, sed do eiusmod tempor incididunt ut labore et dolore magna aliqua. Ut enim ad minim veniam, quis nostrud exercitation ullamco laboris nisi ut aliquip ex ea commodo consequat. Duis aute irure dolor in reprehenderit in voluptate velit esse cillum dolore eu fugiat nulla pariatur. Ex-

cepteur sint occaecat cupidatat non proident, sunt in culpa qui officia deserunt mollit anim id est laborum.

Lorem ipsum dolor sit amet, consectetur adipisicing elit, sed do eiusmod tempor incididunt ut labore et dolore magna aliqua. Ut enim ad minim veniam, quis nostrud exercitation ullamco laboris nisi ut aliquip ex ea commodo consequat. Duis aute irure dolor in reprehenderit in voluptate velit esse cillum dolore eu fugiat nulla pariatur. Excepteur sint occaecat cupidatat non proident, sunt in culpa qui officia deserunt mollit anim id est laborum.

Lorem ipsum dolor sit amet, consectetur adipisicing elit, sed do eiusmod tempor incididunt ut labore et dolore magna aliqua. Ut enim ad minim veniam, quis nostrud exercitation

1. Lorem ipsum dolor sit amet, consectetur adipisicing elit, sed do eiusmod tempor incididunt ut labore et dolore magna aliqua. Ut enim ad minim veniam, quis nostrud exercitation ullamco laboris nisi ut aliquip ex ea commodo consequat. Duis aute irure dolor in reprehenderit in voluptate velit

2. Lorem ipsum dolor sit amet, consectetur adipisicing elit, sed do eiusmod tempor incididunt ut labore et dolore magna aliqua. Ut enim ad minim veniam, quis nostrud exercitation ullamco laboris nisi ut aliquip ex ea commodo consequat. Duis aute irure dolor in reprehenderit in voluptate velit

Correct paragraph spacing.

Paragraphs

Paragraphs are the basic building block of your book, so make paragraphs look their best.

The first paragraph in a chapter or after a headline or subhead should not have an indent—all other paragraphs should.

Indents should not be created by using a tab or by spacing over. Create a style with a first-line indent instead. If you turn your manuscript over to a typesetter full of extra spaces or tabs, he or she will have to remove them which will cost them time and you money.

Set your indent to one-quarter of an inch (.25") and not larger unless you are using big type for the visually impaired. Unfortunately, many word processing programs have the default set to an ungainly half inch (.5").

Never use a double return to create space between paragraphs. Most of the time, you will not need extra space between paragraphs, the indent will give the reader enough of a visual break. If you want more white space on the page, create a paragraph style with slightly more space above each paragraph.

Quotes

If you transcribe a document or quote another author directly, the entire paragraph(s) should be indented from both sides to form a narrower block of text. Create a bit more space above and below quoted paragraphs, as well. Quoted paragraphs should be fully justified (explanation below).

Justified Text

In books, paragraphs should be fully justified not justified ragged right. That is, they should look like a square block of text. In the era of typewriters, ragged right was unavoidable. The type along the right-hand edge of the page was uneven (ragged). Modern software creates much better looking fully justified text blocks.

One potential problem with full justification is the text on the last line of each paragraph. If there are only a couple of words, full justification will spread the words out to the right-hand edge leaving unnaturally large spaces between the words. Most word processing programs give you a way to keep the last line of each fully justified paragraph together on the left.

Use centering and ragged right justification sparingly; in fact, almost never. Poetry with short lines can be centered, but a full paragraph that is centered is difficult to read.

Hyphenation

Most of the time, automatic hyphenation is fine because it avoids creating rivers of white down the page which disturbs the reader's ability to move smoothly from left to right, word to word. On occasion, automatic hyphenation will result

Justified Ragged Right	Justified Ragged Left
Lorem ipsum dolor sit amet, consectetur adipisicing elit, sed do eiusmod tempor incididunt ut labore et dolore magna aliqua. Ut enim ad minim veniam, quis nostrud exercitation ullamco laboris nisi ut aliquip ex ea commodo consequat. Duis aute irure dolor	Lorem ipsum dolor sit amet, consectetur adipisicing elit, sed do eiusmod tempor incididunt ut labore et dolore magna aliqua. Ut enim ad minim veniam, quis nostrud exercitation ullamco laboris nisi ut aliquip ex ea commodo consequat. Duis

Ragged right.   Ragged left.

Fully Justified Correctly	Fully Justified Incorrectly
Lorem ipsum dolor sit amet, consectetur adipisicing elit, sed do eiusmod tempor incididunt ut labore et dolore magna aliqua. Ut enim ad minim veniam, quis nostrud exercitation ullamco laboris nisi ut aliquip ex ea commodo consequat.	Lorem ipsum dolor sit amet, consectetur adipisicing elit, sed do eiusmod tempor incididunt ut labore et dolore magna aliqua. Ut enim ad minim veniam, quis nostrud exercitation ullamco laboris nisi ut aliquip ex ea commodo consequat.

Fully justified correctly (left); Fully justified incorrectly (forced outward spacing) (right).

in lines of hyphens stacked on top of each other (see above left). If this happens, you can artificially hyphenate a few words to make the paragraph look better.

Watch for odd hyphenation breaks. You would not want menswear to become men-swear, or therapist to become the-rapist.

Widows and Orphans

Widows and orphans are bits of text that do not fit neatly into the column grid.

Widows are created when: the last line of a paragraph appears on the following page or at the top of the next column; a headline or subhead is in one column (page) but the paragraph that follows it is in another column (page); or the last bullet in a list is in another column (page).

Page layout programs have much better tools to control widows and orphans than do word processors, including ways to control white space and hyphenation, commands to keep lines together, and the ability to alter the length of a column to force a line into the next column.

If you are using a word processor, one way to control widows is to add a hard return before a widowed headline to force it into the next column or onto the next page. If you have a widowed bullet or a widowed line, see if you can cut the text

Widows and orphans.

above without changing the meaning to allow enough space for the line or bullet to remain with the paragraph or list.

Orphans are created when: the first line of a paragraph appears in one column (page) but the rest of the paragraph appears in the next column (page); the last word of a paragraph is left on a line by itself.

One way to control orphans is to turn on or off automatic hyphenation for the paragraph. This may shift another word onto the last line of the paragraph. Another option is to alter the text without altering the meaning, so there are fewer words to fit in the paragraph.

Initials and Acronyms

How you handle initials and acronyms is a matter of preference as long as you are consistent throughout.

How you handle people known only by their initials is a matter of style. Typically, there are no spaces between initials, so D.S. Yates rather than D. S. Yates.

Acronyms typically do not have periods between the letters, so NASA rather than N.A.S.A.

Some acronyms, such as AM and PM, are typically set in small caps (AM and PM) rather than in full caps, although some style guides use a.m. and p.m. (or am and pm) instead. Small caps are a function of the font, although not all fonts have a small caps option.

Web and Email Addresses

Because we are in the Internet age, your book may include website URLs (website addresses), or email addresses. In electronic books (eBooks), these addresses can be made into hyperlinks so that the reader can click on the link to be taken to the website, or to launch an email program. In printed books, it is up to you whether or not you leave the color and underlining that word processing programs add when addresses are hyperlinked. Most word processors use a bright blue for hyperlinks, which may not be readable in print. Changing them to black will help. Increasing the letter spacing in website addresses also makes them easier to read.

Punctuation

Punctuation can make or break meaning. If you have not already read Lynne Truss's book, *Eats, Shoots & Leaves: A Zero Tolerance Approach to Punctuation*, you should. Single-handedly, she is conducting a rather hilarious war on the proliferation of commas.

Dashes and Hyphens

Hyphens are used to create compound adjectives, such as state-of-the-art computer. Hyphens are used for compound numbers (forty-four books), double last names (Sir Watkin Williams-Wynn), and spelled-out fractions (two-thirds). Hyphens once were used to distinguish all pre-fixes (pre-arranged), but less so today. If eliminating the hyphen would cause confusion with another word (recovered a lost wallet versus re-covered a sofa), then use the hyphen.

Dashes are not hyphens, nor double hyphens. Fortunately, most word processors will turn double hyphens into an em dash. Unfortunately, most word processors do not know the difference between the em dash and the en dash.

An en dash, a dash approximately the width of the letter n, is used to indicate duration, so October–December (October through December), or 10–12 (ten to twelve).

An em dash, a dash approximately the width of the letter m, is used when you want the reader to pause a bit longer than they would for a comma, but not as long as they would for a period. Em dashes are a matter of preference. Many authors will use parentheses to set off a change in thought, others prefer em dashes.

En and em dashes do not have spaces—before or after them.

Ellipses

Ellipses, a series of three periods (...) with a bit of extra space in between, are used to indicate a long pause in thought, or that material was left out of a quote.

Fortunately, if you put three periods in a row without adding a space in between, most word processors will display them correctly.

If you end a sentence with an ellipsis, you still need a period to end the sentence, so there will be four dots.

Ellipses require a full space before and a full space after.

Special Characters

Special characters include bullets, copyright symbols, and accent marks on foreign language words. These special characters are found in glyph or symbols menus. Fortunately, many word processors and page layout programs automatically insert correct accents on common words such as cliché.

Serial Commas

Although Lynne Truss is waging an admirable war on the proliferation of commas, sometimes the serial comma is needed when listing items. For example, you could eliminate the last comma from a list such as bananas, oranges, and apples. If however, you eliminated the last comma from, "To my siblings, Mom, and Grandma," you would be implying that your mother and grandmother were your siblings (i.e. "To my siblings, Mom and Grandma").

It is up to you how you handle serial commas, as long as meaning is clear.

Quotation Marks

Quotation marks are not apostrophes. Quotation marks are the curly-cue-looking marks that face one way at the beginning of a quote, and the other way at the end. Make this simple on yourself by turning on the "smart quotes," in your word processing or page layout program and avoid fonts that do not have true, left and right quotation marks.

Quotation marks should not be used for emphasis. Use italics if you want to get the reader's attention. Use quotation marks for direct quotations, to alert readers that a term is being used in a non-standard way such as for irony or sarcasm, or to replace the words "so-called."

Place commas and periods inside quotation marks. Colons and semi-colons belong outside quotation marks. Place question marks or exclamation points inside if they belong to quoted material, otherwise outside.

Semi-Colons

Semi-colons are used to link two independent clauses together. Most of the time, however, you can use a period and start a new sentence with the same effect.

You can also use a semi-colon to link items in a list together where a comma could cause confusion. For example, "some people choose to go places by motorized vehicles, cars, motorcycles or buses; but others, for different reasons, choose to walk, bicycle or roller skate."

Apostrophes

Apostrophes are used to indicate possession (e.g. John's book), to create contractions (e.g. don't) and to indicate the omission of letters, so Rock and Roll becomes Rock 'n' Roll because both the "a" and the "d" in "and" are replaced with an apostrophe.

A single, straight apostrophe indicates feet (e.g. 125'). A double, straight apostrophe indicates inches (e.g. 3").

In the 80s, means the temperature is in the 80s. In the '80s, means the decade of the 1980s (or 1880s). There is no apostrophe when referring to a decade (1850s) unless you are indicating possession (1850's clothing styles).

Lines, Rules, and Strokes

The terms lines, rules and strokes all mean a line. Most often lines are used in the header to separate the book title or chapter title from the body text.

If you use lines, choose a numbered point size for the thickness of your lines. Avoid the hairline setting, because "hairline" is interpreted differently by each printer's machinery, so the results may be unexpected.

Color

If the interior of your book is color throughout, you can use color for headlines and subheads to make them stand out. Black text is still the easiest to read, so if you use a color for headlines or subheads, choose one that is dark enough to be read easily, and use the same color throughout the book for consistency. Any dark color can work, although people with red-green color blindness will appreciate it if you avoid those two colors.

Cross-References

You may need to include cross-references to chapters, numbered sections, illustrations or pages. The only way to create cross-references without creating a lot of extra work for yourself, is to leave a visual indicator in the text (e.g. [XXXXX]), and wait until the final page proofs are available before adding the appropriate reference.

Most how-to or instructional guides do not need cross-references except in the index. You can accomplish much of the same with good explanations in foot- or endnotes.

Clean Up Your Manuscript Files

Before you begin typesetting, clean up your manuscript files.

One common habit of people who learned to type on typewriters is to put two spaces before the beginning of a new sentence. Modern word processors use proportional spacing at the end of sentences so they do not need the extra space. Use the Find/Replace command to search for two spaces and replace them with a single space. Repeat this task until the software indicates that no more replacements have been made. This will eliminate the extra spaces created by the old typewriter trick of spacing over instead of using tabs, as well.

Remove extra tabs. Paragraphs should not be created by tabbing over. They should be given a style with a first-line indent instead (see Creating Styles below).

Eliminate double returns using Find/Replace. Double returns should not separate paragraphs. The first-line indent in the next paragraph will be enough to distinguish when one paragraph ends and the next begins.

Extra space is used to indicate the start of a new section or a change in topic where a new chapter or headline is not necessary. Double returns are not used to create this extra space. Instead, create a paragraph style to govern this situation, with even more space above the paragraph than that above a subhead, but less than a double return.

Look for odd line breaks, out of place page breaks, and missing punctuation.

Once your manuscript is clean, you can begin creating styles to govern how the text will look.

Create Styles

Most word processing and page layout programs allow you to create styles for different types of text (paragraphs, headlines and so on), and then apply the style when appropriate.

The easiest way to start formatting an entire chapter is to create a style for the majority of the body copy and apply it to the entire chapter. Then you can create new styles for first paragraphs that do not have indents, headlines that could be in bigger or bolder text than the body, and image captions that should be somewhat smaller than the body text.

In most software, each time you encounter a need for a new style, you can manually format the text, and then select that text to create a new style—the software will copy each of the attributes of the new text into the new style. After you create the new style, simply highlight text and apply the new style when needed.

❧❧❧

If you do not believe you can typeset the book yourself, you could hire a book packager to help you.

Working with a Book Packager

Book packagers (designers) offer layout and design services, including book design, typesetting, image preparation, cover design and in some cases indexing. Most book packagers will offer these services together or individually, depending upon your needs.

Interior Design

Provide your manuscript along with a few examples of layouts you like to the book packager so they can understand the type of book you have written, as well as your style preferences. Acquiring good examples may necessitate a trip to a library with a good genealogical collection or to a bookstore that sells a broad selection of how-to guides.

Non-fiction formatting tends to be content specific. Using another how-to or instructional manual as your guide is probably best. A book designer who has worked with these kinds of non-fiction manuscripts before may have suggestions for you.

Most book designers will offer two to three designs plus two rounds of revisions before you pay more than the initial quote. The better you can explain or demonstrate what you want at the outset, the more likely the designer is to create what you are looking for in the first round of designs.

Typesetting

Most of the time, if you have a professional design your book, you will also have them typeset the book because you may not use the same software they use, so there would be no way to hand over the master layout to you. Before you submit your manuscript for typesetting, clean up any overlooked double spaces, tabs and section breaks. Then proofread carefully so you are not paying the typesetter to do that for you.

Print it out. A printout is a way to be sure that nothing is missing or misplaced in the manuscript files. Check it over carefully first. If you find errors and make corrections to the manuscript, print a clean copy for the typesetter.

Image Preparation

You cannot prepare your images for the correct display size at the correct resolution until you have a layout in order to know how big or small each image must be in order to fit into the grid. If you have scanned the images at sizes larger than what will be needed, much of the hard work should already be done. Your book packager can then help you to correctly size the image for the book's layout.

Indexing

Not all book designers offer indexing services, although some do. Using a book packager or a professional indexer can be costly because he or she must read the manuscript in order to determine what should or should not be indexed, and that takes time.

Often called a poor man's index, you can make the job of indexing easy for a book packager by printing a copy of the final layout, and highlighting the items to be indexed. The highlighted copy along with a style sheet of how you want names, places and subjects indexed should be enough for your book packager to take care of the indexing for you.

Another option is to mark the index entries for yourself in your word processor. Index tags from Word import into InDesign, for example, and most book designers accept Word documents. Before you spend the time to index this way, make certain that the book packager can import your index tags.

Cover Design

Every book should have a cover worthy of the work it took to write the book. Book packagers offer cover design services, or you may want to use a cover designer—a graphic artist who only designs covers. Either way, he or she will need to know whether the book will be available for sale. Commercial books have different requirements than books solely for your family's enjoyment. The elements of a book cover meant for commercial sale are described in Chapter 21: Designing the Cover.

The cover will be the last part of your project finalized because spine width is dependent upon the final page count and the paper used, which may be different from printer to printer. In most cases, you will receive a template from your printer after you have a final page count, so that the dimensions and spine width are correct in the template. The designer can assemble the elements ahead of time and make final adjustments to the file when the page count is known.

File Formats

Most book packagers can work with any type of file format generated by one of the common word processors (.doc, .docx, .wpd) as well as plain text files (.txt) or rich text files (.rtf). Most word processors will also convert their native file formats to something more common such as a Microsoft Word file, if that is what the designer prefers.

Ask before converting anything. Converting to a plain text file will eliminate all of your formatting. Converting to a PDF is not helpful either, since PDFs are not easily re-formatted.

PUBLISH YOUR SPECIALTY

Portfolio

Before you ask about cost, look at the designer's work. You want to make sure that he or she has experience preparing books for a printer. Many book packagers have an online portfolio or can send you examples.

Another option is to hire someone who is looking to create a portfolio piece and is willing to do whatever it takes to finish the job to your satisfaction—at a lower price. Students and people who are learning the craft are often willing to work for much less than established book designers.

Cost

Book packagers charge for some services by the piece (image preparation), other services by the page (typesetting), and a few services by the hour (indexing). If you would rather have the designer give you a bid for the whole project, they will need to know the approximate page count and number of illustrations. They will set limits on the number of designs and revisions they will give you on the interior and cover. If you reject the initial round of designs all together, you may have to pay an additional fee to see more designs.

Write a Formal Proposal or Contract

Once you have a cost estimate from the designer, write an additional proposal making your expectations clear about what work will be taken care of by the designer, and what you are responsible for providing to him or her. Include firm deadlines and a do-not-exceed price—the price beyond which you cannot go. Most designers will give you an estimate with a price range since it is difficult to know exactly what you will or will not like until the work is started. You may want to make more changes than what the original agreement calls for, which may necessitate a new estimate. The designer should take care of any errors that are their fault, but be prepared to pay extra if you edit once the typesetting is done.

∼❧❧∼

Typesetting is all about making your manuscript easy to read. Choosing appropriate fonts and type sizes, spacing between letters and lines, and justifying body text are the heart and soul of the typesetting rules. If you can also avoid common punctuation errors, and eliminate any widows and orphans, your book's interior will look like it was typeset by a professional.

Chapter 18

Typesetting the Front Matter

This chapter will take you through the front matter in the order the front matter should appear in your book, from the first item (the endsheets) to the last item (the introduction).

Almost every front matter element should begin on a right-hand (recto) page which means that there may be blank pages within your front matter. Beginning each new section on a right-hand page is a publishing convention—a tradition, but in the interest of saving space, many publishers today are running each successive part on the next available page.

There are not many examples in this chapter because you will find working examples in the front matter of this book.

Endsheets

In hardcover books, endsheets are used to reinforce the attachment from the cloth cover to the sewn-together pages of the interior, so you will find an endsheet in the front and the back of the book. If you are using an offset printer, you may be able to choose the illustration or design for your endsheets. Other printers have stock designs for you to choose from, although many use a common endsheet.

Endsheets are not necessary to hold the covers onto softbound (paperback) books, therefore, are not used. With some printers, it is possible to print an illustration on the inside cover of a paperback book, but it is almost always an extra charge. Most print-on-demand printers do not offer this option.

Frontispiece

A frontispiece is an illustration on the left-hand (verso) side facing the title page. These are common, mostly in high-end coffee table books.

Although an illustration could go on the reverse side of the endsheet, a frontispiece is usually a separate page using the same paper as the interior, rather than the heavier endsheet paper.

Endorsements or Blurbs

Endorsements are also called blurbs. It is common for publishers with commercially available books to solicit short blurbs from well-known authors or experts. The best blurbs belong on the cover or dust jacket flaps. Any others go on pages before the half-title page, and these pages are not numbered.

If you are going to solicit blurbs, five or six will do. Keep them short and sweet. If you are soliciting a well-known author or expert, offer a blurb already written for his or her approval or to edit as he or she sees fit.

Blurbs are typically set in the main body font, in quotes. The name of the blurb's author follows on a separate line either centered or flush right, followed by a line containing any titles, awards or books he or she has written, also centered or flush right. Use italics for book titles.

Half-Title Page

A half-title page was used more than a century ago to identify an unsold book. In those days, books were printed, but not bound until sold, so that the new owner could choose the binding. Today, half title pages are not necessary but if you include one, the reverse side should be blank.

The half-title page should be typeset in whatever font you have chosen for your chapter headers, but big enough to make a statement, placed about one-third of the way down the page.

Ad Card

One option for the reverse side of the title page is to include an ad card—a list of other books you have written. Look at the ad card in this book. It begins with: "Other books by the author" and lists the titles. You could begin with: "Author of ..." or "Also by ..."

The ad card is typeset in the main body font, flush left, but justified ragged right. If you are only listing titles, full justification may stretch the words apart unnaturally.

Title Page

Typeset the title in the same font and size as the half-title page, and place it about one-third of the way down the page. The title should be followed by the subtitle in the same font but smaller. The author's name should be placed about two-thirds of the way down the page, followed by the publishing company, and the city where the book was published (the city of the publishing company not the printer) at the bottom. If you have a logo for your publishing company, it can go on this page, as well.

The reverse side of the title page is the copyrights page.

Copyrights Page

The copyrights page belongs on the back of the title page and should include:

- The title and subtitle
- The author's name
- The publisher's name and physical address
- A copyright notice (the symbol and year)
- The name of the copyright owner
- The expression "all rights reserved" to give you the maximum protection in case of copyright infringement
- A disclaimer, if needed. Most books today include one even if not needed.
- Publishing history (edition or print run if there has been more than one)
- Printed in the United States of America (or wherever the book was printed)

If you plan to sell your book commercially or to libraries, also consider:

Library of Congress (LOC) Cataloging-in-Publication Data [LCC CIP]. The CIP data is bibliographic data prepared by the Library of Congress to help libraries and book dealers correctly catalog the book.

Before the book is published, apply for the CIP Program online (www.loc.gov/publish/cip/).

You can also create your own CIP data, called the Publisher's CIP data, if you do not want to wait months for the Library of Congress to do this for you.

Library of Congress Catalog Number (LCCN or PCN—Preassigned Control Number). A Library of Congress catalog control number (or preassigned number) is a unique identification number given by the LOC, that is included in their national database available to libraries, book stores and other commercial suppliers. Before your book is published, apply for a Library of Congress PCN (www.loc.gov/publish/pcn/).

International Standard Book Number (ISBN). An ISBN is like the Social Security number for you book. It is a unique number assigned by the U.S. ISBN Agency run by the Bowker Company (www.isbn.org). From the website, you can purchase a single ISBN, a block of ten, a block of 100, and so on. A single ISBN costs $125.00. A block of ten costs $295.00.

If you are planning to publish through a print-on-demand printer, many offer ISBNs free of charge. The only drawback to using one of your printer's ISBNs is that the printer becomes the publisher of record, and not you or your publishing company. For many how-to authors, however, using the printer's free ISBN is the simplest way to go.

The copyrights page should be typeset in the main body font, but the majority of the text will be set at a point size small enough to fit all of the above information onto one page. Use the copyrights page of this book as a guide.

Dedication

Many authors use the dedication page to thank whoever has been the greatest influence while writing the book. Most dedications are short. Longer tributes belong in the acknowledgments section.

The dedication page should be typeset in the main body font, in Roman (plain) text or italics.

Dedication pages are optional. If used, they should occupy a right-hand page, and the back should be blank.

Acknowledgments

Acknowledgments are your opportunity to thank the people who helped you research or write the book. Acknowledgments are optional.

If used, be rigorous when checking the spelling of each person's name, and if they have a title, use the correct, most recently earned title.

Acknowledgments begin on a right-hand page, and can be placed after the dedication, after the preface, within the preface, or in the back matter. If your acknowledgments run an odd number of pages, the last page should be blank.

Acknowledgments should be typeset in the main body font, and if there are many paragraphs, should follow the rules for the rest of the book. If there is a single paragraph, it can be set in italics about one-third of the way down the page.

Epigraph

An epigraph is a pertinent quote that sets the tone for the book, and is optional. Epigraphs are sometimes used on the first page of each chapter.

If the epigraph is typeset on a right-hand page, the back of the page should be blank. Epigraphs can also go on the left-hand page facing the table of contents, if that page is blank.

Epigraphs should be in quotes, in the main body font, in Roman (plain) text or italics. The author's name (or anonymous, if not known) should be placed on a line beneath the quote, followed by the source of the quote on another line. If the source is a book title, it should be typeset in italics.

Table of Contents

The table of contents (TOC) begins on a right-hand page. If there is only one page, the reverse side should be left blank. If the contents run more than one page, they are called contents *only* and can be set *either* on a left-right, two-page spread (pages ii and iii, for example), or beginning on a right-hand page with the remainder on the next left-hand page (pages iii and iv, in this case).

The table of contents can be set in either the main body font or the font you have chosen for your headlines and subheads. The page numbers should be type-set with a right-aligned tab to keep the right-hand edges of the page numbers even down the page.

The table of contents should show the number of the first page of each part of the front matter, the parts (or sections), each chapter, the back matter and the index. How much else you include beyond the chapter number, is up to you. You could include the chapter title (if there are chapter titles), and a running list of subtitles to give the reader an idea of what to expect in each chapter. The example (below) from Buzzy Jackson's book *Shaking the Family Tree* uses a running narrative to give readers an idea of what is included in each chapter.

Illustrations

If your book has many illustrations, include a list of illustrations (also called a list of figures). If the illustrations correspond closely with the text, the list is probably not necessary because the information will be provided in the captions, descriptive text or footnotes.

A list of illustrations should include the name (or a description) of the illustration, plus the page number where it occurs. The page numbers should be typeset with a right-aligned tab to keep the right-hand edges of the page numbers even down the page. The back side of a list of illustrations should be blank.

Tables

Lists of tables are common in scientific literature, military histories and occasionally in how-to books. If you need

CONTENTS

Ask Yourself Why You're Doing This; or, Genealogy for Beginners   1
An introduction to the world of genealogy and how I got interested in it. Here I provide an outline of how to do genealogical research and, coincidentally, a map of the book's structure.

They See Dead People But I Stick to the Living; or, Join Your Local Genealogical Society   18
Seeking help from experienced genealogists, I join my local genealogical society. I begin my family research by interviewing my parents and by asking myself how much I really know about my family tree. Answer: not much.

Interview Your Relatives and Go to Your High School Reunion; or, Rust Never Sleeps   39
Having exhausted my parents' fund of knowledge (and my own), I travel to Michigan to conduct interviews with extended family, seek access (mostly denied) to family Bibles, and visit my grandparents' graves for the first time. A few weeks later I attend my twentieth high school reunion, which offers another type of family connection.

Table of Contents.

one, the back of the page should be left blank. A list of tables should be typeset in the same way as a list of illustrations.

Foreword

A foreword is statement about the book written by someone other than the author. Forewords are common in biographies of famous people, but not common in how-tos or instructional guides.

If you include one, a foreword longer than two to three pages should have a title of its own with the author's name at the beginning, rather than at the end, which is typical for short forewords.

The foreword should be typeset in the main body text and follow the same rules as the body as far as paragraphs, headlines and subheads. If your foreword runs an odd number of pages, the next page should be left blank so that the next section will begin on a right-hand page.

Typeset the following using the same rules as the foreword:

Front Matter	Body	Back Matter
Preface	Epilogue	Postscript
Methods	Afterword	About the Author
Contributors		Glossary
Chronology		Colophon
Characters		
Permissions		
Prologue		

Preface

A preface is optional. It is a way for you, the author, to address the reader directly. A preface is one place to explain your research methods, the reasons you undertook this project, or why you are so interested in this subject. Many authors include their acknowledgments in the preface. If you do, there is no need for another section of acknowledgments elsewhere.

Methods

A methods section (also called editorial method) is used in scholarly works where the author's analysis needs explanation. In a how-to or instructional guide, you may want to alert readers to how you arrived at a conclusion if the explanation is important before they begin reading. Much of this could be included in footnotes or endnotes rather than in the front matter.

Contributors

A list of contributors is optional. If someone provided expertise that calls for more than a simple acknowledgment, a list of contributors is the place to give credit along with a short explanation describing how each person or group helped you with this project.

Chronology

A chronology can be helpful if the order of events is not clear, as may happen in a collection of letters, or in a diary with missing entries.

Use a chronology to provide a broader historical context. For example, a list of events preceding the U.S. involvement in the Mexican War and the battles that took place thereafter may be helpful because readers may not be well acquainted with the events of the Mexican War.

A chronology can also serve as a quick reference if your book covers multiple topics with overlapping time lines.

A chronology should begin on a right-hand page, unless it would be simpler for the reader to use a left-right spread.

Characters

Occasionally, in fiction you may find a list of characters. If you need to show relationships between people, you could use genealogical charts.

A list of characters could include: every member of a family or military unit; people who had an influence on your subject but who are not written about in this book; and other people whose work would supplement or complement your book on the subject.

Alphabetize by last name followed by a comma and the first name. To help readers keep people with similar names straight, include birth and death dates as well as a short, descriptive paragraph about the character. Typeset the names in bold or italics either as subheads or run-in subheads.

Permissions

If you have only a few places where you need to acknowledge permissions given to use material for the book, they could be placed in a footnote, an endnote, an image credit or a sidebar. A list may be easier if you have many permissions to acknowledge.

A list of permissions can be placed in either the front or the back matter and should begin on a right-hand page. You can organize the list of permissions in order as the items occur, or alphabetically by repository to avoid repeating information if many items came from one repository. When describing sources, give the location in the book by chapter and (or) page, then use the same style as endnotes or footnotes, typically using either *Evidence Explained* or *The Chicago Manual of Style*.

Prologue

A prologue is used in fiction to set the scene for the story and is told in the voice of one of the characters rather than by the author. Most how-to books do not include a prologue.

Second Half-Title Page

If the front matter is long, you can use a second half-title page to give readers a visual clue where the body of the book begins. The second half-title page should look exactly like the first half-title page.

Introduction

Use an introduction to set the stage. Explain your purpose or goals in writing the book. Make clear the organization and scope of the book. Explain what the book will do, will not do, and what the reader can expect to learn or be able to do as a result of reading the book.

The introduction, although technically a part of the front matter, is the beginning of the book. The introduction should follow the typesetting rules for the body, with one exception. Although the page numbers in the preceding front matter sections are set in lowercase Roman numerals, switch to Arabic numerals when you begin the introduction.

Some publishers will continue the page numbers from the front matter, so if the last page of the front matter was page viii, then the first page of the introduction would be page 9. Others will restart the numbering with page 1 on the first page of the introduction. The first style is more traditional, although the latter style is becoming more common.

۔ೂ؈

Much of what can be included in the front matter is optional. The sections that *are* necessary are the title page, the copyrights page, and the table of contents. Beyond that, it is up to you as the publisher to decide what else to include.

Chapter 19

Typesetting the Body

Most of the typesetting for the body of the book is about the paragraphs, headlines and subheads covered in the previous section. The remainder is how to create first pages different enough to give the reader a visual clue that a new section or chapter is beginning.

Parts or Sections—First Pages

If you have divided the manuscript into parts or sections, you will need an opening page for each. These pages should act as dividers and should be right-hand pages with the reverse side left blank unless you wish to use an epigraph or illustration there.

Typeset the part or section title in large letters about one-third of the way down the page using the same font as your title and subtitle. You can use the part or section title alone, or include a mini-table of contents for the section.

Neither the front nor the back of this page should have a running header or a page number, but these pages contribute to the page count. So even though they should not have page numbers on them, count the pages following a part or section divider as if they did.

Chapters—First Pages

The first page of each chapter should be easy to find while thumbing through a book. Traditionally, chapters begin on a new page on the right-hand side. If you end up with many blank pages because chapters have an uneven number of pages, you can ignore the convention to minimize the number of blank pages—with two exceptions: chapters *must* begin on a *new* page (whether left or right) and Chapter One *must* begin on a *right-hand* page.

Publish Your Specialty

Chapter titles are optional, but numbers are not. If you use titles, they should be consistent in tone from one chapter to the next. In other words, do not use a whimsical title for one, and a serious statement for the next.

Chapter numbers start at one and are consecutive no matter what section they are in, so that chapter numbers are never repeated.

The first page of a chapter should not have a page number or a running header. The chapter number and (or) title should begin at least two inches from the top of the page, but could be as low as one-third of the way down the page with the body text beginning about half-way down the page.

Footnotes or Endnotes

Whether you put your source citations in footnotes or endnotes is up to you. Opinions are divided about whether readers would rather refer to an endnotes page or read footnotes as they occur in the text.

If you use footnotes, leave enough room between the text and the footnote to make it obvious, or use a rule (line) in between. Most word processing and page layout programs create footnotes for you, so they are not technically footers because the amount of space they occupy will change from page to page depending upon how many notes there are on each page.

If you use endnotes, place them either at the end of the chapter, or together in the back matter.

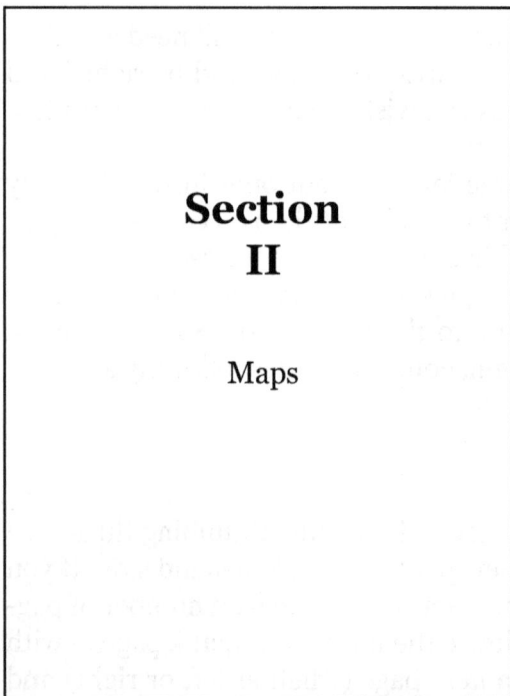

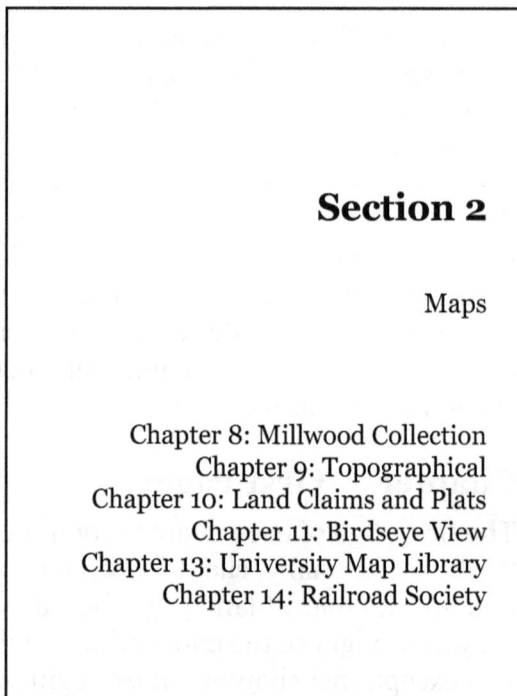

Section II Maps	**Section 2** Maps Chapter 8: Millwood Collection Chapter 9: Topographical Chapter 10: Land Claims and Plats Chapter 11: Birdseye View Chapter 13: University Map Library Chapter 14: Railroad Society

Section divider with number and title (left); Section divider with mini-table of contents (right).

Typical formatting for footnotes or endnotes is as follows:

1. Author (first then last), *Title in Italics* (City of publication: Publisher, date), p. number.

Epilogue

An epilogue is a final note from you, the author, or as a continuation of the main narrative to bring closure to the book.

Afterword

An afterword, is a way for you, the author, to give your final thoughts. Let readers know about additional research you are doing, tell a funny story that wraps up the book, or give the reader an enticing preview of your next book.

Conclusion

If you did not do so in the epilogue, use the conclusion to provide a brief summary of the main points.

Chapter 4

Lorem ipsum dolor sit amet, consectetur adipisicing elit, sed do eiusmod tempor incididunt ut labore et dolore magna aliqua. Ut enim ad minim veniam, quis nostrud exercitation ullamco laboris nisi ut aliquip ex ea commodo consequat. Duis aute irure dolor in reprehenderit in voluptate velit esse cillum dolore eu fugiat nulla pariatur. Excepteur sint occaecat cupidatat non proident, sunt in culpa qui officia deserunt mollit anim id est laborum.

Lorem ipsum dolor sit amet, consectetur adipisicing elit, sed do eiusmod tempor incididunt ut labore et dolore magna aliqua. Ut enim ad minim veniam, quis nostrud exercitation ullamco laboris nisi ut aliquip ex ea commodo consequat. Duis aute irure dolor in reprehenderit in voluptate velit esse cillum dolore eu fugiat nulla pariatur. Excepteur sint occaecat cupidatat non proident, sunt in culpa qui officia deserunt mollit anim id est laborum.

Lorem ipsum dolor sit amet, consectetur adipisicing elit, sed do eiusmod tempor incididunt ut labore et dolore magna aliqua. Ut enim ad minim veniam, quis nostrud exercitation

Chapter 4

Assessor's Cards

Lorem ipsum dolor sit amet, consectetur adipisicing elit, sed do eiusmod tempor incididunt ut labore et dolore magna aliqua. Ut enim ad minim veniam, quis nostrud exercitation ullamco laboris nisi ut aliquip ex ea commodo consequat. Duis aute irure dolor in reprehenderit in voluptate velit esse cillum dolore eu fugiat nulla pariatur. Excepteur sint occaecat cupidatat non proident, sunt in culpa qui officia deserunt mollit anim id est laborum.

Lorem ipsum dolor sit amet, consectetur adipisicing elit, sed do eiusmod tempor incididunt ut labore et dolore magna aliqua. Ut enim ad minim veniam, quis nostrud exercitation ullamco laboris nisi ut aliquip ex ea commodo consequat. Duis aute irure dolor in reprehenderit in voluptate velit esse cillum dolore eu fugiat nulla pariatur. Excepteur sint occaecat cupidatat non proident, sunt in culpa qui officia deserunt mollit anim id est laborum.

Lorem ipsum dolor sit amet, consectetur adipisicing elit, sed do eiusmod tempor incididunt ut labore et dolore magna aliqua. Ut enim ad minim veniam, quis nostrud exercitation ullamco laboris nisi ut aliquip ex ea commodo consequat. Duis aute irure dolor in reprehenderit in voluptate velit esse cillum dolore eu fugiat

Chapter with number (left); Chapter with number and title (right).

PUBLISH YOUR SPECIALTY

❧❧

Because most of the typesetting for the book concerns paragraphs, headlines, subheads and running headers, what is left is to create visual breaks for parts (sections) and the first page of each chapter, and to decide where to place the source citations—in footnotes or endnotes.

Chapter 20

Typesetting the Back Matter

The back matter begins when the stories cease and you have had your last word as the author—well, almost. There is the possibility of a postscript. Back matter typically includes appendices, endnotes, a bibliography and an index. Your back matter could also include a postscript, an about the author section, a glossary, errata, a colophon, an excerpt from another book, and an order form.

The following front matter can be placed in the back matter if you prefer: acknowledgments, lists of illustrations, tables, contributors, and permissions.

Postscript

A postscript is a place to add something you were unable to include in the book. If you came across additional research, for example, give a brief synopsis.

About the Author

An about the author section is optional. It is an opportunity to tell the reader who you are and why you wrote the book. It should include a brief biography and a photograph is customary. Often, a brief version is placed on the back cover, or a longer version on the dust jacket flap of a hardcover edition.

Appendices

Items in an appendix may explain, elaborate or clarify information that do not fit neatly into the narrative. Each appendix needs a title, a number or a letter. The first appendix should appear on a right-hand page. Each subsequent appendix could begin on the next available page, right or left, to avoid blank pages.

Addendum

An addendum is a section of new material that was unavailable when the book was written. Often, an addendum is added in a subsequent edition, updating information without a complete re-write.

Glossary

A glossary is optional, but appreciated if you use: foreign words; jargon or technical phrases (common if you are describing a process or a profession from a century or more ago); words used during an earlier era but not used today; or unfamiliar slang (e.g. military slang).

Alphabetize glossary terms followed by a brief explanation.

Endnotes

If you want to place endnotes in the back matter, they should begin on a right-hand page, be organized by chapter, and then by note number. Leave extra space before the start of each chapter's endnotes to create a visual break.

Bibliography

While a formal bibliography is optional in a how-to or instructional guide, readers may be interested in what books and articles you consulted in addition to any original source material you used.

You will find standard bibliographic style guides for published materials in *The Elements of Style* by William Strunk and E.B. White, or *A Manual for Writers of Term Papers, Theses, and Dissertations* by Kate L. Turabian.

Your bibliography could be organized by family, location, research facility or topic. If you organize in a way other than alphabetical by author's last name for the whole list, use a subhead to indicate the start of a new section, alphabetize within the section, and leave space before the subhead as a visual break.

Index

All non-fiction books must have an index. Fortunately, most word processing and page layout software makes it possible to create index tags electronically within the body text, which are compiled into an index once the final layout is finished. It is important to compile the index last, however, to make certain text has not shifted from one page to the next during any final editing or touch ups to the layout.

Unfortunately, there is not one, single set of rules for creating an index. Most publishing houses have their own criteria, as do professional indexers. As the publisher, you have a great deal of latitude in what you will include.

Indexing takes time and adds pages to the book, but, first and foremost, it should be a useful tool. Be careful not to let the task of indexing determine the contents. It is not uncommon to find books where material in the beginning is over-indexed, and material at the end is under-indexed because the indexer tired of the process.

There are three types of index listings to consider: names, places and subjects.

Every person mentioned should be included in the index. A full-name index has become the standard for genealogical works thanks to the persistence of genealogists such as Birdie Holsclaw. Your index should adhere to this standard.

Indexing places is helpful to other people researching the area, if the subject of your book is a location. Who knows, you may find yourself quoted or footnoted in another author's work.

Indexing subjects is a little trickier because it is hard to know what subjects are the most important to include. If you have spent time talking about battles, or the details of a profession, or have discussed the manufacturer of a product, those are the kinds of subjects worth including.

An index is not merely a list of names and places, it is a way for people to retrieve information quickly, so any subject you think would help the reader find what they are looking for will be appreciated.

Index the whole book—everything from the dedication to the appendices—with a couple of exceptions. There is no need to index the colophon or copyrights page, nor the bibliography because it is already alphabetical by author's name and therefore easy to search. Endnotes or footnotes may be a different matter, if you have included other explanatory material in the note. If there are relevant entries in the explanatory material, then index it.

Basic Index Formatting

The index should begin on a right-hand page and be typeset in the body font, one or two points smaller. Each page should have a running header and page numbers, the same as the rest of the book. Use hanging indents to keep the alphabetical first letter flush left, but the remainder of the listing along with the page numbers, indented about one-quarter of an inch. Use a slightly larger space between listings than the line leading for wrapped text to create a visual break or to add a bit of white space to the page.

When you begin a new letter in your alphabetical list, use a subhead in bold that is slightly larger than the index body text.

Some publishers use bold page numbers to indicate illustrations, and bold italicized page numbers to indicate boxed text or tables. If you have created a list of illustrations or tables in the front matter, there is no need for this type of formatting in your index.

Page numbers are formatted according to long-standing tradition. Information that occurs on sequential pages is formatted with an en dash in between the numbers, but only if the discussion of the subject is continuous across those pages. For example, a person may be mentioned on page 140 and again on page 141, but there is *not* a continuous discussion of this person, so the formatting would be 140, 141. If there had been a continuous discussion of that person, the formatting would be 140–141. This is a subtle difference and not crucial.

Most software-generated indexes will create a list of numbers separated by commas. You can save space in the index by combining a long list of consecutive page numbers (140, 141, 142, 143, 144), into a shorter run of 140–144. Whether you follow the long-standing convention of using the en dash only to indicate a continuous discussion of the subject, is up to you, although using the en dashes correctly is more accurate.

Depending upon your subject, there may be chapters where the same individual is mentioned on every page. Another way to cut down on the number of pages where an individual is indexed, is to give the reader the first page plus a symbol (e.g. * or # or +) on which a major player is mentioned in a chapter, but no subsequent page numbers. If you shorten the number of listings this way, explain it at the beginning of the index—true of any deviation from convention—so that the reader knows what to expect.

There is no need to indicate how many times an individual, place or subject is listed on a single page. An index points the reader to the page, it does not absolve the user of reading what is there.

Formatting Subjects

Main subjects should be flush left, then broken down into minor subjects. The minor subjects should be indented one-quarter of an inch using a hanging indent so that any wrapping page numbers fall at half an inch. Main subjects are capitalized; minor subjects are not unless they begin with a proper noun. If you include a cross-reference, the word "see" should be in italics before the cross-reference subject. The following is an example:

Wagon
    Conestoga   33, 70, 104
    repair, *see* wainwright
    trains 21-24, 47

Formatting Place Names

Formatting place names can be tricky if the place is known by more than one name during different time periods. The New Netherlands is a good example. If you discussed people who lived in the Manhattan area during Dutch rule, they would have lived in New Netherlands, not New York. If you are unsure whether your readers will be acquainted well enough with the location to know that New Netherlands became New York, you may want to include a cross-reference.

New Netherlands, *see also* New York.

Another way to deal with place names where the location is the same but the name is not, is to include an explanation, such as:

Denver, Denver County (then Arapahoe County), Colorado
Denver, Arapahoe County (now Denver County), Colorado

Index geographic names the way a reader would look for them, so:

The Dalles, Oregon.
  The Dalles, Oregon, not Dalles, The, Oregon because "The Dalles" is recognized as the place name.

Elms, The.
  However, if you have a property name such as The Elms, it would be indexed as Elms, The and not The Elms. (Indexing can be tricky.)

Florence, Italy.
  Florence not Firenze (for an English-speaking audience)

Pear Cottage.
  Pear Cottage, not Cottage, Pear

If you use abbreviations in your place names, do so consistently, such as:
  St. Louis or Saint Louis, but not a mixture of the two
  Ste. Genevieve County for Sainte Genevieve County
Or:
  Ste. Genevieve Co. (if you also consistently abbreviate county using Co.)

Formatting People's Names

Surnames are not universal, and they can be inconsistent over time. That makes them tricky to index if you have included people whose families are the same, but whose surnames are different. In general, whatever rule you followed for the text, repeat in the index, except where alphabetizing by your software becomes a problem. Not all software alphabetizes the same way. Microsoft Word, for example, will treat De la Rosa differently than de la Rosa, giving priority to the capitalized version. The index will show both versions, but the capitalized version will come first.

Most software will treat names with spaces in them differently than names without, so these words would be alphabetized as:

De la Rosa
Deify
Delarosa
Detrimental
Di Larosa

If the number of listings between the two versions of De la Rosa is substantial, use a cross-reference (e.g. *see* Di Larosa or *see* Du Larosa) so that the reader knows to look for another spelling. A different way to deal with this is to explain at the start of the index that you have made all versions of Vandergard (Vander Gard, Van Der Gard, van der Gard) the same for the purposes of indexing only.

If there are people with the same name, do something to distinguish them in the index, for example:

      Josiah Smith (1830–1899) 33, 89, 90
      Josiah Smith (1864–1919) 60, 71, 90
      Josiah Smith (1880–1956) 78, 91, 106

Or:

      Josiah Smith (the elder)   33, 89, 90
      Josiah Smith (the baker)   60, 71, 90
      Josiah Smith (the son)   78, 91, 106

If you have many people listed with the same surname, so you will list the surname once, flush left, then alphabetize the first names indented one-quarter of an inch (.25") with the hanging indent leaving any wrapping page numbers indented one-half inch (.5"). For example:

Foster
    Allen 71, 77
    Bruce 50
    Carter 44

If you have a long list of people under the same surname, when you reach the next column or page, repeat the surname followed by (cont.).

Foster (cont.)
    Wesley
    William, Jr.
    William, Sr.

Women's names can be problematic because in order to create the most useful index, you need to refer to women by both their maiden and married names, if appropriate, and on occasion, by multiple married names. The following are examples of how to handle this.

If a woman's name was Mary Jane Jones Rankin Scarborough, meaning she was born as Mary Jane Jones, married a Rankin and subsequently married a Scarborough, she should be listed as:

    Jones, Mary Jane (*see* Rankin, Mary Jane, *see* Scarborough, Mary Jane)
    Rankin, Mary Jane (Jones)
    Scarborough, Mary Jane (Jones) (Rankin)

People with hyphenated surnames should be listed under both names as well. For example:

Gowan-Saroyan, Jane (*see* Saroyan, Jane Gowan)

If there are women who are referred to by *only* their married names, they should be listed as:

Brice, William (Mrs.)—not, Brice, Mrs. William.

If there were many women named Mrs. Brice, for example, they would all alphabetize under Brice, M (for Mrs.) and not under the letter of their husband's first name where they should.

Incorrect:
Brice, Keith
Brice, Mrs. Adam
Brice, Mrs. William
Brice, Nathan

Correct:
Brice, Adam (Mrs.)
Brice, Keith
Brice, Nathan
Brice, William (Mrs.)

The use of titles such as Miss and Dr. is a matter of preference in the index, unless Miss Shaw or Dr. Reynolds is the only name you have for those individuals. If you have only a last name and a title, then the titles belong in the index.

In a transcription, using a name as you find it is proper; in an index, not necessarily. For example, if you find the name Daniel, Dan'l and Dan in the body text, in the index, you may not wish to have three listings for the same person under each of these iterations. If it is clear that you are referring to the same person, use the best, most complete name—Daniel.

If there are people who are referred to by only one name, or by none at all, include whatever you need to, to reference that individual:

Horace (the watchmaker)
Negro girl (b. ca 1850)
Susannah (the neighbor)

The same goes if you have a surname but no first name, for example:

Halford (cotton buyer)
Rosenkranz, Miss (housekeeper)
Surry, Miss (teacher)

If you have people who used a nickname that does not suggest their formal name, and then use a cross-reference, such as: Rogers, Buzz (*see* Rogers, Alden).

Formatting Institutional Names

Formal names should be indexed as they are presented:

>All Saints Cathedral
>Miss Porter's School
>Van Pelt Cemetery

These places could also be indexed under subject headings:

Cemeteries
>Van Pelt Cemetery

Churches
>All Saints Cathedral

Schools
>Miss Porter's School

Institutions with the same name should include a way to differentiate one place from the next:

>Old Burying Ground (Boston, MA)
>Old Burying Ground (Waverly, NH)

Institutions using people's names can be tricky, as well. For the most part they should be indexed as written, so either:

>Harrison Trimble High School

Or:

>Trimble, Harrison. *See also* Harrison Trimble High School

But not:

>Trimble, Harrison (High School)

In the 19th century, it was common for people to name their businesses after themselves. The best way to list them is both as they appear *and* by the founder's last name, for example:

>C. Madison & Co.
>Madison, Charles. *See also* C. Madison and Co.
>Madison (C. Madison & Co.)

Index legal cases the same way as business names above. First by the full name of the case, usually plaintiff versus defendant, and then by the surname of the defendant followed by the full case name, so:

Delaney vs. Richards
Richards (Delaney vs. Richards)

Index consistently using listings that help readers find information quickly and easily.

Errata

An errata section is used to alert the reader to any errors that were discovered during production that are uncorrected in the narrative. For publishers who run thousands of books in a single press run, these sections are necessary because the publisher will not issue a corrected edition until the print run is sold out. Fortunately, if you use one of the print-on-demand printers that does not charge to upload a new version, you can correct errors as you find them by uploading a new interior file. There would be no need for an errata section.

An errata section is organized in order of the errors with the chapter number and page number, followed by what is listed and the correction. For example:

Chapter 2, page 26: 21 May 1767 should read 21 May 1867
Chapter 2, page 33: Richard S. Burton should read Richard L. Burton

Remember: Each time you make changes that move words from one page to another, you must re-create the index.

Colophon

A colophon is the design and production credits for the book: who created the cover and interior, the fonts and paper used, and the name of the printer. This information can also go on the copyright page above the copyright notice and cataloging data.

Excerpt

If you have written other books, or are writing or planning to write additional books, include an excerpt from another book at the end of this one, especially in an electronic version. In an electronic version you can also include a live link to your website, a blog where you will update readers on the progress of a new book, or to a place where the other book(s) is sold. Include the full links in your print edition as well so interested readers can find you online.

Include something exciting or useful in the excerpt. Then, tell the reader why they may be interested in other books you have written. Ask readers to check out the link. This is referred to as a "call to action" in marketing. You could also include a line such as, "If you enjoyed this book and would like to purchase a copy for a friend, family member or your local library ... "

Format the excerpt the same way as the body text. If you have many other books, list them at the end of the excerpt so that interested readers can browse your list of titles. Include links for each of those titles as well.

Order Form

Including an order form is one way to make sure an interested person who has found your book in a library has a way to contact you to buy their own copy. Not everyone uses the Internet to place orders, even today.

An order form should occur on the last page, and should include:

- Your name or your company name
- Your address (where they should send the order)
- Your website address
- A call to action ("If you enjoyed this book and would like to buy a copy for a family member [or your local library] ...")
- All titles available (cross-sell your other books)
- The price of each item
- Shipping and handling charges for each item
- A discount for ordering more than one book (free shipping perhaps)
- Any additional merchandise you have to offer (photographic reprints or family tree charts, for example)
- A place to total the order
- A place to fill out their name, address, email address (make this area big enough for the person ordering to write legibly)
- An explanation of the payment methods you will accept (check, money order, PayPal or credit card)

Creating order forms can be tricky. Find a good catalog order form and use it as your guide.

❧❧❧

In the back matter, you have an opportunity to include whatever did not fit easily into the body of the book, or to clarify terms used or mistakes discovered after the typesetting was finished.

The most important item in the back matter is the index. Every non-fiction book must have one, including a how-to or instructional guide. Even if you forgo the place names and subject entries, an every-name index has become the standard.

As the publisher, everything else in the back matter is up to you.

❧❧❧

Working with an Indexer

Most how-to or instructional guides do not need the services of a professional indexer. You know your material as well as any indexer could. Professional indexing is often necessary for complex non-fiction or scientific works, but you should be able to either create the index yourself as you typeset, or be able to work with your book packager to do so. If you choose to hire an indexer, consider the following:

Portfolio

A professional indexer should be able to give you the titles of books he or she has indexed, and an electronic copy of an index or two.

What to Include

Your index should include every name mentioned in the book, along with the names of groups or institutions. Include place names that are significant. The indexer may be able to suggest subject headings to you, since subjects are more commonly what professional indexers categorize, rather than names.

Fees

Professional indexers charge either by the page, or by the hour. If your indexer does not have much experience, pay by the page. Pay by the hour, only when hiring an accomplished indexer. Using a professional indexer can often run as much as book packaging or editing costs. If you have to choose, put the money into editing first, and then into the layout and design. Leave the indexing for last.

Final Layout

A professional indexer must work from your final layout—with all of the typesetting in place and pages established—in order to create an accurate index. Before you give the final layout to the indexer, make certain all revisions or corrections have been made. Then, print a final copy.

After the indexing is complete, if you make revisions to the text that alters on which page the indexed words appear, you will pay dearly to have the indexer make corrections.

Write a Formal Proposal or Contract

Use a formal proposal to indicate how the index is to be returned to you or your book packager—as a Word document, or an unformatted plain text document, for example. Make your expectations for the index and deadlines clear. If you have agreed to pay by the hour, include a do-not-exceed price to keep the indexer from running wild with your budget.

❧❧

It may seem as if there are a lot of rules to follow for typesetting, but it is the attention to detail in the typesetting that will make your book look as if it has been professionally published.

Chapter 21

Designing the Cover

It would be nice to think that readers do not judge books by their covers, but in reality, they do. Not only do they judge whether they want to buy the book, but often a book with a poor cover will go unread, simply because it looks uninviting. If you have not given much thought to your book's title while you were writing, once you start designing the cover, you must. In fact, choosing the right title and making it look good on the cover may be the most difficult element of cover design. Fortunately, there is a fairly simple formula for the other elements expected on the front and back covers as well as on the spine.

Choosing a Good Title

The title will affect the perception readers have of the book and as such, the title should be the most prominent item on the cover. A non-fiction title is like a promise you are making to the reader for what they will experience reading the book. While it is tempting to use a title that is also a clever play on words (e.g. Deep Roots and Long Branches), if you want potential buyers to know which subject you are writing about, it is best to be specific in the title or subtitle.

Most online bookstores will list both your title and subtitle in the short listings, so, if you prefer, you can use a shorter title followed by a more lengthy, explanatory subtitle.

The following are examples of good titles:

Up the Mississippi: The Little-Known Records of the Mississippi River Plantations, 1820-1900

Researching World War I Women: Where to Find Their Enlistment, Service and Discharge Papers

Handcarts Across the Plains: How to Research the Mormon Migration from 1840-1900

These titles are not as good:

A Treasure-Trove of Records
Inside the Courthouse
The University Archives

On the cover, typeset the title in a font large enough to be readable in a small thumbnail online. Online bookstores and eReaders will display your cover this way and often the small image is all a potential buyer has to evaluate the book.

Cover Layout Basics

How your cover is designed depends upon how it will be bound—hardbound, hardbound with a dustcover, or softbound (paperback).

A paperback cover is printed on a single sheet that wraps from the front around the spine to the back. It will be printed at a size larger than the book's pages, and then attached to the book with glue and trimmed so that the page and cover edges are smooth and even.

Hardbound covers can be made from either cloth or paper. They are glued to stiff boards to form a solid cover. A paper cover for a hardbound book will look like modern textbooks—full color with a glossy coating. Paper covers for hardbound books are designed even larger than those for softbound books because they must wrap around the edges of the boards and glued down to form part of the inside cover. An endsheet will be glued over the edges of the cover.

Cloth covers are made of anything from linen to leather, depending upon the printer's equipment and how much you are willing to pay. Cloth covers, typically, do not have much more than the title and the author's name. Many cloth-covered books also have a full-color, paper dust jacket that wraps around the cloth cover. The dust jacket uses flaps inside the front and back covers to keep it secure.

Whether you are designing a paper cover or a dust jacket, your printer should have a template for you to follow. Many printers have template generators that will give you an exact size based upon the number of pages in the book, which will determine spine width. You can assemble the elements at any time, however, and create the final cover once you have a page count.

Cover templates will have three areas defined by the edge of the element: the bleed edge, the trim edge and the safe area.

The *safe area* is the innermost area that allows for any slippage when the printed cover is attached to the book's interior. Most templates will give you three safe areas, one each for the front cover, the back cover and the spine. The

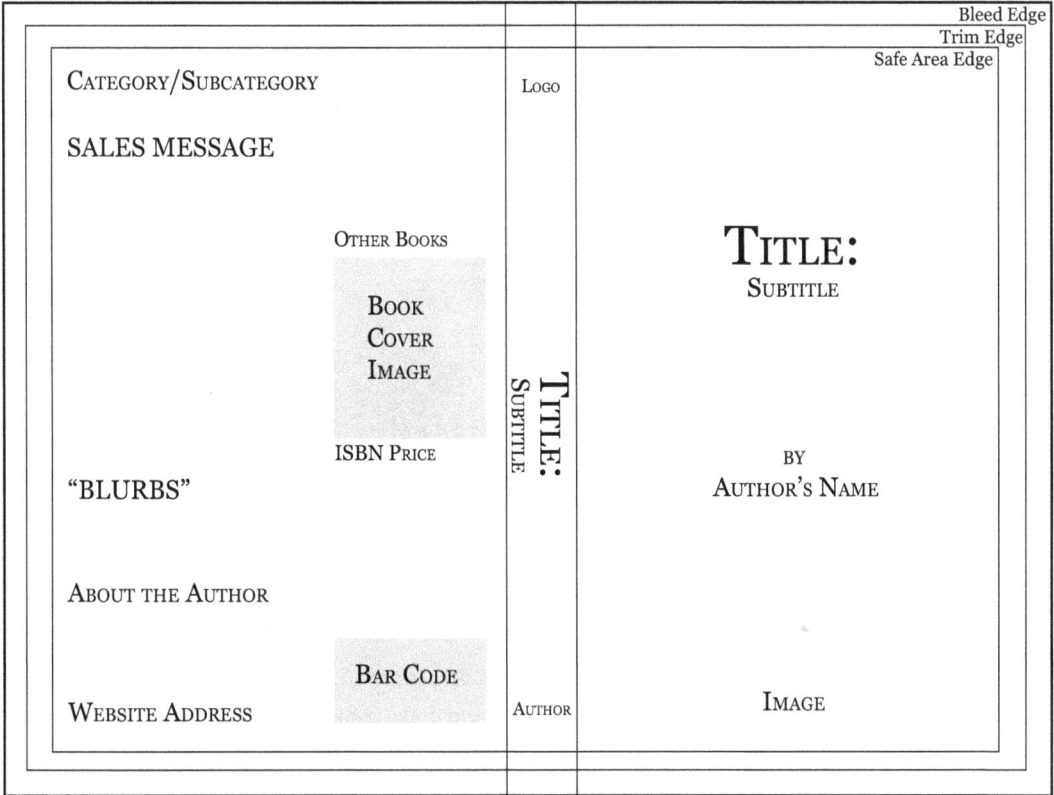

CATEGORY/SUBCATEGORY		LOGO		Bleed Edge

The diagram shows cover elements laid out:

Back cover (left):
CATEGORY/SUBCATEGORY

SALES MESSAGE

OTHER BOOKS

BOOK COVER IMAGE

ISBN PRICE

"BLURBS"

ABOUT THE AUTHOR

BAR CODE

WEBSITE ADDRESS

Spine (middle):
LOGO

TITLE: SUBTITLE

AUTHOR

Front cover (right):
Bleed Edge
Trim Edge
Safe Area Edge

TITLE:
SUBTITLE

BY
AUTHOR'S NAME

IMAGE

Cover elements.

safe areas are away from the edges of the spine and the front and back covers. Keep all text, as well as the barcode, and any logo images within the safe areas.

The *trim edge* is where the book will be trimmed once the cover is applied to the interior pages so that the finished book will have clean, smooth edges.

The *bleed edge* is the area where photographs or solid background color should reach, so that when the book is trimmed, there is no danger of leaving a white line around an edge because nothing was printed in that area.

Cover Elements

Covers have three elements: the front, the spine, and the back. Most covers are designed in a single piece, and when laid flat, the front cover will be on the right-hand side, the spine in the middle and the back cover on the left.

If you use a print-on-demand printer that has an online cover generator—not a template but a design tool—you may be able to design the cover in three separate parts. Using one of these cover generators, however, will give you fewer options than designing the cover yourself.

If you design your own cover, create it as a single piece. You can use a word processor (although not ideal), an image editing program, a page layout program

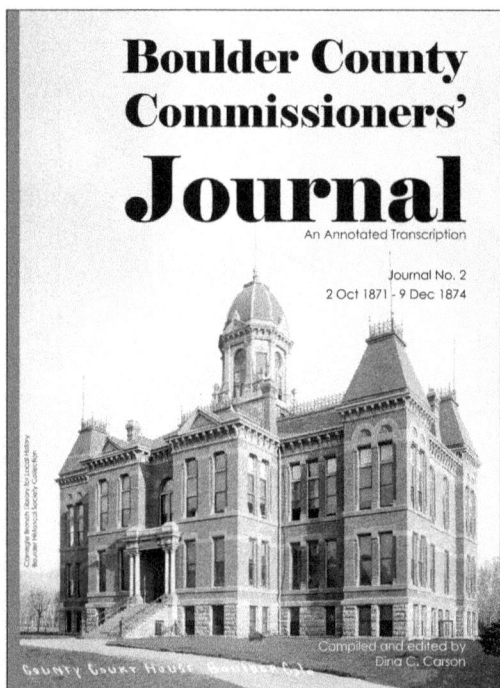

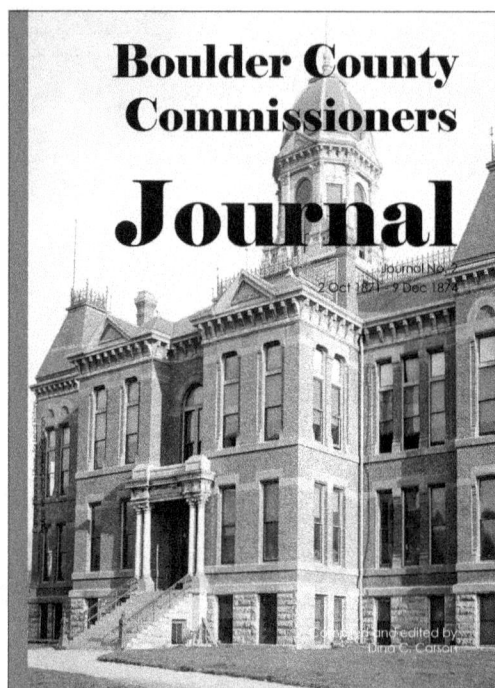

Cover photograph properly placed (left); Cover photograph making the title difficult to read (right).

or a vector graphics editor such as Adobe Illustrator. One of the benefits of using a page layout program or a vector graphics editor is that they are built for creating cover files—to combine images with crisp, sharp type.

For ideas, take a look at Book Cover Archive (www.bookcoverarchive.com). This website offers a gallery of book covers created by professionals.

Front Cover

The front cover should get the reader's attention. The title should be the most prominent element on the cover, set in a font that is easy to read. The following are popular cover fonts: Baskerville, ChunkFive, Franchise, League Gothic, and Trajan.

For the background, use a photograph, a color, or a texture as long as the area where the title and subtitle are placed is plain (subtle) enough that the reader has no trouble reading the text at a glance. Avoid background elements that are too busy and those that do not create enough color contrast with the title text.

If you use an image, choose one that says something about the contents. The illustration shows two covers with the same title, but uses the background photograph in a different way. The key to making a book cover image look great is finding one that leaves a large, nearly solid area where you can place the title in a contrasting color. The cover on the left has enough plain sky to read the title and subtitle clearly. The closeup cover image does not.

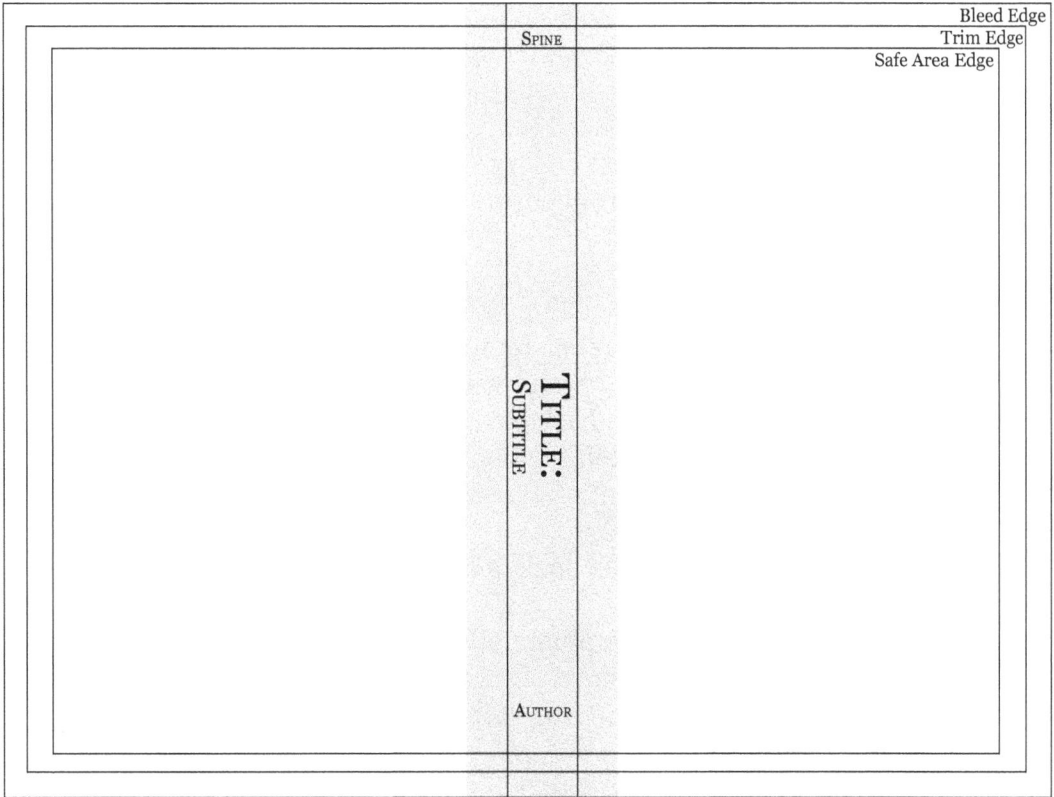

Spine wrap.

If you do not have an appropriate photograph in your own collection, you may be able to find a historical photograph that you could license, or you could purchase an image from one of the online rights-managed image companies for a few dollars.

Size and resolution matter and your cover image is likely to be the largest image you use for this project. The resolution should be 300 ppi at a size big enough to cover the bleed area. A cover with a 2.5" spine, for example, would measure 19.5" x 17.5" which is 5850 pixels by 5250 pixels.

If you cannot find the perfect photograph for the cover, blocks of color or subtle patterns also work.

The Spine

The spine will contain your title, your name as the author (full name, initials plus last name, or last name only), and a publishing company logo, if you have one.

The lettering on the spine goes from top to bottom—never the other way—so that all of the titles read the same way when books are spine out on the bookshelf.

The tricky part about designing the spine is making the elements (background image) stop at precisely the point at which the cover bends, either to the front or back. One way to avoid this is to use a solid color, a texture, or a photograph that continues across the entire cover. Another option is to create a spine wrap, where a graphic element or color continues onto the front and back covers to disguise a little slippage if the cover is not placed perfectly during production.

The typeface on the spine must be large and legible, and typically, the same one you used for the title on the front cover.

Back Cover

The back cover does most of the selling. It should explain why the reader will want your book and gently asks the reader to buy a copy.

If you have solicited blurbs or endorsements, your best endorsement(s) should go on the back cover. The back cover should include a bit about you as the author, or why you have written the book. If there are other books you have written, there may be room to mention those books, or to show their covers, page count, ISBNs and price.

If you have a website where the book is sold, the URL should appear prominently on the back cover.

If you plan to sell your book commercially through a print-on-demand printer (such as Lulu or Amazon), you must place an ISBN barcode at the bottom right corner about one-quarter inch from the spine. The barcode can also include the price, although price is optional.

Some printers will include the barcode for you in their template. If you are using one of the ISBNs belonging to your print-on-demand printer, the barcode will be placed on the cover as you create it. If you are printing through an offset printer and must purchase an ISBN barcode, you can do so online. There are many companies offering barcodes for as little as $10. You will receive an EPS (.eps) image by email to use in your design. If you are purchasing your own ISBNs from the Bowker Company, they also offer barcodes for sale.

The other element you will need if you plan to sell your book to libraries or bookstores is a subject heading in the top left corner of the back cover. This is to give the librarians or bookstore employees an idea where to categorize the book.

Book Industry Standards Advisory Committee (BISAC) codes are the standard across the industry for subject headings. If you search online for BISAC codes, you will find a complete list. For most genealogical specialties, the code will be Reference/Genealogy. If you are using a print-on-demand printer, this question will come up as you are creating a listing for your book. Some printers make it easy to search for the BISAC code, others do not. Some printers allow you to list two or more categories, others do not. Search online for the complete list, then use the best subject heading on the back cover.

Advanced Cover Design

The following are additional tips for designing effective covers:

First, go to Amazon.com and take a look at Todd A. Stone's book, *Novelist's Boot Camp*. This is a simple cover, in two colors, black and olive, but it says something about what is in the book, and does so simply.

Now take a look at *Virginia Historical Genealogies* by John Bennett Boddie. This is a black-and-white cover that is about as simple as is possible, but it does not re-produce well as a thumbnail on screen. Arguably, this is a well-written book, but does the cover give you that impression? This book has been around for more than fifty years, so it is hard to be critical of a cover that was designed before major printing technology changes. However, the contents are deserving of a better cover.

Using Color

To make areas of solid black (such as your title text) look its best, use the formula for rich black, which is: 40% cyan, 40% magenta, 40% yellow, 100% black. You will notice that these are in CMYK colors. CMYK is the color palette most printers prefer. If you are designing your cover in your word processor or image editing program, you may not be able to choose the CMYK color palette, so the colors you are seeing on screen in the RGB palette may look slightly different when printed. Page layout and vector graphics programs are designed for working in CMYK.

Limit the cover's color palette to two or three colors and their various tints. That should be a sufficient variation unless you are using a photograph. If you are, choose colors from the photograph for other elements such as the subhead "About the Author" on the back cover. As with interior text, black text is still best for most elements on the cover.

If you need help choosing colors that look good together, use a good color picker. There are apps and online color wheels available, or buy one of Jim Krause's books, *Color Index*, or *Color Index 2*. If you want to go all out, buy one of the Pantone Color Guides (www.pantone.com).

Selecting great color combinations is not easy. If your spouse will not let you choose your own shirts, ask for help choosing colors for your book cover.

Other Cover Considerations

Once you have a cover design in mind, scale it down to a small thumbnail of one inch by one and a half inches (1" x 1.5"). This is how your cover will appear to people shopping at an online bookstore. A thumbnail image is how you will present the cover on your blog, website, Facebook, on a bookmark, or business card to give away to interested buyers. If the title is not easy to read at the thumbnail size, then revise the cover for those uses with bigger, bolder text.

Save your cover in different sizes. You may need an eBook version (600 pixels x 800 pixels), an online bookstore version (Amazon's requirement is 1880 pixels x 2500 pixels), one for your blog or social media (400 pixels x 600 pixels), and a small thumbnail 90 pixels x 108 pixels (the standard cover size in Amazon's email promotions).

If you have plans for writing more than one book, consider using a branded look, that is, the same layout with different colors or photographs so that the books look like they belong together.

෮ᘰ

If you cannot design a cover yourself, the following are tips for working with a cover designer.

Working with a Cover Designer

Before you hire a cover designer, ask about the designer's experience. Cover design is a specialty, and most graphic designers have never designed a book cover. Most book packagers, however, either have cover designers on staff, or use freelancers who are familiar with book cover design.

Take a look at Book Cover Archive (www.bookcoverarchive.com). This website offers a gallery of book cover designs. Show the prospective designer four or five styles that you like, but be open to suggestions.

In addition to cover ideas, bring along a two or three paragraph synopsis, to help the designer understand the content of your book. The cover design should complement the content.

Portfolio

Ask to see the designer's book cover portfolio. Evaluate the full covers, front, spine and back, to make sure the designer is familiar with the elements needed for a commercially available book.

Estimate

Ask for an estimate. Most cover designers will offer two or three designs, plus two rounds of revisions before you start paying more than the initial estimate. You may even find that the cover designer has a few standard layouts that you can choose from to save money. Include a do-not-exceed price in the agreement, so the designer cannot go wild with changes before you have a chance to revise the estimate.

Deadlines

Make your expectations clear and set firm deadlines. Let the designer know when you will have a final page count, and when you expect the final cover finished once the page count is given. The designer should have the cover essentially ready, needing only a few minor adjustments once the page count is final.

File Type and Resolution

Let the designer know what type of file and resolution you need (usually a PDF) and any special instructions provided by your book printer. In addition, ask for web-ready book cover images in the different sizes you may need—an eBook version (600 pixels x 800 pixels), online bookstores (Amazon's requirement is a cover of 1880 pixels x 2500 pixels), and a small thumbnail 90 pixels x 108 pixels (the standard cover size in Amazon's email promotions). Make sure the final cover looks good and that the title is readable, even at the smallest thumbnail size.

Write a Formal Proposal or Contract

Use a formal proposal to indicate how and when the cover should be delivered to you—on a thumb drive, an external hard drive, an archival DVD, or through a file sharing service. Make sure deadlines for payment and a finished cover are clear. Include all prices and payment terms.

⁋⸙⁊

Your cover is the ambassador for your book. Your family members may want a copy even if it comes as loose leaf sheets wrapped in newspaper. Most readers, however, will form an impression of the book's contents by looking at the cover. When designing your cover, you should be able to find many suitable possibilities from the hundreds of thousands of non-fiction books already published. Use one as your guide. Bottom line: all of your hard work writing the book deserves to be covered in something beautiful, and representative of the quality of the contents.

Chapter 22

Preparing the Final Files

Most how-tos or instructional guides are printed. However, some of your readers may prefer an electronic version, or, if you are not interested in selling the book, an online version may be a good choice to distribute it as widely as possible. You may choose to do all three or some combination of the three.

While this book focuses mainly on print publishing, there are ways that you can use what you have produced for print to also publish electronically or online. What follows are brief descriptions of the differences in setup between print and electronic or online versions. For complete instructions, please consult *Set Yourself Up to Self-Publish: A Genealogist's Guide.*

Final Files for Print

How you prepare your final files depends upon your printer. Most printers want PDF files because they are the least problematic. If you send a file in a word processing format such as Word, and you have used a font that the printer does not have, the text may re-format in a way you do not intend. By creating a PDF, there are rarely any font issues because the process of creating the PDF embeds the fonts into the document. Creating a PDF is, in some ways, like taking a snapshot of your manuscript. It will create a file that looks exactly like your manuscript file whether you created it in a word processing program or a page layout program. Most word processing and page layout software will save documents as PDFs.

Create Final PDFs

If you are using one of Adobe's software products to create your PDF (Acrobat or InDesign, for example), there are different PDF settings, including press quality or high quality print (what we want for a printed book), smallest file size (appropriate for emailing the book), and several other settings in between. The best settings for printed material are: Press Quality, High Quality Printing or PDF/X 1a:2001. Most page layout programs will give you a choice in PDF settings, your word processor may not. In most cases, the printed book will still look fine.

If you use a digital or offset printer, ask for their preferred PDF settings before saving your files. Most print-on-demand printers, on the other hand, will accept whatever file you upload, so the responsibility for creating a file that will look its best when printed is up to you.

After creating the PDF, print it out and check it over carefully by comparing the printed version to your original to make sure nothing shifted or was lost in the conversion. This is the process of typescript editing (mentioned in Chapter 15: Editing Your Manuscript). This is the time to catch widows and orphans, captions that do not match images, and other errors. Take a ruler and scan each line one at a time for errors. You may be surprised at what crept in as elements were typeset. The following are common post-typesetting errors:

- Widows and orphans
- Missed or incorrect formatting styles
- Hard returns mid-sentence
- Missing punctuation
- Incorrect quote marks (the symbol for inches)
- Spacing around images
- Spacing between different types of text blocks
- Images that fade into the page (missing outlines)
- Images that do not fit the grid
- Placeholder images not final images (at resolutions too low for print production)
- Pages that are mis-numbered

Uploading Files for Print

If you have created your final layout in chapters so that they are easier to work with, it is safer to send the printer a single file so there is no chance the files could be printed out of order. Programs such as InDesign will take your individual files and combine them into a single book-length PDF. The full version of Adobe Acrobat will also combine individual PDF files into a larger book-length file.

If you must upload your manuscript files individually, the best way to make sure they are printed in the correct order is to begin each file name with a number so that the computer arranges them in the correct order. If you followed the advice in Chapter 14: Writing a First Draft, you should be ready to go.

If you need to number your files now, the following is another way to make sure the computer arranges them in the correct order.

Unfortunately, if you number your files starting with a one (1), and you also have an eleven (11), the computer may order the files this way: 1, 11, 2.

The only way to avoid this is to count the total number of files, and use a sufficient number of zeros preceding the file number to force the computer to put the files in the correct order.

If there are fewer than ten files, there should be no issues, as the computer will number those files from one (1) to nine (9) in order. If there are ten or more files but fewer than one hundred, create two digit numbers from 01 to 09, so that subsequent numbers will be in the correct order. If there are more than one hundred files, file names require two zeros in front of the numbers from one (001) to nine (009), and a single zero before each and every number from ten (010) to ninety-nine (099). Numbers greater than one hundred will fall in order correctly.

Once you upload the files, the best way to see whether or not the files were placed in their proper order is to order a proof copy. Many print-on-demand printers offer a digital PDF proof for you to download. This should not cost you anything, but proofing on screen and proofing in print are different. You will catch different errors. It is worth the money to print a proof copy as well.

Examine the digital and print proofs carefully page by page. You may be surprised what you find. Missing punctuation and incorrectly applied styles are common errors. Watch for places where widows or orphans were created by text shift. It happens. Make sure your illustrations remain in place along with any captions or credits.

Other Information About Your Book

Once you start the process of uploading files to a print-on-demand printer, requesting ISBNs or creating marketing materials for your book, you will need the following information. Keep it gathered in a convenient place so that you can cut and paste whatever is required by vendors or websites.

If you have purchased your own ISBNs, much of this information will inform the book-buying community about your book. If you use a print-on-demand printer, they will ask for much of this information when you upload your files. Each printer has slightly different requirements. What follows is the information asked for most often.

Title

Title. Keep the title and subtitle separate.

Subtitle. Keep the title and subtitle separate.

Author and Publisher

Primary Author. List your name as the primary author. If you have co-authors or other contributors, you should have a chance to add their names.

Author Biography. Write a few paragraphs about yourself as the author and why you wrote the book.

Publisher. If you are acting as your own publisher, you have a choice whether to create a publishing company, or not. For tax and legal reasons you may wish to do so. One sign that you are a self-publisher, however, is naming the publishing company after yourself.

Language and Printing Location

Language. The primary language of the book.

Country. The country in which the book was published, not printed.

Important Dates

Copyright Year. The year in which the book was finished. Although your copyright existed from the time you put pen to paper, most publishers use the most current year as the copyright date, so that readers know that the information is current.

Publication Date. This is a fictional date used by the publishing industry to schedule book reviews ahead of the book's official launch. Use the date when your book is available for sale.

Audience

Target Audience. Unless you are writing a children's book, the audience will always be "Trade."

Metadata

Together, the title, license, description, category and keywords make up the metadata—cataloging information about your book that is key to book sales. Any mis-matches in the metadata will make it difficult for the big databases (online book catalogs) to place your book in front of the right potential buyers.

License. Indicate that you own the copyright to your work, that you are not re-packaging a work already in the public domain.

Description. This is your sales language, your chance to interest potential readers. Some sites use descriptions as short as 200 characters, others as long as 4000. Have several descriptions ready with the most important information wrapped up in the shortest description, and additional detail in the longer descriptions. If you want to sell your book, the description may be one of your most important marketing tools. Lulu describes "providing too little detail in the description" as the greatest mistake of new authors.

Category. Many printers will use the BISAC codes, others have a search option, still others make it as confusing as humanly possible. When in doubt, if

Genealogy is not a main category, look for Reference/Genealogy & Heraldry. A secondary category could be Reference/Handbooks & Manuals or Reference/Research.

Keywords. Most sites allow five or more keyword phrases separated by commas. Choose the five most important and put those first. For most how-to books, the keywords should be about the subject(s). For example, school records research, land records genealogy, or world war I records research. If you are able to add more keyword phrases, do. More keywords will help potential readers find the book. Think of the phrases another researcher would use to find the book. There are keyword search programs online that can help with this, such as Google Adwords Keyword Planner (adwords.google.com). This tool is free, but you must create an account to use it.

ISBN and Price

ISBN. If you have your own ISBN, use it. If you do not, leave this blank and the printer will assign one of theirs to you.

Price. Choose a price higher than the wholesale price if you want to make money. Another reason you may wish to choose a price higher than the wholesale price is to give the distributor (printer) the opportunity to price the book at a discount. Book buyers love bargains, but if you price the book at the wholesale cost, the distributor cannot sell the book for less than what it costs to manufacture it.

The following are a few items particular to Amazon (CreateSpace), Lulu and Bowker (the ISBN Agency).

Amazon (CreateSpace)

Distribution. Amazon offers the following outlets for distribution: Amazon.com, Amazon Europe, Create Space eStore, Bookstores and Online Retailers, and CreateSpace Direct. If you are using one of their ISBNs your book is also eligible for distribution to libraries and academic institutions—a plus for non-fiction books.

Prices. If you have chosen distribution outside of the United States, choose US Dollars, Euros, and British Pounds. Google's online currency calculator can help convert U.S. dollars to English pounds or euros. Round the prices up to the nearest .99 or .95, as prices ending that way have become customary.

Option to Publish on Kindle. If you use CreateSpace to publish your print book they will give you the option to create a Kindle version.

PUBLISH YOUR SPECIALTY

Lulu

Private Access. One of my favorite features of Lulu is that you can publish a book and keep it completely private, meaning that only you can order copies. This may be appropriate for books that have information about living people you would not want distributed widely.

Direct Access. Direct Access gives you a private URL to direct people to buy the book for themselves. This option gives you less control over distribution than private access, but it is a good option if you have a select group spread out all over the country, and you want them to be able to buy their own copies and have the books delivered directly to them.

General Access. Any book you assign as general access will become available through Lulu's catalog as well as other online booksellers' catalogs.

Bowker Company (ISBN Agency)

ISBN 10. Older ISBNs had only 10 digits. If you have a newer ISBN it will have 13 digits. There is a calculator on the site to convert it to the older 10 digit version. This site asks for both, and checks one against the other for accuracy.

ISBN 13. The ISBN for your book.

LCCC. A Library of Congress Catalog Number.

Medium. Medium is the format of the book, usually print or eBook, unless you have chosen to distribute it as an audiobook, or on CD or DVD instead.

Format. In most cases the format will be paperback or hardbound.

Title Status. If you want the book industry to know that your book is available for sale, use Active. You can use the term Forthcoming, if you are months away from publishing. Be sure, however, to come back and change the status. The big databases that the book sellers use will show the book as unavailable until you change the status to Active.

Price Type. Choose Retail Price.

Keep a file with this information gathered in one place. When you are ready to let others know that you have a book available, having these details handy will save time.

SECTION 5

For most genealogical how-to or instructional manuals, marketing is not as much about making sales as it is about contacting the people who would be interested in using your book or adding it to a library collection, and providing information about where interested readers can obtain a copy. Marketing—spreading the word—is about using methods that get results at a cost you can afford, in both money and time.

Baby Steps

If your intent for writing your book is solely to put your expertise down in writing for the benefit of a few interested people, then once they have copies, you can stop marketing.

Next Steps

If, however, you would like your book to remain available well past the current generation, contribute it to the major genealogical collections around the country, and establish a sales channel that will last awhile. Creating a website for the book or selling the book through an online bookseller such as Amazon are two ways to keep the book out in the marketplace long after you have turned your attention to other projects.

Giant Leaps

If your expertise would be of interest to the general public, then by all means, market the book wherever you can. Your work may be what inspires a young historian to find out more about the subject, or a new genealogist to explore new records. It may help seasoned genealogists who need your expertise to proceed with their own research. There may be many people who are interested in your book that you will remain unaware of unless you spread the word far and wide.

Note: In this section, the expression "pitch" means to make an appeal or to make your case about your book.

Chapter 23

Creating a Marketing Plan

Quite often, when I speak to groups about marketing anything related to genealogy, I get moans and groans about not wanting to "sell" something. Not all selling is the equivalent of selling used cars. Some of you will generously give your books away. If you have the means to do so, hooray.

Many of you will sell your book, if for no other reason than it is more practical for interested readers to order a copy online and have the printer ship the book to them directly, than for you to buy hundreds of copies, store them (and dust them), and have to run to the post office every time someone orders one.

In this section, marketing (and its side-kick, selling) is more about getting the word out that you have a book available, than becoming a tycoon selling books to unsuspecting people.

Marketing 101

Marketing has five elements: identifying the target market, determining a method to reach out to the target market effectively, giving interested people a reason to buy, showing them where they can buy, and asking them to do so.

Identify the Target Market

Most of you will have more than one target market. For this discussion, a target market is a group of people with similar interests. The reason you want to narrow down a wide group of potential buyers into narrow target markets is to be able to reach them effectively. People who have similar interests tend to gather in the same places, belong to the same (or similar) groups, read the same books or magazines, and use the same websites. Once you identify where you can reach the target market, you can let them know the book is available.

Reach Out to the Target Market

Let us use your immediate family as an example. Most people have multiple ways to reach parents, grandparents, siblings and children. You have phone numbers, email, and home addresses. That gives you many ways to reach this audience. You could call each person and discuss the book. You could create an email list and send a group email, or you could write a letter or create a sales sheet and send it to each family member's home. You could make an announcement on the social media your family follows. You could talk about the book at the next family gathering. Contacting your family should be easy. Unfortunately, you may not have as many easy options with other target markets.

Every target market has a way to contact the group and its members. You may have to decide, however, whether the effort or expense of reaching out to each target market is worth the cost.

Give the Target Market a Reason to Buy

In most cases, it is not enough to simply tell someone you have a book available. While your Mom will buy a copy without hesitation, other buyers will want to know what they will get out of reading your book. The most important part of your marketing plan is putting together a list of benefits.

Benefits are the reasons why a person will want to read your book. Distinguishing benefits from features can be confusing. The following are common book *features*:

- The book is 396 pages long.
- The book has 16 complete lessons.
- The book has over 100 illustrations.
- The book contains images from a Civil War re-enactment.

By contrast, this is an example of a benefit-rich statement: "With cinematic power and beauty, bestselling author David Laskin brings to life the upheavals of the twentieth century through the story of one family, three continents, two world wars, and the rise and fall of nations." That description, taken from the dust jacket flap of David Laskin's *The Family*, sounds much more like an enticement to read the book than a list of facts, does it not?

Remember back in Chapter 22: Preparing the Final Files in the discussion about your book's description and how vital the description can be to sales? It is worth your time to write a compelling enticement to read the book. In fact, it is worth writing, and re-writing, if necessary. Once you have a vivid, enticing description, you can use it in all of your marketing materials.

Show the Target Market Where They Can Buy

Let potential book buyers know where they can buy a copy, whether by contacting you directly, by buying from your website or at an online bookstore such as Amazon. If you have multiple options for sales, give the buyer a choice. Not everyone is comfortable purchasing items online. And, if you want to offer autographed copies, state where those copies are available, as well. For some people, autographed copies are an additional inducement to buy.

Include a Call to Action

One of the biggest mistakes in marketing is forgetting to ask for the sale. You do not have to include an obnoxious, flashing "Buy Now!!!" button. A simple, "purchase your copy today" will do. Or offer free shipping if the buyer purchases a book by a certain date. Enticements to act sooner rather than later often work.

Setting the Price

Before you can sell your book, you have to determine its price. If you do not plan to make any money on the book, you can set the price a few cents over your wholesale cost.

In the publishing industry, the standard price is set at eight times (8x) the wholesale cost to account for the cost of marketing and fulfillment. That cost is based upon long print runs, however, that keep the wholesale cost of each book very low.

Realistically, your wholesale costs will be a bit higher and depending upon which type of printer you have chosen, the cost may be substantially higher. You will have to decide which is more important to you, making the book widely available—meaning keeping the retail price low—maximizing the amount you make on the sale of each book, or something in between. The higher you set the price, however, the fewer you will sell.

If you plan to offer an eBook version, understand that eBook readers do not expect to pay the same price for their electronic version as they would for a printed book. Amazon has recognized this fact and has structured their royalty payments to reflect what readers want. Amazon pays a royalty of 70 percent to any eBook priced under $9.99, but only a 30 percent royalty for books priced at $10 or higher. Amazon has analyzed a lot of buyer data to discover that $9.99 price point. Consider pricing your electronic version under $9.99.

For most how-to or instructional guides, making the book more widely available at a lower cost is the best way to get your hard work out there to the people who are interested in learning from your expertise.

The Offer

Use the following formula to build your marketing pieces: attention-catching headlines and sub-headlines, text that supports the headlines while giving readers details, and a call to action. I have added bullets and keywords to the formula to make your offer easy to scan, and easy for the search engines to find if you post the offer online.

Headline

The headline should get the reader's attention and interest them enough to read more. For most how-to or instructional guides, this would include the main subject(s) covered in the book (e.g. New Book Reveals Hidden Treasures in the University Archives).

Sub-Headlines

Sub-headlines break up the rest of the text into small, easy-to-read sections. Subheads also make it easy to scan the piece from beginning to end. Subheads are an opportunity for you to catch and keep the reader's attention (e.g. Local Man Left Scandalous Scrapbook to the University).

Supporting Text

After each headline and sub-head, give the readers details from the book. Tell a quick story, allude to the contents, give something to pique the reader's interest.

Bullet Points

Give the reader a bulleted list of the book's main features:

- Subjects covered
- The most important places or events covered
- Number of pages
- Number of photographs or illustrations (you could name any that are especially enticing [e.g. The only known photograph of Madame Lacy S. Park, 1890.])
- Price (include shipping and handling charges)
- ISBN (if you have one)

Keywords

If you will place your marketing piece online, include a few important keywords within the text to help the search engines find it. Using the example above, keywords could include: University Archives, Roger Mills Scrapbook, Madame Park Photograph 1890, and so on.

Call to Action

A call to action is a marketing term for asking the reader to buy (e.g. "Buy by November 1st and receive free shipping").

Pre-Publication Offers

One method publishers use to jump-start their sales is to send a pre-publication offer letting potential readers know that the book will be available soon, while offering a discount of some type as an enticement to buy before the book's release.

Before print-on-demand, the proceeds from a pre-publication offer was a way to pay for the first print run. It was also a way to fill the time between when the book went to the printer, and when the books were delivered. With print-on-demand, there is no longer much of a delay or the need to pay for an initial print run. Today, a pre-publication offer is more a thank-you to the people who purchase right away.

Ongoing Offers

Continue to market your book for as long as you want readers to buy it. How-to or instructional guides do not go out of style although they can become dated, so you could repeat your offer every now and again for the next several years. Even after interested researchers have copies, there will always be a new generation of interested researchers who were unaware of their interest in your expertise when the book was released.

Check Out the Competition

If you are ever at a loss for how to get the word out about your book, look for ways in which other authors are marketing their books. Check out book-related websites. Read the About the Author pages. Sign up for book-related emails. Check YouTube for book trailers. Spend some time on Amazon and other online booksellers' sites and read the description of similar books. Read blurbs about the authors.

Create a Marketing Plan

For many authors, once a book is complete and that huge project is off the desk, it may be difficult to jump right back in to create awareness for the book. If you will create a plan with just one marketing technique per week over the first six months after your book is finished, you will be surprised at how many people you will reach. Like many things, you are more likely to accomplish your marketing goals if you write them down and schedule them on the calendar.

❧❧❧

The most important thing about marketing is being able to identify your target market, finding a way to contact these potential buyers, and describing your book in such a way that they simply cannot resist placing an order. That goes for librarians, too.

Chapter 24

Reaching Your Audience

One of the biggest mistakes novice marketers make is believing that "everyone" will want a copy of your book. With a how-to or instructional guide, that is not likely. With most books, it is better to identify the people who are the *most* likely to buy in order to save marketing money and time. The natural markets for your book are a starting point. There may be other, unanticipated buyers, however, who surface through your marketing efforts.

Genealogical Researchers

The most obvious target market for a book describing a genealogical specialty are other genealogical researchers. The key to finding the people in this target market is to evaluate where they gather and make an announcement where they are likely to see it. In the announcement, do not try to sell directly. Let the group know that there is a new book out and where they can go for more information.

Genealogical Forums

Many of the major genealogical research sites have forums by topic or location. You can leave a message for members in the forum. Use an informative headline (e.g. New Book Explains the Value of Justice of the Peace Records in Genealogical Research). Within the post, use your description of the book. And, if you are posting in a locations forum, make ties to the location clear (e.g. New Book Gives Research Tips for Justice of the Peace Records in Springfield, Illinois).

Some of the older forums have stopped accepting new posts, but their older posts remain online and contain contact information. Although you can no longer post a message, you could contact anyone who is researching your subject.

Blogs

Finding a topic-based blog will be relatively easy because so many people are blogging, but finding a topic-based blog that is also researching genealogy is not. My best suggestion is that you use both "[your topic]" and "genealogy" in your keywords when you search.

If you find an appropriate blog, ask to become a guest blogger, or set up a blog-interview where regular readers can ask questions for you to answer.

Groups by Topic

Look at Cyndi's List (www.cyndislist.com) for topics and groups studying your topic. The categories list alone will keep you busy. Some links will take you to personal websites, and others to societies or newsletter websites.

Conferences

Ascertain whether there are genealogical conferences where you could post an announcement for attendees. Most conferences sell inexpensive advertising space in their giveaway bags or programs that you could use to make your book announcement.

Family Members and Friends

Your family and friends may be interested in reading your book. The following are marketing techniques you can use with family members and friends.

Email Campaign

Send an email announcing the book. Add a signature to your regular email so that each time you correspond, a message will go out showing you as the author, the title, a link back to your website or a place where the book is sold and any social media you are participating in that concerns the book. If you include "http://" before any website address, the link will become click-able within the email.

Ask family members and friends to forward your book announcement email to anyone else who may be interested in the book. This is a good way to have them help spread the word.

Family Gatherings

Bring a few books with you to each and every family gathering in case there are people who have been waiting to buy directly from you.

Autographed Copies

Autographed copies are a nice touch when you know the buyer personally. They also make some books more valuable. In order to offer autographed copies, you must purchase enough books to keep a few on hand to fulfill the orders, or ask family members to bring their copies with them to reunions, or other family gatherings for you to sign.

Make an Announcement

Make an announcement on any social media sites where your family and friends participate. Google+ has a new service called Google Hangouts (LIVE) that enables you to hold a town meeting of sorts with friends and family using the Internet. (More on the workings of Google Hangouts in Chapter 25: Generating Publicity.)

Send a Card

Some of your family members may not use email. There are services such as Send Out Cards (www.sendoutcards.com) that enable you to create a personalized card that the company will print and send through the postal service. Use your cover image and images from the book to create your personalized card. Have the description and buying information for the book ready to copy and paste into the card. Write a quick personal note, as well. Personal notes take only a few seconds to compose but mean a lot to the recipients.

Local Historians

How much you can interest local historians or history buffs in your how-to depends upon the topic of the book. If you have conducted extensive research on a particular area or time period, or if your interest is in something more universal such as stagecoaches or early furniture-making techniques, contact local historians and make your pitch.

Historical Societies and Their Museums

Societies appreciate being able to offer special deals to their members, so offer to give society members a discounted price in exchange for mentioning the book in their member newsletter and on the society's website. Set up a special landing page on your website where society members can go to place a discounted order.

The most likely opportunity for in-store sales may be at a local historical museum bookshop. There you will find like-minded local history buffs who buy how-to books on historical subjects.

Offer a small discount if the museum shop buys only one book, and a larger discounted price if they buy three or more books. Most museum shops will not stock an abundance of any one book until they see how well the book will sell.

Not every historical museum is connected to a historical society. The independent museums in the area may be willing to sell your book, as well.

Living History Societies and Re-Enactors Groups

Re-enactors are individuals who are so fascinated with how people lived during an era that they spend time and money re-enacting what life was like then. If your instructional guide includes detailed research about an era, a profession, war-time, or military groups or any object of interest to re-enactors, there may be a society of like-minded historians who may be interested.

One of the most interesting re-enactors I have found is a Victorian Photographer who demonstrates historically accurate wet-plate photography to interested photographers, and who takes photographs of re-enactors in Victorian dress. Check out Alex Burnham's website (historic-photographer.co.uk).

Collectors Groups

Although collectors will rarely refer to themselves as re-enactors, many of them have an interest in the historical era from which their collections came. As an example, consider the Winchester Arms Collectors Association (winchestercollector.org). They feature historical articles and host events for collectors. Collectors groups may be willing to feature an article about your book if there is a significant tie from the book to their members' interests.

Complete Strangers

"Complete strangers" is a difficult target market to define, but there are a few ways in which to reach interested individuals without knowing who they are.

Website

Host your own website with enough information about the book that someone who is doing similar research could find the site using a search engine. Use appropriate keywords in the copy and the metatags to help the search engines correctly categorize the site. Look back at the cheat sheet of "Other Information About Your Book" you should have standing by and pump up the keywords to include the same type of information that other genealogical researchers, history buffs or collectors would use to find the website. (More about hosting your own website in Chapter 27: Selling Online.)

Email Signup

One way to make contact with complete strangers is to ask them for an email address when they visit your website. Many companies use this technique to send product or service offers. If you are not planning a regular newsletter, indicate that you will only be contacting them with news of the book, either when it is finished or when a second edition is offered so that they will not be fearful of dozens of emails a day clogging their email box.

Book Trailer on YouTube

Create a quick book trailer on YouTube showing some of the photographs or instructions from the book and giving a little taste of how helpful the instructions in the book will be. You can create a book trailer quite easily using movie or slideshow software such as Windows Movie Maker or iMovie for the Mac. Watch a few episodes of Ken Burns's *Civil War* to see how the master uses still photographs and voice-overs to tell a compelling story. Search for book trailers on YouTube to see other examples.

Social Media Page or Group

Create a specialty page (fan page) or group for the book or a part of the contents that would appeal to other researchers, local historians or collectors. The expectation with a fan page or group, however, is that you will contribute to it regularly enough to keep members interested. If you do not have the time to commit to updating it at least once every couple of weeks, you may want to skip this step. I would give you the same advice about establishing a blog for the book. The expectation of people who read social media or blogs is that you will provide updated content often.

Make Yourself Available to Answer Questions

If you are able to help other researchers and are willing to answer questions about your expertise, say so on your website, a public blog, or a post to your social media account. The same goes for letting genealogical and historical societies know that you are willing to help their members, and give them a way to contact you. Being helpful can translate into book sales.

Libraries

Most libraries have limited budgets, and the books they want to buy are ones that patrons will check out over and over. In other words, libraries will buy the latest bestsellers but may not be interested in buying a how-to unless they have a genealogical or historical collection.

It would be a grand gesture to send the local library a free copy, along with a note about how your research or the subject is connected to the area (if it is). To go the extra mile, help the library's indexer by sending a synopsis of the book's contents or how to properly categorize the subject.

If you are planning to sell to the library market, however, the following are a few things to consider:

Obvious local ties. Libraries are more likely to buy if you have strong ties to the area, or if your research is about the local area.

General appeal. If the subject of the book has broader, general appeal, make sure your description of the book includes that information.

Price. If you are able, offer the library a discount on the book or sell it to them at cost plus shipping. Librarians must look after their budgets.

Bookstores

In general, bookstores are lousy places to sell books. Bookstores play by a different set of rules than other retail outlets. Bookstores expect to put your books on their shelves, wait ninety days to see if the books sell, and if they do not, to return them to you for full credit. You pay the shipping to get the books to them; they return the books, and oftentimes, you get back books in no condition to re-sell.

Bookstores can be a good place to sell books if you can be there to give a talk about your book to an eager audience. Book signings are a long-standing tradition in publishing, but the only people who make money by signing books, are celebrities. If you are well known, you can sit and sign books for a couple of hours and make some money. If you are not well known, you must create a reason for people to come into the store, usually by offering a free, informative talk.

In either case, a bookstore hosting a book signing or a talk will expect to buy the books from you at a discount of about fifty percent. You will be expected to bring enough books to the store to satisfy the expected crowd, and the bookstore will sell the books at full price to the audience. Afterward, the bookstore will pay you the negotiated price for each book sold.

Non-Book Stores

The list of non-book stores is nearly endless. Any retail outlet that you can establish a tie with could sell your book for you. Books are sold at restaurants, tire stores, copy shops, outdoor stores, indoor stores, bait and tackle shops—nearly everywhere there is a cash register.

The best news regarding selling to non-book stores is that they do not expect to return the books. They will expect the same deep discount as bookstores and will likely take only a few copies to see how sales go. They also may expect a counter-top display. Fortunately, you can pick up an easy-to-assemble cardboard display form online or at most office supply stores.

Complimentary Copies

For the sake of posterity, other genealogical researchers, and the possibility that some major catastrophe will happen somewhere at some time, please send a complimentary copy of your book to the following major genealogical collections:

The Library of Congress
101 Independence Ave, SE, Washington, DC 20540

The Family History Library
35 North West Temple St, Salt Lake City, UT 84150

The DAR Library
   1776 D Street, NW, Washington, DC 20006

The Denver Public Library
   10 W 14th Ave Pkwy, Denver, CO 80204

The Allen County Public Library
   900 Library Plaza, Fort Wayne, IN 46802

The Wisconsin State Historical Society
   816 State St, Madison, WI 53706

The Midwest Genealogy Center
   3440 S Lee's Summit, Independence, MO 64055

The New York Public Library
   31-11 Thomson Ave, Long Island City, NY 11101

If you are able, add to your list the local libraries in the places covered by your research (if appropriate). I have often been surprised by the amazing collections of local history in even the tiniest of local libraries.

‰‰‰

Reach out to people who may want to buy a copy of your book, and to stores that could sell the book for you. Start with the natural target markets. If you are interested in expanding your reach, the next few chapters will show you how.

Chapter 25

Generating Publicity

There is an old saying in marketing: "When you advertise, you pay for the privilege of saying good things about yourself. Publicity allows other people to say good things about you free of charge." Publicity often sets the "word-of-mouth" train in motion, but it is not without work. If you want to gain publicity for your book, you will need to pitch it to the people who can help spread the word.

Gaining publicity for a how-to or instructional guide is going to be a stretch, except in certain genealogically-based publications and websites. This chapter is primarily for those books with information that would be interesting to the public, or are of such an extraordinary nature that they will generate interest in the news. You can use some of these same techniques with genealogical publications.

Book Reviews

Book reviews are a long-standing publishing tradition. Unfortunately, the most widely read book reviews are out of reach for a how-to unless you write for a major magazine or newspaper.

Book Review Magazines

The book publishing industry fills the review pages for *Kirkus Reviews*, *Publishers Weekly*, *Library Journal*, *Booklist* (American Library Association), *Library Review*, and the book review columns in the major newspapers. The likelihood of being able to get a how-to reviewed in one of these outlets is slim.

Local Newspapers

You are much more likely to have success with your local newspaper if they feature local authors. There are two approaches you can use when pitching a local newspaper: one is to ask for a book review; the other is to offer something useful, of interest to the general public, or an anecdote that features local people. Most newspapers today, even small local papers, have online editions. To make the pitch to the right person, check the online edition for book reviews and local human interest stories. If the newspaper runs a local history column, even better.

Online Bookstores

Most of the major online bookstores such as Amazon and Barnes&Noble offer reader reviews. Whether or not your book appears in these catalogs is largely a function of which print-on-demand printer you use.

The best thing about online reviews is that friends and family can easily post them. Ask people who have read the book to write an online review. If you asked people to write blurbs for the book, ask them for a review, as well.

Your Associations

You may belong to associations, clubs or organizations that would feature a review of your book in their member newsletters. Consider school groups and alumni associations, sororities or fraternities, civic groups, philanthropic groups, religious organizations, sports teams—any group you have an affiliation with that would be willing to let their members know that you have written a book.

The Press

The key to working with the press is making it easy for them to help you while meeting their deadlines.

Help a Reporter Out

One way to get the attention of busy reporters is to join the website, Help a Reporter Out (www.helpareporter.com). Every day, reporters seek information from experts. To use the site effectively, do not overstate your expertise and respond to the digest of queries in a timely manner. The free account will send queries in your field of expertise three times a day. There is a paid option as well, if you want to become known to a wide range of journalists as an expert in a particular field. Help a Reporter Out is not the only press leads website available, but it offers a free option where many others do not.

Google Alerts

One of the easiest ways to keep track of events that are happening in the news is to set up Google Alerts (alerts.google.com) for the places and events that occur in your book. For example, if you have researched the Battle at the Alamo, and a re-enactors group is conducting a demonstration at the Alamo, you could pitch the local newspapers, any societies associated with the Alamo, and the re-enactors group to include stories from your book, or a mention of your book in their coverage of the event.

Press Releases

The standard pitch tool for the media is a press release. The key to an effective press release—first and foremost—is sending it to the correct person or media outlet. The likelihood of getting any attention by sending a fax to the *Chicago Tribune* is a lot lower than sending an email to a local reporter who covers events for a small town.

Press releases follow a formula. The following is the standard formula for most press releases:

The Header. The header should include the line "For Immediate Release" unless you wish the news outlet to hold the release until a specified date.

Headline. The headline often includes a hook that helps the journalist provide something of value to the readership, usually in the form of entertainment, information, analysis or assistance. So, a curiosity piquing headline could go something like this: "Mrs. O'Leary's Cow Started the Great Chicago Fire ... Or Did She? New Book Offers Eye-Witness Testimony of Arson and Murder."

First Paragraph. The first paragraph after the headline backs up the headline with facts and should include the who, what, where when, and why of the story.

Subheads. Subheads help journalists skim through the press release quickly.

Body Paragraphs. The body paragraphs contain more about the book, perhaps a quote from you as the author, or a quote from an expert concerning the substance of the book, all of which support the main headline's promise of content.

Contact Information. If a journalist is on a deadline and wants a quick quote from you, he or she must be able to reach you quickly. Include your email address and cell phone number.

Distributing Your Press Release

Once you have a press release ready to go, make it available one or all of the following ways: by sending it directly to a journalist from a local news outlet, posting it on a free online press release site, paying a press distribution site to deliver it to targeted journalists, and including it in your own media kit (more on media kits shortly).

If you have done your homework and found the correct journalist from a local newspaper, email the press release to him or her directly. If you do not hear anything back, wait a few days, and then send an email asking whether he or she received the release. If nothing happens after that, there is no sense in pestering the journalist. Not every journalist has the time to respond to every press release sent to him or her.

Free Online Press Release Sites

At one time, there were dozens of free online press release sites. Many of those sites have become subscription sites. CyberAlert, a media monitoring service (www.cyberalert.com), posts its top free press release distribution services list every so often, and these are the top three from their latest list:

- PRUrgent (www.prurgent.com)
- PRLog (www.prlog.org)
- Newsvine (www.newsvine.com)

Paid Press Release Services

Book Publicity Services (bookpublicityservices.com) has a list of the best paid and free press release services. Unfortunately, paid distribution services are expensive and may not yield worthwhile results for a how-to or instructional guide. Regardless, the following are the top three paid sites from their list:

- PRWeb (www.prweb.com)
- eReleases (www.ereleases.com)
- PRNewswire (www.prnewswire.com)

Media Kit

The purpose of a media kit is to answer questions for the media quickly. At bare minimum, your media kit should include: a press release, an author biography and suggested interview questions in case the media person would like to conduct a quick interview about the book. You could also include: links to any social media you are using for the book, a link to your YouTube book trailer, story ideas, a fact sheet, current event tie-in ideas, quizzes, a resource list, FAQs, a review copy request form, any honors or awards the book has received, reviews and a list of interviews you have given.

Keep these items together as a PDF to attach when you reply to email queries that come from the media. Each piece of the media kit should have your full contact information in case only one page from the PDF is printed for reference.

Your online media kit (or media room) should go one step further. In addition to the media kit as a quick PDF to download, also provide each page of your media kit in plain HTML so that the text is available to the search engines. In the online version, also provide: low and high-resolution images of your book cover, an image of you as the author, and any interesting images from the book—low resolution for the Internet, high resolution for print; any media clips—audio, video or a link to the media outlet where you have given interviews; as well as your speaking schedule or author events you have planned.

Bloggers

For those of you who are unfamiliar with blogs, blogs are web-logs—a type of website. Blogging software makes blogs easy to update. The most recent post (information) remains at the top of the page until the next post comes along and moves the older information down or into an archive.

Blogs are popular because they are easy and inexpensive to set up. If you can use email, you can post (add information) to a blog. That said, for a blog to become popular, it must be fed and followed. In other words, you must add useful, helpful, interesting information to the blog regularly enough to satisfy the audience—the blog's followers. (You will find detailed instructions for creating a blog in *Set Yourself Up to Self-Publish: A Genealogist's Guide*.)

There are two primary ways to encourage bloggers to help get the word out about your book: to provide content for the blog, or to become a guest host providing interesting information to or answering questions by the blog's audience.

First, however, you must locate blogs that are appropriate to a conversation about your book. Any aspect of your book may be interesting to a blogger's audience. If, for example, you studied recipes that your 19th century ancestors would have used, then you may have information of interest to a historical cooking blog, or a blog that features unusual recipes.

Finding an Appropriate Blog

Use a search engine to locate a blog by searching for your subject (i.e. historical recipes) and the word "blog," or you can use a blog directory. A search engine is likely to return individual blog posts that contain your keywords, whereas a blog directory is more likely to return entire blogs dedicated to the subject. The Search Engine Journal (searchenginejournal.com) keeps a current list of the top blog directories. The following are a few of the most popular blog directories:

- Blog Nation (www.blognation.com)
- Best of the Web Blog Search (blogs.botw.org)
- Bloggeries (www.bloggeries.com)
- EatonWeb Blog Directory (portal.eatonweb.com)
- Blogged (blogged.com)
- Blog Search Engine (www.blogsearchengine.com)

Providing Content

If you want a blogger to include your information on his or blog, it has to be of value to their readers. It pays to spend some time looking through the archives of the blog to see what has interested readers in the past before you contact the blogger and suggest content.

Become a Guest Host

Guest hosting on numerous blogs is a way to create a virtual book tour. Instead of going from city to city signing books in bookstores, you become a guest on blogs. To become a guest host, ask the blogger to set up an author interview. The blogger will let his or her audience know in advance when the interview will take place, and the audience will submit questions for you through the blog. At a set date and time, you will become available on the blog (from your computer) to answer the audience's questions. The best thing about an author interview by blog, is that you can remain in your office to participate. No traveling is necessary.

Provide Something of Value

Another way to encourage a blogger to help you is to offer something of value to their readers. Offer a discount on your book, or free shipping, or a free sample (recipe, chapter, quiz) by email. Or offer a copy of the book as a prize for your guest appearance. Allow the host to choose the winner.

Social Media

There are two ways to use social media to spread the word: you can post (write short tidbits of information) on your social media pages, or you can comment on other people's pages.

Many people use social media as a private way to communicate with friends and family. If you are going to generate any publicity about your book, however, you must establish a public page. On some sites, that means creating a different account for you as an author, or creating a business or fan page about the book. Each social media site is different, so you will need to establish an account and test it out to see what will suit you and your book best.

Social Media Sites

The following are, currently, the most used social media sites. Trends on social media change over time, so do not be surprised if a year from now, something new has come along to grab the interest of the public. To use these sites, establish an account, give yourself a public profile and post.

- Facebook (www.facebook.com)
- Twitter (www.twitter.com)
- LinkedIn (www.linkedin.com)
- Pinterest (www.pinterest.com)
- Google+ (plus.google.com)
- Tumblr (www.tumblr.com)
- Instagram (www.instagram.com)
- Flickr (www.flickr.com)

There are specialized social media sites such as: regional sites (e.g. VK is a European site); subject-based sites (e.g. GenealogyWise is a genealogy social network); format-based sites (e.g. YouTube is a site for video); or activity-based sites (e.g. MeetUp is a site that puts people together for activities such as running).

Post to Your Own Page

The best social media posts are brief—two to three sentences, max. Share links if there are websites that have more information on the topic of your post. Use hashtags to enable people interested in the subject to find the post. A hashtag is the symbol "#" followed by a subject (e.g. #StagecoachHistory).

Use an image. Images get attention and posts with images are more likely to be read. If you want to spread the conversation, include the names of followers. On some social media sites such as Facebook, typing another person's screen name is enough to alert them that they have been tagged (written about) in a post. On others such as Twitter, using the symbol "@" plus their screen name is necessary.

Most social media sites give viewers a chance to:

- Like (indicate their interest)
- Share (re-issue the post on their own timelines)
- Comment (write something about the contents of the post)

The terms for each of these activities may vary in different social media sites, but the effect is the same. Ideally, you will write something that is interesting enough to your followers (the people reading your posts) that they will pass the information along to their followers. Or, you can encourage them to share by asking that they do so.

Brand Your Social Media Account

Most social media platforms allow you to upload a cover (banner) image. Use this opportunity to show your book cover. In most cases, your cover image may be too small for most people to easily read the title, so place the title in a larger font beside the cover image, along with your name as the author and your website address.

Link Back to Your Social Media Pages

Once you establish social media accounts, you will have a unique URL (website address) that you can link to, on your website, social media accounts, blog or email signature to direct viewers to other information you have posted online.

Comment on Other People's Posts

Commenting on other people's posts can be a great way to introduce yourself as an expert on a subject. Unfortunately, it can be a potential minefield. Be positive, choose your words carefully so that they cannot be misinterpreted, and offer something helpful to the discussion. Leave controversial topics alone. There are people who revel in the worst, base culture of the Internet. There is no sense in painting your book with that kind of brush. Take the high road.

Book Lovers

There are a host of websites devoted to book lovers and posting an announcement on these sites is a good way to spread the word about your book. There are three types of sites for book lovers—sites devoted to readers, books, and book promotion.

Reader Websites

Each of the following sites provides information for readers, and each has its own rules of participation. What you will be allowed to post about your book varies from site to site. Please read the rules before you post.

GoodReads. GoodReads (www.goodreads.com) is a social media site for book lovers that allows you to share what you are reading with your friends. GoodReads also has an author program similar to Author Central on Amazon where you can post information about your book (www.goodreads.com/author/program).

LibraryThing. LibraryThing (www.librarything.com) is a social media site for book lovers and a place to catalog your books.

BookTalk. BookTalk.com (www.booktalk.com) describes itself as "all the buzz about books." BookTalk.org (www.booktalk.org) a free book discussion group.

Shelfari. Shelfari (www.shelfari.com) is Amazon's "encyclopedia for avid book lovers."

ReadingGroup Choices. ReadingGroup Choices (www.readinggroupchoices.com) helps book clubs choose their next book. It may be hard to break into book clubs, but you will not know unless you try.

Discussion Groups

Many eReader platforms have their own discussion groups (forums) for book lovers. The following are three of the most popular:

Kindle Boards. Kindle Boards (www.kboards.com) is a discussion forum for all things Kindle.

NookBoards. NookBoards (www.nookboards.com/forum/) is a discussion forum for Nook users.

MobileRead. MobileRead (www.mobileread.com) is a cross-platform forum for people who use eReaders.

Book Sites

There is a growing list of book search engines, including:

Open Library. Open Library(openlibrary.org) is building an enormous encyclopedia of books by devoting "one web page for every book." You may as well have your book listed on this site.

BookHitch. BookHitch (www.bookhitch.com) is a search engine for books and authors.

Book Promotion Sites

Every place you can leave a mention of your book is a book promotion site, but the following are free sites where you can upload your cover, leave a sample of your writing, and other promotional materials.

Nothing Binding. Nothing Binding (www.nothingbinding.com) allows you to upload cover images, excerpts, reviews, an author image and other promotional items.

The Book Report. The Book Report (www.bookreportradio.com) is a digest of radio stations where author interviews are conducted. Listening to other authors give radio interviews can be helpful if you are planning to do any interviews of your own.

News Feeds

It is difficult to get a mention on a NewsFeeds site, but they are valuable if you want to follow social trends or breaking news to provide a hook for a pitch about your book to a local journalist.

Mashable. Mashable (mashable.com) follows the headlines, social media, tech and business, but also has a "watercooler" section of interesting headlines. One recent headline detailed how easy it is to get lost in the New York Public Library's Massive Map Collection.

Alltop. Alltop (alltop.com) has a good range of categories to follow that will digest the news across the Internet for you. While there is no genealogy subject heading, there is a history section.

Digg. Digg (digg.com) collects headlines across the Internet including headlines from social media sites and uploaded video.

StumbleUpon. StumbleUpon (www.stumbleupon.com) describes itself as "a giant collection of the best pages on the Internet." They will evaluate your interests and recommend pages for you to explore.

Google+

If there was ever a way to shout out to the world that you have a book available, Google+ may have figured it out.

Google+ has a feature entitled Hangouts on Air (www.google.com/+/learnmore/hangouts/onair.html) where you can "broadcast to the world for free." The live streaming feature allows you to create live video and have it broadcast on Google+, YouTube, and your website. It will be recorded and automatically saved to your YouTube channel.

You must establish a Google+ account, a YouTube channel (also a Google product) and have a webcam in order to record your broadcast. You can let others know about your broadcast, and they can view it on their computers, tablets or smartphones.

✥

Most publicity you can do for yourself, if you are willing to learn the ins and outs of what media outlets require. If your book would benefit from national publicity, you may want to hire a publicist, because they specialize in gaining the attention of hard-to-reach, national media outlets.

Working with a Publicist

The only time you should consider working with a publicist is if you have a family history that is of interest to the general public. Publicists are specialists in enticing media to cover you and the stories in your book. They perform a valuable service, and they charge accordingly.

Find the Right Publicist

Most publicists are specialists in one aspect of the media or another. Find a publicist who specializes in books and authors, and one who can conduct whatever type of media campaign you are interested in—online, newspaper, television, radio or all of the above. Publicists offer a multitude of services including: writing press releases, posting to blogs and social media, arranging for public appearances, scheduling interviews on television or radio, pitching feature stories, and locating media outlets appropriate to your media plan.

Research other book campaigns the publicist has worked on. The publicist should be able to tell you which books have gotten what kind of coverage.

Ask About Fees

Some publicists charge a retainer for a certain number of hours worked, others charge by the package. What the package includes can be a matter of negotiating. Many publicists offer a starter book package that includes: sending your book to a specific list of reviewers; sending press releases to a select group of media; scheduling you for interviews on radio, TV or blogs; and seeing that you get media training before any interviews take place. You may be able to find a publicist who will offer even smaller packages such as a single press release or a media kit.

Create a Media Plan

Before you approach a publicist, create a rough media plan so that you have a general idea of what you want the publicist to do for you. Where do you want your book mentioned? Local newspapers and journals? On local radio or television? Or do you think you can interest a national newspaper, radio show or television program in covering your book? If you are shooting for the moon, understand how hard it is to reach it. A local campaign may be a better way to start.

Be Realistic About Your Expectations

Before you add a media outlet to your plans, do your homework. If you think a *New York Times* book review is in order, then head to the library and read the reviews over the last month. Is there anything resembling your book in those reviews? If there is, great. Look at the way the book was covered and see how it could apply to your book. If there is nothing resembling your book in the reviews, there is a reason. The same goes for other media outlets—local or national. Asking a publicist to do the impossible will waste their time and your money.

Prepare the Publicist

Before a publicist can prepare a media campaign, they will need a copy of your book and any marketing materials you have generated.

Expect Criticism

Publicists are marketing experts. If you hire one, trust them to do what is right for you and your book. There may be a more effective way to get the word out than the marketing materials you prepared yourself. On occasion, using a good graphic designer to make your marketing materials look more professional is all it takes.

Ask How the Publicist Would Pitch Your Book

Publicists know how to sell ideas to the media and how to phrase a hook to pique interest. If a publicist struggles with how to describe your book to a journalist, there is little possibility that a journalist will be interested enough to interview you or write a story about your book.

Work With the Publicist's Schedule

Publicists work around the deadline schedule of the media. Your publicist should welcome input and questions, but ask for the best time to call or send your questions by email so that there is time for a thoughtful response.

Educate Yourself

The best way you can help your publicist help you is to learn how to market books by attend publishing association meetings and conferences, giving public talks to make yourself a better public speaker, and training to interview well on television and radio.

♥♥

Publicity is another way to describe word of mouth. For most books, word of mouth does not happen naturally. It must be generated and encouraged.

Chapter 26

Expanding Your Audience

Expanding your audience will help you reach potential buyers. The following are many of the same steps a business would use to reach out to new prospective customers, and a few techniques used primarily to market books.

Promote Yourself as an Author

For many authors, promoting one's self is uncomfortable, but your book sales will be the better for it if you do. The following are a few ways to promote your book while you promote yourself.

Promote Yourself Whenever You Can

Carry a few copies of your book wherever you go. You never know when you can strike up a conversion about your book or yourself as an author. Carry a few collaterals, such as bookmarks or business cards as well. (More about collateral materials shortly.)

Amazon's Listmania

Amazon allows users to create lists of books and other products within the Amazon catalog. When a user searches for a product that fits your list, the name of your list will pop up in the right-hand bar letting the user know that there are other similar products available in the list. This is one way to show what other books or products you found on Amazon that helped with your research, along with your book, of course, at the top of the list.

Amazon's Author Central

If your book is listed on Amazon, you can sign up for Author Central (authorcentral.amazon.com). Even if you do not use Amazon (CreateSpace) as your print-on-demand printer, your books could show up in the Amazon catalog a number of other ways—as a Kindle edition (through an eBook aggregator), Amazon's link to your POD printer's catalog (print books), or as a re-sale item. Many people re-sell their books on Amazon. In fact, you can sell your own books as a re-seller.

However your book made the list, you can use Author Central to promote yourself as an author. You can add book extras such as their "ridiculously simplified synopsis" or a longer excerpt. Your profile can include up to eight photos, eight videos, your speaking engagements calendar, a "from the author" note, reviews sent to you, additional details about the book, and your blog's RSS feed (more on RSS feeds in Chapter 27: Selling Online).

One of the best features of Author Central is that readers can see everything you have written in one place, which may generate additional book sales. One way to direct interested people to your Author Central page is to include a link to it on your author's website, in your profiles at social media sites, or anyplace online where you have your book listed.

You could get the URL (domain name) for yourself as an author (e.g. www.your-name-author.com) and redirect the URL to your Author Central page. You could also include a link in your email signature so that every time you send out an email, you encourage readers to check out your author's page.

Pixel of Ink Author's Corner

Pixel of Ink (www.pixelofink.com) also has an author's corner if you have a book for the Kindle and are willing to sell the book at bargain prices for a short time. Selling your book for $0.99 or giving it away free can spur other sales when the time for the deal has elapsed.

Create an Author's Website

Host a website that focuses on you, the author. There are a couple of ways to do this, and the next chapter will provide more details for creating websites, blogs and using URL re-directs to establish a presence online. For now, include the following in your author's website:

A Photograph (or Two). Invest in a decent head shot (portrait photograph). If you want to let your personality show a bit more, include a few candids.

A Biography. Write a quick biography about yourself, including the story of why you wrote the book. Provide a few details of expertise, describe any discoveries or difficulties you encountered during your research, and explain why the book is a "must read."

The Media Kit for the Book

In the last chapter, I described what should go into a good media kit. The media kit for your author website should include the book's media kit, examples of any articles you have written, lectures you have given about your book, and interviews you have given to the media.

Content

Provide a few book excerpts. Give away a tip or two. If you have written additional articles from your expertise or research, include them.

Lectures List

If you speak to groups frequently, include a lectures list. Interested historical or genealogical societies may be interested in one of your talks and ask you to speak to their group.

Ask for Reader Feedback

Ask people who have read your book to comment on it, and then post their comments. This is similar to asking for a testimonial about a business.

Links for Purchase

Make sure that anyone who is interested has an easy way to purchase the book. Provide a link to websites where the book is sold, or provide an order form. If you book is sold in more than one format (print and electronic), or is sold through different outlets, use an icon for the format (i.e. Kindle or iBooks) as a link to the sales venue.

Email Subscription List

If you would like to contact readers about future books, or if you are planning to write additional articles about your book, ask readers to subscribe to your email list. An email list can be valuable in the event you write another book.

Contact Information

Make sure readers have a way to contact you, either through a form on the website, an email address, a mailing address or a telephone number.

If you are serious about promoting yourself as an author, there are companies such as @uthors on the Web (www.authorsontheweb.com) who produce author-centric websites for big-name authors such as David Baldacci and Debbie Macomber. If you want to take a look at a good author's website, look at David Baldacci's website (davidbaldacci.com). His site includes the following categories: Home, About David, Books, Author Events, FAQ, Photo Gallery, In The News, Philanthropy (The Wish You Well Foundation), and Contact. He used to have a full-blown press room at this site, but has opted for a contact form for readers, and contact information for his speaker's bureau, publicist and the director of his foundation.

Author David Louis Edelman (science fiction novelist, www.davidlouisedelman.com) has an interesting list of other places to find him online including: Amazon, DeepGenre, Facebook, FiledBy, GoodReads, Google Profile, LibraryThing, LinkedIn, LiveJournal, MySpace, Nextcat, Picasa, Red Room, SFNovelists, Shelfari, Twitter and Wikipedia. David Edelman created his website using WordPress. His list of all the places he can be found online is a good example of promoting one's self as an author.

Start a Blog

Another way to expand your audience is to start a blog. Blogs are popular because they are so easy to set up and get going. One advantage to using a blog to spread the word about your book is that you do not have to seek out readers. If you publish a blog, readers can find you using a search engine based upon similar interests. The downside of establishing a blog for marketing, however, is that you have to provide content regularly in order to keep followers happy.

If you are interested in establishing your own blog, you will find detailed instructions in *Set Yourself Up to Self-Publish: A Genealogist's Guide*.

Join a Publishers Association

I believe that there is always something to learn from other people who have blazed a trail, and that is especially true when it comes to marketing books. Attending local publishers association meetings may inspire you to keep up your marketing efforts, and offer ideas for new avenues that have worked for other members of the association.

Many associations have negotiated special deals that can help with your marketing efforts, such as: annual conferences, cooperative mailings or catalogs, awards, advocacy in disputes or lawsuits, networking, freight discounts, rights negotiations, legal or financial services, distribution channels, reviews, networking and printing.

The following are publishers associations that you may find helpful:
- Small Publishers Association of North America (www.spannet.org)
- Independent Book Publishers Association (www.ibpa-online.org)
- Christian Small Publishers Association (www.christianpublishers.net)
- Association of Publishers for Special Sales (www.spanpro.org)

There are local and regional associations that may be helpful to you, as well.

Collaterals

Businesses rely upon collateral materials to get the word out to potential new clients. Everything a business would use can be useful to book marketing. The cost of full color printing has come down so much that I consider a box of 1,000 business cards a starting point, and I challenge myself to give them all away within a few weeks of a book launch.

Consider the following printed collaterals:

Business Cards

Use your book cover for one side of the business card and the other side to give a quick list of benefits, the ISBN, the price and a website where the book is sold.

Bookmarks

Think of a bookmark as an oversized business card. It should include the same information as a business card, along with quotes or images from the book.

Postcard

If you have a large list of people to contact by mail, create a postcard announcing the book to send to your list.

Rack Cards

Rack cards are the size of about one-third of a sheet of paper (4" x 9"). If you have more than one book to announce, use a rack card. Rack cards will fit inside a standard #10 business envelope. Use the extra real estate on a rack card to offer a discount, excerpts, tips, or images from the book.

The following are sites where you can order business cards and other collaterals at a reasonable cost. There are undoubtedly many others online.

- GotPrint (www.gotprint.com)
- VistaPrint (www.vistaprint.com)
- Moo (us.moo.com)

Leave Behinds

If you have a larger budget, the following are a few ideas for leave-behinds: flyers, postcards, mini cards, stickers, refrigerator magnets, note cards, sticky notes, table tents, or calendars. Use your book cover image or title on these products.

You can "leave behind" these items wherever people gather or wait—doctor's offices, community bulletin boards, chambers of commerce, public building lobbies—any place that will allow you to leave your materials behind.

Swag

If you have lotto winnings to throw at your book marketing, step up to items commonly found in swag bags at conferences, such as: key chains or other photo gifts, thumb drives, phone cases, tote bags, mugs, mousepads, tape measures, pens or calendars.

The following are promotional products companies where you can purchase leave-behinds and swag to give away:
- VistaPrint (www.vistaprint.com)
- 4Imprint (www.4imprint.com)
- Positive Promotions (www.positivepromotions.com)

Attention Getters

If you want to garner attention, consider the following products: banners, yard signs, window decals, window clings, car door magnets, posters, bumper stickers, t-shirts—even aprons. You can put a photograph on just about anything with a surface, and your book cover is a good image to place on items that will be seen by the general public. Car door magnets promote your book(s) while you are out and about, wherever you go.

The following companies provide customized products:
- CafePress (www.cafepress.com)
- Zazzle (www.zazzle.com)
- VistaPrint (www.vistaprint.com)

There are hundreds of companies around the country that supply printed and promotional products. You may find local providers as well.

Speaking Engagements

There are ample opportunities to speak to groups about your book. Groups often looking for speakers at their meetings include: historical or genealogical societies, clubs, church groups, PTAs, or service groups (Kiwanis, Elks, or Optimists).

Consider educational opportunities such as life-long learning programs or other adult education providers in your community. Teachers welcome speakers if you can talk about a subject that would tie in with their lesson plans. Some businesses offer learn-at-lunch opportunities. Businesses such as cruise ships and ski lodges invite speakers to entertain their patrons.

If you are uncomfortable with public speaking, Toastmasters International (www.toastmasters.org) has groups in nearly every community where you can test out your talk on people who will offer constructive criticism. The more you practice, the more comfortable you will be in front of a group.

Community Events

Community events are good places to sell books with local ties. Consider book fairs, farmer's markets, local festivals, town or county fairs, and holiday events. Check with the local historical society as well as civic and service groups for their event schedules. Many times, you can rent a booth at one of these events for little money, giving you and your book exposure to hundreds, if not thousands, of potential book buyers.

Articles, Columns, and Blog Posts

One way to give your book exposure and re-use the research you have already done is to write articles for magazines, columns for newspapers, or posts for blogs. Every media outlet is looking for content, and they are under pressure to find good material before every deadline. Their need creates an opportunity for you to obtain a mention of your book.

Write a Query Letter or Email First

Before you write any article, it is worth your time to query the media outlet with your idea first. A good query is similar to a good press release in that it uses a hook to gain attention, and then gets to the idea quickly. Boil it down to three paragraphs: the who, what, where, when and why; the meat of the idea; and why you are the perfect person to write the article. End with a thank you for considering your idea and your contact information.

Find an Appropriate Media Outlet

Before you submit a query, do your homework. The article should be appropriate for the media's readers. A genealogical magazine, for example, may be interested in an article about research methodology, but a local newspaper would not. An article about the history of the county fair may interest a local newspaper, but may not be right for a Revolutionary War blog. Some media outlets have specific submission guidelines. Look for the guidelines and follow them closely. Submissions outside of the guidelines likely will be tossed.

Article Ideas

Become a curator of information or website links. Most people do not have time to search for everything they may like to know for themselves, so your article could comprise something along the lines of: "The Top Ten Websites for Local History" or "The County's Best Historical Museums and Why You Should Visit."

Write about your experience writing the book. There are fledgling writers in nearly every audience.

Write about your passion for your expertise. If you have an interesting story to tell about how you got involved with your specialty, tell it.

Write about your research methodology. If you discovered a record set that most genealogists, family or local historians are unaware of, write about it and why it provided such good information.

Write in-depth stories of the neighborhood, city, area, region, time period or how tasks were accomplished.

Write a how-to article. If you learned enough about tatting to describe your great-grandmother's winter pastime, show others how they can learn too.

Proofread and Fact Check

Before you submit anything, proofread carefully and check your facts. It never hurts to give an article a thorough going over for spelling, punctuation, grammar and accuracy. The most common reason editors reject article submissions is sloppy copy editing.

Include a Signature with Your Article

At the end of each submission, include a signature (also called a resource box) with as much information as the magazine, newspaper or blog will allow.

Your signature could include:

- A photograph (of you or an image from the book)
- Your Name, Author of (the title of the book)
- Available at (local bookstore or online bookstore)
- Your website address (include the "http://" in any electronic communication to create a live link)

YouTube

YouTube can be useful to your marketing efforts beyond just a video book trailer. Consider filming each of your author events and posting those clips on YouTube. Look at the list of article ideas in the last section. Each and every idea for an article could also be an idea for a quick YouTube video.

YouTube is a Google company, and you can establish your own YouTube channel using your Google account. Google accounts are free and they give you access to Gmail (email), Google+ (social networking), Blogger (a free blog platform), Picasa (image editing), GooglePlay (apps), Google Books, Google Maps and more.

Brand your YouTube channel the way you did for other social media sites by uploading a cover (banner) image with your book cover, the title, your name as the author and your website address. Your YouTube channel will also have a unique URL (website address) that you can link on your website, social media accounts, blog or email signature to direct viewers to your videos.

Partner Up

One way to sell many books at a time is to partner up with a group that is willing to either let their members know your book is for sale, or to give your book to members as a membership perk.

If your book would interest the members of a local historical society, for example, ask the society to include a mention of your book along with a discounted price in their next email to members.

Asking the society to buy a book for each member is a little tougher sell, but with the right book, it is possible.

Stretch your imagination a bit to find partners. For example, if your book has information about a person who also happens to be a famous local musician, you may be able to partner up with the local philharmonic to give members the book if they renew their season tickets. Expect to offer the book at a significant discount to interest a group in partnering with you in this way.

Cross Promotions

Cross promotions are similar to partnering. You will offer to promote a group, business or society in your social media pages and on your website if they agree to promote your book to their members. Consider cross promotions with family associations, genealogical and historical societies, or local groups or businesses with ties to the subject or the people in your book.

Viral Marketing

Another way to expand your audience is to offer something that others will be willing to share with their friends, family, and colleagues. In marketing, these offers are called viral marketing tools. Usually, these tools come in the form of information—a helpful article that readers would pass along to someone who would also benefit from reading the article.

One way to offer viral marketing tools is to put them on your blog or website with a download link to a PDF document. Another way is to set up an autoresponder in your email program. Most email programs offer a way to send an automatic response based upon the email address or a subject line. Gmail, for example, calls autoresponders "canned responses" but it works the same way as an autoresponder.

To use autoresponders effectively, set up a new email box as an autoresponder, with an email greeting along with your PDF attachment. Anyone who sends an email, for example, to "5Tips@mycompany.com" will receive back a thank you for the inquiry along with the PDF containing the 5 Tips article. The other way to set up an autoresponder is to use your email box with a filter that catches the subject line and returns an automatic response. So, for example, you would tell interested readers to send an email with the subject line "5 Tips" to youre-mail@yourcompany.com and your email program would receive the email and automatically send a return email with your PDF attachment.

Make sure the PDF has your signature (resource box) or contact information on it, in case someone passes along the article to another person. You will want every person who receives the article to know how to contact you or where to go to order your book.

Ongoing Communication

One way to market your book(s) continuously is by maintaining some ongoing communication with your readers.

The most popular method of ongoing communication is an email list, often referred to as an email blast or an eZine (electronic magazine). Keeping in touch is particularly helpful if you plan to write another book. It is also a way for you to ask for stories and photographs while writing the next book.

You could ask interested readers to sign up for your email newsletter on your website, your blog, or in the signature in your email.

To make ongoing email communication easy, consider using an email service. One advantage to using a service is that they cue up the email from your list one at a time to avoid triggering the spam filters in most email programs that catch any email with more than eight to ten recipients. Group emails get sent to the spam filter most of the time. Using an email service means your email is more likely to be delivered, and most email services have tools that allow you to see which emails are being opened and which are not. Analyzing which emails are going unopened should help you write more attention-getting subject lines in the future.

The following are email services to consider. Some are free (or have free options); others charge a monthly fee based upon the number in your list.

- MailChimp (www.mailchimp.com)
- AWebber (www.awebber.com)
- Constant Contact (www.constantcontact.com)
- iContact (go.icontact.com)
- ActiveCampaign (www.activecampaign.com)
- Benchmark (www.benchmarkemail.com)

❧❦❧

There is almost no limit to the ways in which you can reach out to the general public to raise awareness for your book. A little bit of effort and creative thinking goes a long way.

Chapter 27

Selling Online

Selling your book online is a convenience for many readers, but also the most practical way to sell books. Bookstores are only interested in books that sell quickly, and convincing a bookstore to carry a how-to or instructional guide can be difficult unless the subject is of interest to the general public. Not to mention, that once the book is in the store, you must inspire interested readers to go there to purchase the book.

Fortunately, there are a multitude of ways to offer your book for sale on the Internet.

Create a Website

If you want to sell your book online at your own website, you will need a domain name, a web host with server space to hold your website files, a way to build the website, a method of sending files to the server, and a way to allow customers to pay for the book.

Domain Name

A domain name (also called a URL—Uniform Resource Locator) is the address where web browsers will locate your website in order to display it. Google's domain name, for example, is www.google.com. If you know a website's domain name, you can type it directly into the search bar.

You can obtain a URL through one of the many registrars online, such as:

- Register.com (www.register.com)
- Domain.com (www.domain.com)

Registering a domain name will cost anywhere from a few dollars per year to about twenty-five dollars per year. If you stop paying the annual fee, you will lose the domain, and Internet users will no longer be able to find your website.

Web Hosting

The files that make up your website must sit on a server (computer) that is connected to the Internet all the time.

You can obtain free server space for a website. The most popular free website hosts are:

- Weebly (www.weebly.com)
- Wix (www.wix.com)

The following are sites where you can obtain free space for a blog. The sites marked with an asterisk also have paid options. You can use a blog to sell your book online instead of a website, if you prefer.

- Blogger (www.blogger.com)
- WordPress (www.wordpress.com)*
- Squarespace (www.squarespace.com)*
- Tumblr (www.tumblr.com)

There are hundreds of others. Free websites or blogs include a domain name, although, it may be a subdomain of the company, such as, www.yourname.webhostingcompany.com. If you have your own domain name, you could employ domain forwarding to point your domain name to the site. For example, your domain could be something simple such as www.SuffolkMassLandRecords.com. That is the URL you would print on your business cards or use in your email signature because it will re-direct anyone who types that address into their web browser to the site which may be located at a more complicated address such as www.suffolksmasslandrecords.domainhostingcompany.com.

Note: Domain mapping is a bit more detailed than simply forwarding. Once you establish the domain map, all of the interior files that the site creates will use only the shorter, easier domain name, rather than the complete URL. For example: www.suffolksmasslandrecords.domainhostingcompany.com/10-Best-Examples.html will become *www.suffolksmasslandrecords.com*/10-Best-Examples.html using domain mapping.

Many free website hosts offer simple HTML editing tools to help you create a website. How much control you will have over the look and the organization depends upon the type of tools offered. Blogs work a little differently than HTML sites. Blogs are built primarily upon templates that hold the code for the blog posts so that the latest post goes to the top until it is replaced with something newer. Most blogging software also allows you to create static pages, and to add widgets (code) to a sidebar so that readers can click a button to go to your payment system or shopping cart.

Free sites often place advertising on your web pages. Some free sites limit the number of pages you can create. Others limit server space (often impacting the number of images you can use on the website) or traffic (the number of people visiting the site at a time and in a single month). Free is fantastic, as long as the hosting company stays in business.

Another option is to purchase hosting for your website from an Internet Service Provider (ISP). Three of the biggest ISPs are:

- HostGator (www.hostgator.com)
- NetworkSolutions (www.networksolutions.com)
- GoDaddy (www.godaddy.com)

There are thousands of local and regional ISPs offering different levels of services at all price ranges.

Some ISPs offer web-building tools, many of which are drag and drop which means you do not need to know much about creating websites in order to use them. Most ISPs charge for a certain amount of server space before you have to buy more. If you have many large files, such as videos, you may need more space. Some ISPs also charge for traffic, so if you have a popular website, you may pay more for the number of people visiting the site. Thankfully, most ISPs allow a generous amount of space and traffic in their basic (least expensive) packages.

HTML Editor

If you do not have the option of using your ISP's website building tools, or want to have more control over the look and contents of your website, you will need a way to build it. The most common way to build a site is in the computer coding language HTML, using an HTML editor. HTML editors come in all levels of sophistication and price from free downloads found on the Internet to Adobe Dreamweaver (www.adobe.com). For the most part, you do not need the most sophisticated program available to sell your book online.

Note: If you choose a blog-based site, you will not need an HTML editor. The blog software contains all of the editing tools you will need.

Uploading Files

If you build a website using an HTML editor, you must upload your files to the server space reserved for your site by your Internet Service Provider (ISP). Some ISPs have file transfer protocol (FTP) tools available from your account dashboard. Others will give you an FTP address and you must use an FTP program to upload your files from your computer to the ISP's server. The following are some of the most popular FTP programs. Those with an asterisk are free.

- WS_FTP Pro (www.ipswitchft.com)
- SmartFTP (www.smartftp.com)*
- CuteFTP Pro (www.cuteftp.com)
- WiseFTP (www.wise-ftp.com)
- FileZilla (www.filezilla-project.org)*

Uploading files to or downloading files from the Internet is simple. To send new files to the Internet, you choose files from the panel showing your computer, and hit the arrow key pointing to the side showing the server's files. If you want to download files from the server to your computer, you choose files from the server side, and hit the arrow key pointing to the files on your computer.

Payment Method

If you want to sell your books online, you must provide a way to receive payment. You can use a simple form that readers can print and send to you in the mail with a check, but most people who shop online expect to pay online. The simplest way to accomplish this is to set up a business PayPal account. These accounts are one step up from personal accounts in that they allow you to pay for items, but also receive payment. And, the site will create the code for a unique "buy now" button for each product you wish to sell, that you can copy and paste into your website or blog allowing readers to make a purchase online.

Organizing Your Website

Organizing the website well is key. At a glance, readers should be able to look at the home page and understand what to do next.

Banner Images. Most websites use a banner across the top to identify the website, display a logo, and tell viewers what the website is about. Use the banner to show your book cover and give the title, subtitle and your name as the author.

Navigation. Every page of the website should have essential navigation (links or buttons), so that readers can go from place to place within the website without losing track of where they are, and without having to use the back button on their web browser repeatedly to access other sections of the website.

Place the essential navigation in a vertical column down the left-hand side of the website or across the top beneath the banner. These are the two most common areas for navigation, and where the reader will expect to find links.

Website Real Estate. Most websites are wider than they are tall to keep viewers from having to scroll. If you can, keep whatever information you wish to impart on each page short enough to keep scrolling to a minimum.

What to Include in Your Website

Once you have the essentials—the domain name, hosting space, a way to build the site, and a payment method—there are other elements that will help potential readers find your site, and obtain enough information to purchase the book.

Home Page. Your home page should let readers know enough about the book to make them want one. Include a book cover image (even if you have one in the banner area), along with a "buy now" button, and the same type of information you used in your press releases—headline with a hook, follow up paragraphs with who, what when where and why, as well as a call to action (asking the reader to purchase the book).

Autographed Copies. If you plan to offer autographed copies, let readers know how to request one. This should be a different process than your "buy now" button so that you can tell which books must come from your stock and be autographed, and which ones you can ship directly from your book printer to the buyer. If you are using PayPal to create your "buy now" buttons, simply set up a different button to indicate a request for an autographed copy.

Author. Use this page to promote yourself as the author, or to explain why you wrote the book and how you went about the research. Show your event schedule or give a list of lectures you have prepared about the book, and give interested readers a way to contact you to book a lecture.

Excerpts. Include an excerpt or two so that readers get a feel for the contents.

Reviews. If you have good reviews, put a few on your website or blog.

Social Media Links. If you are using social media to promote the book, use an icon for each of the social media sites where you are active (Facebook, Twitter, YouTube or others) to link to your page on those sites. If you have a video book trailer, you can use the YouTube icon to link to your YouTube channel (where viewers can see all of your videos), but the site also produces the code to embed a small video window into your website or blog.

Ask for an Email Address. If you are planning any ongoing communication with readers, ask them to give you an email address. You could also capture email addresses by adding some viral marketing pieces to the site. Viral marketing was discussed in the last chapter.

Media Kit. If you are doing any publicity for the book, put your media kit online.

Contact Information. Give readers, people who may want to book you as a speaker, or members of the media a way to contact you.

Bookstore. Give readers information about other books you found helpful in writing your book. You can make a few dollars with your bookstore by becoming an affiliate of other online bookstores (see Affiliate Programs below).

Search Engine Optimization (SEO). In order for the search engines to correctly categorize your site so that users can find them you need the following:

Good Content. Search engines will look for matches between the content (the words on the page) and the keywords (metatags in the background). The closer the match, the more "relevant" the page is to the search term. In other words, if a person is searching for "Greene County Land Records" and you include that phrase in the content and the keywords, your site will show up higher in the search engine's list than a site using "Greene County History" in the text.

Clean Design. Clean design means error-free code. If you use blogging software or your ISPs website building tools, you should not have to worry about the code. If you use an HTML editor, as long as you follow the software's basic design process, you should have clean code. If you edit the code on your own—all bets are off. If you edit the code yourself, be sure to check each page for missing images or bad links.

Keywords that Make Sense. Most website-building software allows you to add keywords (metatags) to the code of the website that will remain unseen by the user. Keywords are used by the search engines to help determine relevance. By choosing your keywords or phrases wisely, you will help boost your website's rankings in the search engines. Keywords are separated by commas, and can include more than one word (e.g. Greene County Land Records, Greene County Homestead Records, etc.). Do not stuff the keywords with anything that is irrelevant to your book or the search engines will push your page rank down. Also, use the best eight to ten keywords or phrases. Any more than that, the search engines will ignore them.

Description Tags. Keywords are one metatag; the description is another. The description tag is what appears in search engine results underneath the headline link. It should give the viewer an idea of what the site is about in one sentence. Look at the first sentence of the description you wrote for your book. That sentence should hook the reader or pique his or her curiosity about the book, and is probably the best description for your website as well.

Title Tags. Each page in your website should contain a title tag. The title tag is what appears in the top left-hand portion of the web browser when visitors are on the site, but also is used as the click-able headline in the search engine results. A good title tag for the home page should be short and sweet (e.g. New book. Greene County Land Records, 1802–1896: How to Locate Them).

Image Tags. Image tags are used by the search engines to determine relevance. Image tags can boost your ranking by adding more keywords to the page. Image tags are also used by the "Images" tab on the major search engines, so if you tag an image with the names of each person in the image, anyone searching for those names may find your image which will lead them back to your website.

Image Basics Online

The goal when preparing images to use on the Internet is to keep the file sizes small enough that web pages load quickly. One way to accomplish this is to use thumbnail images with links to full-sized images so that readers have the option of looking at a photograph or a document at full size or downloading the larger image for themselves. Full-sized images can be used to order prints, as well.

If you place a full-sized image online, however, expect that people will save the image for themselves. If you do not want your images saved or used in ways you cannot control, there are ways to disable right clicks and copy/paste, or use thumbnail-sized images only, and give interested people a way to contact you for a full-sized image.

If your thumbnails are linked to larger images, explain that somewhere on the home page. Not everyone will understand that the thumbnails are click-able links unless you explain. Also post a warning about large file sizes so that readers are prepared for how long a full-sized image may take to download. Oftentimes, large images will take a minute or two to appear in a web browser making the viewer believe that nothing is happening and close the window prematurely.

Book Cover Image

Use your book cover image in the banner or in the right-hand column of the page. To keep pages loading quickly, convert your book cover image as you would any other image for the website. If you use a small thumbnail which can make the title hard to read, you can link it to a larger image or add your title, subtitle and author's name in the banner area in a larger font.

File Formats

Save full-sized images as smaller thumbnails using the "for the web" setting in your image editor, or at 72 ppi because the monitor cannot display an image at any higher resolution anyway. While web browsers will recognize and display TIFF, BMP, JPG, GIF, and PNG files, you will achieve the best quality with the fewest compatibility issues if you stick to JPG or PNG. Use PNG if you want to maintain a transparent background if the image is an icon or a logo, for example, with sharp lines and distinct areas of color. Use JPG for photographs, maps or illustrations. Play with the image format for your documents to see what gives you the best results. Typically, documents or illustrations that are fairly clean, with easy-to-read handwriting will look fine as a JPG.

Animation

While you can include animated graphics, such as animated GIFs or flash animations on your website, please do so sparingly. Flashing or rotating graphics have fallen out of fashion and tend to annoy viewers.

If you have many images to share, create an animated slide show. The most common website building software have simple plugins that create slideshows, or you can use stand-alone software such as Adobe Flash (www.adobe.com) to create a file that plays like a video. Microsoft Movie Maker comes pre-installed on most Windows machines or is free to download. Macs have iMovie that is similar. Both iMovie and Movie Maker create web-ready video slideshows.

Another option is to find (or purchase) a flash gallery where the slideshow is already built, you just add the images. Search for "free photo gallery download" on the Internet and you will find hundreds of sites with flash galleries to download. One you have a flash gallery filled with images, upload it to the server and create a link to it in the navigation of the website.

Video

If you have video, you may want to use a thumbnail or link to take readers to a full-screen version of the video. If you create a "channel" on YouTube, you can store your video files there (saving server space that you may have to pay for), and YouTube will give you the code to bring a small video window into your website. You will copy and paste the code into the page on your website. Viewers will then click on the video window to play the video from your website.

Audio

Audio files also can be large. While audio alone can generate memories, you could use your audio as the soundtrack behind a slideshow, and load it on YouTube.

Websites can be a dynamic way to showcase what is in the book, add extras, share photographs and documents, and provide an easy way to sell books online.

Online Ads

Typically, I do not recommend that you purchase ads to sell your book because there are an infinite number of ways that you can plug your book without having to purchase advertising. However, there are a few ways that you can do so without busting your budget.

Adwords

Adwords is a Google company that sells advertising which appears in the Google search engine results (usually the top three listings on the page, plus the top ten items in the right-hand sidebar), and on selected websites that have allowed an advertisement window to be placed on the site. To purchase an ad, you will set up an account, choose the keywords you would like to bid on and set a budget for how much you are willing to pay per day to let the ad run. The best thing about Adwords is that you only pay if a viewer clicks on the ad and goes to your website. Because the best keywords for a how-to are not often searched, you may not pay a great deal to get interested people to your website to buy the book.

Note: Adsense is also Google company that pays for advertising if you allow an advertisement window to be placed within your website. It is a way to make a few dollars, but unless you have an often-visited website, do not expect much more than dinner or movie money.

Facebook Ads

Facebook advertisements show up in the news feeds on individual's facebook pages based upon what they have "liked" on other pages. In other words, if you choose "genealogy" in the likes and interests field, your ad will be shown to other people interested in genealogy. A recent search showed that choosing "genealogy" as an interest returned more than two million interested people. A search for "genealogy family history" returned only eighteen thousand, and "genealogy research" only sixteen thousand. Unfortunately, there is no way to know more specifically if any of these people are interested in your expertise. Select the option to only pay for clicks to your website, which will narrow the number of people down considerably. The fewer clicks through, the lower the cost of the ad.

Trade an Ad

Make an offer to a local historical or genealogical society to trade ads. You host an ad for the society on your website, while they host an ad for your book on theirs. Agree to a length of time you will keep each other's ads up.

Book-Related Sites that Sell Ads

There are several book-related sites that sell advertising. The following are two of the most popular:

Ereader News Today. Ereader News Today (ereadernewstoday.com). This site sends emails to its subscribers daily that offer readers free and bargain books for their Kindles. This site also spreads the word through their Facebook page. If you want to price your book at $2.99 or less in order to reach their enormous audience, buying an ad on this site will help you do so. They also offer a Bargain

Books ad that takes 25 percent of whatever you sell through the ad, measured by their affiliate code through Amazon.

BookBub. BookBub (www.bookbub.com). This site offers bargain eBooks to their subscribers across many eReader platforms. You coordinate the sales price with each of your retail outlets (Amazon, Barnes&Noble, BooksaMillion, etc.) or through your eBook aggregator, if you used one. You purchase an ad based upon the genre and the sales price. Their primary focus is on fiction and, unfortunately; there is not a category listed for family histories. There are categories for Biographies and Memoirs as well as Advice and How-To, which may fit your book.

Online Bookstores

There are many bookstores besides Amazon that sell books online. If you are using one of the big print-on-demand printers, chances are good that your book will be included in the catalogs of:

- Amazon (www.amazon.com)
- Barnes&Noble (www.bn.com)
- Books-a-Million (www.booksamillion.com)
- Powell's Books (www.powells.com)
- Alibris (www.alibris.com)
- Abe Books (www.abebooks.com)
- Biblio (www.biblio.com)
- The Tattered Cover (www.tatteredcover.com)

If your book is not included in these catalogs automatically, look for the "publisher" information on their websites to see what you must do to have your book added. Amazon, however, remains the largest online book seller. As long as your book is listed there, you may not want to go to a lot of trouble to have your book listed in other online stores.

Wherever your book is listed online, use every tool available to enhance your listing. Make sure each site has a cover image. Enable all features that allow readers to get a feel for what the book entails. Add a description, an author biography or an excerpt. Everything you can do to help buyers find your book will increase book sales.

Amazon

The three most important sales tools on Amazon are the "Look Inside the Book" function, reviews that come from readers, and Author Central, where you can showcase yourself along with the book. These features have been discussed, but here is one more. On your book's listing, below the cover is a link to "share your own customer images." If you have other photographs related to the book that would entice readers to buy, by all means, add the photographs.

Affiliate Programs

One way to earn a little bit more for selling your own book is to join an affiliate program. Affiliate programs give you credit (and a percentage of the sale) every time someone goes to your website or opens your email, clicks through to the online bookstore, and makes a purchase. Amazon has one of the most comprehensive affiliate programs online.

One way to be helpful to your readers is to suggest other books (or products, if appropriate) to enhance the reader's experience. For example, if you have a travel guide, you could recommend travel gear or a translation guide that would be helpful while visiting the area your travel guide describes. For a family history, you could recommend other books about the area or era. Amazon does this expertly with their "customers who bought this item also bought" feature.

Amazon also has a "recommended for you" feature based upon your prior purchases. You could set up a "recommended reading" list with links to the books you used in your research.

If you think viewers would appreciate buying from their favorite online bookstore, or in different eReader versions (Kindle, Android, etc.), set up multiple affiliate links giving readers a choice.

Each affiliate program will give you a coded link to the products on their website so that when viewers on your website make a purchase using the affiliate link, you get credit for the sale.

Online Non-Book Stores

Bookstores are not the only places books are sold online. There are online sales outlets such as eBay (www.ebay.com) where you can set up an account and sell items directly to eBay's buyers. There are also museum shops and historical or genealogical organizations that sell books.

Conduct a quick search for Chambers of Commerce, independent bookstores, colleges or universities, local libraries, and tourist attractions where people may have an interest in your specialty. Depending upon your subject, you may be able to sell books through a local hotel or bed & breakfast.

You can negotiate with any place that has a website where products are already being sold to list your book on their website. They will collect the full retail price, send you payment for the wholesale price through PayPal or a wholesale page on your website, and you will ship the book to the reader.

∝৶৽

Selling online is one way to expand your audience because potential readers can find your book using a search engine. You will make the most per book if you sell directly to the reader, but there is something to be said for gaining access to the customer base of an existing group or online store. You may make more money by selling books at a discount through an association, for example, because of the larger volume of sales, than selling one book at a time through your website.

Conclusion

Whether you took only the baby steps or jumped headlong into the giant leaps, I am sure that your experience deserves to be written about and published for other interested researchers to read and appreciate.

I am confident that if you can do the research and follow the steps outlined in this guide, you can publish. Although most how-tos or instructional guides are published in print, if you choose to publish electronically, let me encourage you, once again, to publish at least a few copies in print to contribute to the major genealogical collections around the country. Your hard work deserves to be preserved and available for years to come.

If you are just beginning, I trust you are inspired enough to pick a project to publish. In fact, I hope to have inspired half a dozen projects you cannot wait to begin, and caused many more ideas to tumble around in your imagination.

If the research is underway but the writing is not yet complete, I anticipate that you will reach out to others who can be of assistance to gather new research, find or create illustrations, and finish the book.

If the research is sitting in your computer yearning to bust out of the bytes and into the hands of less learned researchers, I trust this guide has made you believe that you *can* publish and get the word out that you have a helpful, informative guide available.

About the Author

Dina C. Carson has been involved in publishing and genealogy for more than two decades. She brings her experience with all phases of book publishing to help first-time self-publishers create quality family or local histories, and research guides that are both believable and achievable.

She is the coordinator of the Boulder Pioneers Project, a comprehensive look at the original source documents for Boulder County during the territorial period (1858–1876) and is the author of more than a dozen annotated indexes of Boulder County source materials.

She lectures frequently to genealogical, historical and philanthropic societies, gives workshops on publishing, pioneers and other topics, and is working with the Colorado State Archives on state-wide records indexing projects.

Although her formal education is in international law and economics, she owns Iron Gate Publishing, a publishing company that focuses on genealogy, local history and reunion planning. She is also a partner in Imagination Technology, a graphic design and marketing firm working with local businesses.

When she's not at a computer working on a publishing project, you can find her photographing the pioneer cemeteries of Colorado.

Bibliography

RESEARCH

Blumenson, John J-G. *Identifying American Architecture: A Pictoral Guide to Styles and Terms, 1600-1945*. New York, NY: W W Norton, 1981.

Butchart, Ronald E. *Local Schools: Exploring Their History*. Nashville, TN: American Association for State and Local History, 1986.

Carpenter, Will. *The Life and Times Of ...: Researching and Writing American Local History*. Cookeville, TN: HistoryWorks, 2009.

Carson, Dina. *Directory of Genealogical and Historical Societies, Libraries and Museums in the U.S. and Canada, 2014*. Niwot, CO: Iron Gate Publishing, 2014.

Danzer, Gerald A. *Public Places: Exploring Their History*. Nashville, TN: American Association for State and Local History, 1995.

Davidson, James West and Mark Hamilton Lyle. *After the Fact: The Art of Historical Detection*. Boston: McGraw Hill, 2000.

DeBlasio, Donna M. *Catching Stories: A Practical Guide to Oral History*. Athens, OH: Swallow Press, 2009.

Dudley, Roger L. *In Their Time: A Timeline Journal for Placing Family Events into Historical Context, 1000-2076*. Denver, CO: Warfield Press, 2013.

Evans, Tonya Marie and Susan Borden Evans. *Literary Law Guide for Authors: Copyright, Trademark and Contracts in Plain Language*. Philadelphia: Literary Entrepreneur Series, 2003.

Field, Marion. *The Writer's Guide to Research: An Invaluable Guide to Gathering Material for Features, Novels and Non-Fiction Books*. Oxford, England: How to Books, 2000.

Filby, William. *A Bibliography of American County Histories*. Baltimore, MD: Genealogical Publishing Company, 2000.

Foster, Gerald. *American Houses: A Field Guide to the Architecture of the Home*. Boston, MA: Houghton Mifflin, 2004.

Hart, Cynthia and Lisa Samson. *The Oral History Workshop: Collect and Celebrate the Life Stories of Your Family and Friends*. New York: Workman Publishing Company, 2009.

Henderson, Nancy. *The Genealogist's U.S. History Pocket Reference: Quick Facts & Timelines of American History to Help Understand Your Ancestors*. San Diego, CA: Family Tree Books, 2013.

Howe, J. and Delores A. Fleming, Emory L. Kemp, Ruth Ann Overbeck. *Houses and Homes: Exploring Their History*. Walnut Creek, CA: Alta Mira Press, 1997.

PUBLISH YOUR SPECIALTY

Hunt, R. Douglas. *American Farms: Exploring Their History*. Malabar, FL: Krieger Publishing Co., 1996.

Jacobson, Judy. *History for Genealogists: Using Chronological Time Lines to Find and Understand Your Ancestors*. Baltimore, MD: Clearfield Publishing Co., 2009.

Jones, Thomas W. *Mastering Genealogical Proof*. Arlington, VA: National Genealogical Society, 2013.

Kammen, Carol. *On Doing Local History: Reflections on What Local Historians Do, Why and What it Means*. Nashville, TN: The American Association for State and Local History, 1986.

Kammen, Carol. *The Pursuit of Local History: Readings in Theory and Practice*. Walnut Creek, CA: Alta Mira Press, 1996.

Kerr, K. Austin and Amos J Loveday, Mansel G Blackford. *Local Businesses: Exploring Their History*. Nashville, TN: American Association for State and Local History, 1990.

Kyvig, David E. and Myron A. Marty. *Nearby History: Exploring the Past Around You, 2nd Edition*. NY: Alta Myra Press, 2000.

Lynch, Daniel. *Google Your Family Tree*. Baltimore, MD: FamilyLink, 2008.

McAlester, Virginia and A. Lee McAlester. *A Field Guide to American Houses*. New York, NY: Knopf. 1984.

Mills, Elizabeth Shown. *Evidence Explained: Citing History Sources from Artifacts to Cyberspace*. Baltimore, MD: Genealogical Publishing Co, 2007.

Ritchie, Donald A. *Doing Oral History*. New York: Oxford University Press, 2003.

Szucs, Loretto Dennis and Sandra Hargreaves Luebking. *The Source: A Guidebook to American Genealogy, 3rd Edition*. Provo, UT: Generations Network, 2006.

Urend, James P. *Places of Worship: Exploring Their History*. Nashville, TN: American Association for State and Local History, 1990.

Yow, Valerie Raleigh. *Recording Oral History: A Guide for the Humanities and Social Sciences, 2nd Edition*. Walnut Creek, CA: AltaMira Press, 2005.

WRITING

Ackerman, Angela and Becca Puglisi. *The Emotion Thesaurus: A Writer's Guide to Character Expression*. Jupiter, FL: JADD Publishing, 2012.

Ackerman, Angela and Becca Puglisi. *The Negative Trait Thesaurus: A Writer's Guide to Character Flaws*. Jupiter, FL: JADD Publishing, 2013.

Ackerman, Angela and Becca Puglisi. *The Positive Trait Thesaurus: A Writer's Guide to Character Attributes*. Jupiter, FL: JADD Publishing, 2013.

Amato, Joseph A. *Rethinking Home: A Case for Writing Local History*. Berkeley, CA: University of California Press, 2002.

Barany, Beth. *The Writer's Adventure Guide: 12 Stages to Writing Your Book (for Novelists and Creative Nonfiction Writers)*. Oakland, CA: Barany Pub, 2009.

Beckett, John. *Writing Local History*. Manchester, England: Manchester University Press, 2007.

Bickham, Jack M. *The 38 Most Common Fiction Writing Mistakes (And How to Avoid Them)*. Cincinnati, OH: Writer's Digest Books, 1997.

Blake, Gary and Robert W. Bly. *The Elements of Technical Writing: The Essential Guide to Writing Clear, Concise Proposals, Reports, Manuals, Letters, Memos, and Other Documents in Every Technical Field*. NY: Simon & Schuster Macmillan Company, 1993.

Block, Lawrence. *Spider, Spin Me a Web: A Handbook for Fiction Writers*. NY: William Morrow Paperbacks, 1996.

Block, Lawrence. *Telling Lies for Fun and Profit: A Manual for Fiction Writers*. NY: William Morrow Paperbacks, 1994.

Block, Lawrence. *Writing the Novel from Plot to Print*. Cincinnati, OH: Writers Digest Books, 1985.

Borg, Mary. *Writing Your Life: An Easy-to-Follow Guide to Writing an Autobiography*. Fort Collins, CO: Cottonwood Press, 1990.

Bowerman, Peter. *The Well-Fed Self-Publisher: How to Turn One Book into a Full Time Living*. Atlanta, GA: Fanove Publ, 2007.

Boyer, Carl III. *How to Publish and Market Your Family History, 4th Edition*. Santa Clarita, CA: Carl Boyer, 1993.

Brohaugh, William. *Write Tight: How to Keep Your Prose Sharp, Focused and Concise*. Cincinnati, OH: Writer's Digest Books, 1993.

Browne, Renni. *Self-Editing for Fiction Writers: How to Edit Yourself Into Print*. New York, NY: Harper Paperbacks, 2004.

Carpenter, Will. *The Life and Times Of ...: Researching and Writing American Local History*. Cookeville, TN: HistoryWorks, 2009.

Casagrande, June. *It was the Best of Sentences, It was the Worst of Sentences: A Writer's Guide to Crafting Killer Sentences*. New York: Ten Speed Press, 2010.

Cheney, Theodore A. Rees. *Writing Creative Nonfiction: How to Use Fiction Techniques to Make Your Nonfiction More Interesting, Dramatic and Vivid*. Berkeley, CA: Ten Speed Press, 1991.

Chicago Manual of Style, 16th Edition. Chicago: University of Chicago Press, 2010.

Clark, Roy Peter. *Writing Tools: 50 Essential Strategies for Every Writer*. New York, NY: Little, Brown and Company, 2008.

Clausen, John. *Too Lazy to Work, Too Nervous to Steal: How to Have a Great Life as a Freelance Writer*. Cincinnati, OH: Writer's Digest Books, 2001.

Cleaver, Jerry. *Immediate Fiction: A Complete Writing Course*. NY: St Martin's Griffin, 2005.

Collier, Oscar and Frances Spatz Leighton. *How to Write & Sell Your First Nonfiction Book*. NY: St. Martin's Press, 1994.

Collins, Brandilyn. *Getting Into Character: Seven Secrets a Novelist Can Learn from Actors*. NY: John Wiley & Sons, 2002.

Dalton, Judy. *The 29 Most Common Writing Mistakes and How to Avoid Them.* Cincinnati, OH: Writer's Digest Books, 1985.

Dibell, Ansen. *Plot: How to Build Short Stories and Novels that Don't Sag, Fizzle, or Trail Off in Scraps of Frustrated Revision—and How to Rescue Stories That Do.* Cincinnati, OH: Writer's Digest Books, 1988.

Dickson, Paul. *War Slang: American Fighting Words and Phrases since the Civil War.* Washington, D.C.: Brassey's, 2004.

Edgerton, Les. *Hooked: Write Fiction That Grabs Readers at Page One and Never Lets Them Go.* Cincinnati, OH: Writer's Digest Books, 2007.

Einsohn, Amy. *The Copyeditor's Handbook, 3rd Edition: A Guide for Book Publishing and Corporate Communication.* (Berkeley, CA: University of California Press, 2011).

Ellis, Sherry. *Now Write! Nonfiction: Memoir, Journalism and Creative Nonfiction Exercises from Today's Best Writers.* New York, NY: Tarcher, 2009.

Embree, Mary. *The Author's Toolkit: A Step-by-Step Guide to Writing and Publishing Your Book (Revised Edition).* New York: Allworth Press, 2003.

Finley, Carmen J. *Creating a Winning Family History.* Arlington, VA: National Genealogical Society, 2010.

Franklin, Jon. *Writing for Story: Craft Secrets of Dramatic Nonfiction.* New York, NY: Plume, 1994.

Friedlander, Joel. *A Self-Publisher's Companion: Expert Advice for Authors Who Want to Publish.* San Rafael, CA: Martin Bookworks, 2011.

Fruehling, Rosemary T. and N. B. Oldham. *Write to the Point! Letters, Memos, & Reports that Get Results.* New York, NY: McGraw-Hill Book Co, 1988.

Garrison, Webb. *The Encyclopedia of Civil War Usage: Everyday Language of Soldiers and Civilians.* Nashville, TN: Cumberland House, 2001.

Gaughran, David. *Let's Get Digital: How to Self-Publish, and Why You Should.* US: Arriba Arriba Books, 2011.

Genealogy Publishing Service. *How to Write & Publish Your Family Book.* Franklin, NC: Genealogy Publishing Service, 1992.

Gerard, Philip. *Creative Nonfiction: Researching and Crafting Stories of Real Life.* Cincinnati, OH: Waveland Pr Inc, 2004.

Goldfarb, Ronald L. and Gail E. Ross. *The Writer's Lawyer: Essential Legal Advice for Writers and Editors in All Media.* NY: Times Books, 1989.

Gouldrup, Lawrence P. *Writing the Family Narrative.* Salt Lake City: Ancestry Publishing, 1987.

Gutkind, Lee. *In Fact: The Best of Creative Nonfiction.* New York, NY: W. W. Norton & Company, 2004.

Gutkind, Lee. *Keep it Real: Everything You Need to Know About Researching and Writing Creative Nonfiction.* New York, NY: W. W. Norton & Company, 2009.

Gutkind, Lee. *The Art of Creative Nonfiction.* New York, NY: Wiley, 1997.

Hale, Constance. *Sin and Syntax: How to Craft Wickedly Effective Prose*. New York, NY: Broadway, 2001.

Hart, Jack. *Storycraft: The Complete Guide to Writing Narrative Nonfiction*. Chicago: University of Chicago Press, 2011.

Hatcher, Patricia Law. *Producing a Quality Family History*. Salt Lake City: Ancestry, Inc., 1996.

Howard, V. A. and J. H. Barton. *Thinking on Paper: Refine, Express, and Actually Generate Ideas by Understanding the Processes of the Mind*. New York, W Morrow, 1986.

Kawasaki, Guy and Shawn Welch. *APE: Author, Publisher, Entrepreneur—How to Publish a Book*. US: Nononina Press, 2013

Kempthorne, Charley. *For All Time: A Complete Guide to Writing Your Family History*. Heinemann, NH: Boynton/Cook Publishers, 1996.

Kidder, Tracy and Richard Todd. *Good Prose: The Art of Nonfiction*. New York: Random House, 2013.

Kitchel, Dwain L. *Writing and Marketing a Family History in the 1990s*. Knoxville, TN: Tennessee Valley Publicatiions, 1990.

Kramer, Mark. *Telling True Stories: A Nonfiction Writer's Guide from the Nieman Foundation at Harvard University*. New York, NY: Plume, 2007.

Krull, Kathleen. *12 Keys to Writing Books that Sell*. Cincinnati, OH: F&W Publications, Inc. 1989.

Lashier, Kathleen. *Grandma [Grandpa], Tell Me Your Stories*. Waverly, IA: Cq Products, 1992.

Lashier, Kathleen. *Mom [Dad], Share Your Life With Me*. Waverly, IA: Cq Products, 1992.

Lashier, Kathleen. *To the Best of My Recollection*. Waverly, IA: G&R Publishing, 1996.

Leland, Christopher T. *The Creative Writer's Style Guide*. Cincinnati, OH: Writer's Digest Books, 2002.

Levin, Donna. *Get that Novel Started and Keep it Going until You Finish*. Cincinnati, OH: Writer's Digest Books, 1992.

Lopate, Phillip. *To Show and to Tell: The Craft of Literary Nonfiction*. New York: Free Press, 2013.

Lukeman, Noah. *The First Five Pages: A Writer's Guide to Staying Out of the Rejection Pile*. New York, NY: Fireside, 2005.

Lukeman, Noah. *The Plot Thickens: 8 Ways to Bring Fiction to Life*. New York: St. Martin's Griffin, 2003.

Marshall, Carl and David Marshall. *The Book of Myself: A Do-it-Yourself Autobiography in 201 Questions*. New York, NY: Hyperion, 2007.

Marshall, Evan. *The Marshall Plan for Novel Writing: A 16-Step Program Guaranteed to Take You from Idea to Completed Manuscript*. Cincinnati, OH: Writer's Digest Books, 1998.

McCutcheon, Marc. *Building Believable Characters*. Cincinnati, OH: Writer's Digest Books, 1996.

Merriam-Webster's English Usage Dictionary. New York: Merriam-Webster, 2010.

Morris, William. *Morris Dictionary of Word and Phrase Origins, 2nd Edition*. New York, Collins Reference, 1988.

Noble, William. *The 28 Biggest Writing Blunders (And How to Avoid Them)*. Cincinnati, OH: Writer's Digest Books, 1992.

Noble, William. *Noble's Book of Writing Blunders (And How to Avoid Them)*. Cincinnati, OH: Writers Digest Books, 2006.

Noble, William. *Writing Dramatic Non-Fiction*. Forest Dale, VT: Paul S Eriksson, 2000.

Nuwer, Hank. *How to Write Like an Expert About Anything: Bring Factual Accuracy and the Voice of Authority to Your Writing*. Cincinnati, OH: Writer's Digest Books, 1995.

Obstfeld, Raymond. *Fiction First Aid: Instant Remedies for Novels, Stories and Scripts*. Cincinnati, OH: Writer's Digest Books, 2002.

Orion, Dean. *Live To Write Another Day, A Survival Guide for Screenwriters and Creative Storytellers*. US: Sky Father Media, 2013.

Perl, Sondra. *Writing True: The Art and Craft of Creative Nonfiction*. Boston, MA: Wadsworth Publishing, 2006.

Plotnik, Arthur. *Spunk & Bite: A Writer's Guide to Bold, Contemporary Style*. New York, NY: Random House Reference, 2007.

Polking, Kirk. *Writing Family Histories and Memoirs*. Cincinnati, OH: Betterway Books, 1995.

Poynter, Dan. *Writing Nonfiction: Turning Thoughts into Books*. Santa Barbara, CA: Para Publishing, 2007.

Pyne, Stephen J. *Voice & Vision: A Guide to Writing History and Other Serious Nonfiction*. Cambridge, MA: Harvard University Press, 2011.

Q&A a Day: 5-Year Journal. New York, NY: Potter Style, 2010.

Rampolla, Mary Lynn. *A Pocket Guide to Writing History*. Boston, MA: Bedford-St Martin's, 2007.

Raymond, Stuart A. *Genealogical Jargon for Family Historians*. Bury: Federation for Family History Societies, 2005.

Reminiscing: 21st Century Master Edition. Itasca, IL: TDC Games, n.d.

Rodale, J.I. *Synonym Finder, Completely Revised*. New York: Grand Central Publishing, 1988.

Roerden, Chris. *Don't Murder Your Mystery: 24 Fiction-Writing Techniques to Save Your Manuscript from Turning up D. O. A.* Rock Hill, SC: Bella Rosa Books, 2006.

Rubie, Peter. *The Elements of Storytelling: How to Write Compelling Fiction*. NY: John Wiley & Sons, 1995.

Rubie, Peter and Gary Provost. *How to Tell a Story: The Secrets of Writing Captivating Tales*. Cincinnati, OH: Writer's Digest Books, 1998.

Schmidt, Victoria Lynn. *Story Structure Architect: A Writer's Guide to Building Dramatic Situations and Compelling Characters.* Cincinnati, OH: F&W Publications, 2005.

Sellers, Heather. *Page After Page: Discover the Confidence and Passion You Need to Start Writing and Keep Writing (No Matter What!).* Cincinnati, OH: Writer's Digest Books, 2005.

Silverman, Sue William. *Fearless Confessions: A Writer's Guide to Memoir.* Athens, GA: University of Georgia Press, 2009.

Smith, Michael C. and Suzanne Greenberg. *Everyday Creative Writing: Panning for Gold in the Kitchen Sink, 2nd Edition.* Lincolnwood, IL: NTC Publishing Group, 2000.

Stewart, James B. *Follow the Story: How to Write Successful Nonfiction.* NY: Touchstone, 1998.

Strong, William S. *The Copyright Book: A Practical Guide, 4th Edition.* Cambridge, MA: MIT Press, 1993.

St. Maur, Suzan. *How to Write Winning Non-Fiction: The Complete Writing and Publishing Handbook for Non-Fiction Authors.* London, England: Publishing Academy, 2010.

Stone, Todd A. *Novelists' Boot Camp: 101 Ways to Take Your Book from Boring to Bestseller.* Cincinnati, OH: Writer's Digest Books, 2006.

Strunk, William and William Strunk, Jr. *The Elements of Style (Updated 2011 Edition).* New York: The Style Manual Press, 2011.

Szucs, Loretto Dennis. *Family History Made Easy.* Salt Lake City: Ancestry Publishing, 1998.

Truss, Lynne. *Eats, Shoots & Leaves: A Zero Tolerance Approach to Punctuation.* New York, New York: Gotham, 2004.

Tuchman, Barbara W. *Practicing History: Selected Essays.* New York: Ballantine Books, 1935.

Turabian, Kate L. *A Manual for Writers of Research Papers, Theses, and Dissertations, 8th Edition.* Chicago, IL: University of Chicago Press, 2013.

Walsh, Bill. *Lapsing into a Comma: A Curmudgeon's Guide to the Many Things that Can Go Wrong in Print—And How to Avoid Them.* New York: McGraw-Hill, 2000.

Walsh, Bill. *The Elephants of Style: A Trunkload of Tips on the Big Issues and Gray Areas of Contemporary American English.* New York: McGraw-Hill, 2004.

Walsh, Bill. *Yes, I Could Care Less: How to Be a Language Snob Without Being a Jerk.* New York: St Martin's Griffin, 2013.

Wilson, Lee. *Make it Legal.* NY: Allworth Press, 1990.

Zinsser, William. *Inventing the Truth: The Art and Craft of Memoir.* NY: Mariner Books, 1998.

Zinsser, William. *On Writing Well.* New York, NY: Harper Paperbacks, 2006.

Zinsser, William. *Writing About Your Life: A Journey into the Past.* New York, NY: Da Capo Press, 2005.

Zuckerman, Albert. *Writing the Block Buster Novel*. Cincinnati, OH: Writer's Digest Books, 1994.

EXAMPLES

Howe, Barbara J. and Delores A. Fleming. Houses and Homes: Exploring Their History. Walnut Creek, CA: AltaMira Press, 1995.

Jones, Thomas W. *Mastering Genealogical Proof*. Arlington, VA: National Genealogical Society, 2013.

Levenik, Denise May. *How to Archive Family Keepsakes: Learn How to Preserve Family Photos, Memorabilia and Genealogy Records*. Cincinnati, OH: Family Tree Books, 2012.

Morgan, George G. *How to Do Everything Genealogy, 4th Edition*. New York: McGraw-Hill Education, 2015.

Morgan, George G. and Drew Smith. *Advanced Genealogy Research Techniques*. New York: McGraw-Hill Education, 2013.

Neagles, James C. *U.S. Military Records: A Guide to Federal & State Sources, Colonial America to the Present*. Provo, UT: Ancestry Publishing, 1994.

Reid, Judith Prowse and Simon Fowler. *Genealogical Research in England's Public Record Office: A Guide for North Americans, 2nd Edition*. Baltimore, MD: Genealogical Publishing Company, 2000.

Schaefer, Christina K. *The Center: A Guide to Genealogical Research in the National Capital Area*. Baltimore, MD: Genealogical Publishing Company, 2009.

Szucs, Loretto Dennis, et al. *The Source: A Guidebook Of American Genealogy, 3rd Edition*. Provo, UT: Ancestry Publishing Company, 2006.

Thorndale, William and William Dollarhide. *Map Guide to the U.S. Federal Censuses, 1790-1920*. Baltimore, MD: Genealogical Publishing Company, 1998.

PRODUCTION

Ashford, Janet and John Odam. *Start with a Scan: A Guide to Transforming Scanned Photos and Objects into High-Quality Art, 2nd Edition*. Berkeley, CA: Peachpit Press, 2000.

Blatner, David and Glenn Fleishman, Steve Roth. *Real World Scanning and Halftones: The Definitive Guide to Scanning and Halftones from the Desktop*. Berkeley, CA: Peachpit Press, 1998.

Bonura, Larry S. *The Art of Indexing*. New York, NY: John Wiley & Sons, 1994.

Bringhurst, Robert. *The Elements of Typographic Style*. Point Roberts, WA: Hartley & Marks, 2008.

Carter, David, ed. *Big Book of Design Ideas*. New York, NY: Harper Collins, 2000.

Cohen, Sandee and Robin Williams. *The Non-Designer's Scan and Print Book: All You Need to Know About Production and Prepress to Get Great-Looking Pages*. Berkeley, CA: Peachpit Press, 1999.

Ctein. *Digital Restoration from Start to Finish*. London: Elsevier, 2010.

de Bartolo, Carolina. *Explorations in Typography: Mastering the Art of Fine Typesetting*. 101 Editions, 2011.

Evans, Poppy. *Designer's Survival Manual: The Insider's Guide to Working with Illustrators, Photographers, Printers, Web Engineers, and More ...* . Cincinnati, OH: How Design Books, 2001.

Felici, James and Frank Romano. *The Complete Manual of Typography: A Guide to Setting Perfect Type*. San Francisco: Peachpit Press, 2002.

Hendel, Richard. *On Book Design*. New Haven: Yale University Press, 1998.

Hoff, Henry B. *Genealogical Writing in the 21st Century: A Guide to Register Style and More*. Boston: New England Historical and Genealogical Society, 2002.

Krause, Jim. *Color Index—Revised Edition*. Cincinnati, OH: HOW Books, 2010.

Krause, Jim. *Color Index 2*. Cincinnati, OH, HOW Books, 2007.

Lee, Marshall. *Bookmaking, 3rd Edition: Editing, Design, Production*. New York: Norton & Co., 2004.

Lupton, Ellen. *Thinking with Type: A Critical Guide for Designers, Writers, Editors and Students, 2nd Revised and Expanded Edition*. NY: Princeton Architectural Press, 2010.

Masterson, Pete. *Book Design & Production: A Guide for Authors and Publishers*. El Sobrante, CA: AEonix Publishing Group, 2007.

McClure, Rhonda R. *Digitizing Your Family History: Easy Methods for Preserving Your Heirloom Documents, Photos, Home Movies and More in a Digital Format*. Cincinnati, OH: Family Tree Books, 2004.

Pantone Graphics. *Formula Guide: Solid Coated & Solid Uncoated*. Carlstadt, NJ: Pantone Graphics, 2014.

Smith, Brian R. *Dollarhide Numbering for Genealogists—An Authorized Guide for the Serious User*. Orting, WA: Family Roots Publishing, 2011.

Spaltro, Kathleen. *Genealogy and Indexing*. Wheat Ridge, CO: American Society of Indexers, 2003.

Sperry, Kip. *Abbreviations & Acronyms: A Guide for Family Historians*. Orem, UT: Ancestry, 2000.

Steinhoff, Sascha. *Scanning Negatives and Slides: Digitizing Your Photographic Archive*. Santa Barbara, CA: Rocky Nook, 2009.

Tally, Taz. *Avoiding the Scanning Blues: A Desktop Scanning Primer*. Upper Saddle River, NJ: Prentice Hall, 2001.

Wellisch, Hans H. *Indexing from A to Z*. Bronx, NY: The H. W. Wilson Company, 1991.

Wheildon, Colin. *Type & Layout: How Typography and Design can Get Your Message Across—Or Get in the Way*. NY: Strathmoor Press, 1995.

White, Jan V. *Great Pages: A Common-Sense Approach to Effective Desktop Design.* London: Serif Publishing, 1990.

Williams, Robin. *The Mac is not a Typewriter, 2nd Edition.* San Francisco, CA: Peachpit Press, 2003.

Williams, Robin. *The Non-Designer's Design Book, 3rd Edition.* San Francisco, CA: Peachpit Press, 2008.

Williams, Robin. *The Non-Designer's Type Book.* San Francisco, CA: Peachpit Press, 1998.

MARKETING

Amir, Nina. *Authorpreneur: How to Build a Business around Your Book.* Los Gatos, CA: Pure Spirit Creations, 2014.

Daffron, Susan C. *Publishize: How to Quickly and Affordably Self-Publish a Book That Promotes Your Expertise.* Logical Expressions, 2011.

Eager, Rob. *Sell Your Books like Wildfire: The Writer's Guide to Marketing and Publicity.* Cincinnati, OH: Writer's Digest Books, 2012.

Gaughran, David. *Let's Get Visible: How To Get Noticed And Sell More Books.* US: Arriba Arriba Books, 2013.

Kremer, John. *1001 Ways to Market Your Books: For Authors and Publishers.* Taos, NM: Open Horizons, 2006.

Levinson, Jay Conrad. *Guerrilla Marketing, 4th edition: Easy and Inexpensive Strategies for Making Big Profits from Your Small Business.* Wilmington, MA: Mariner Books, 2007.

Miller, J Steve. *Sell More Books! Book Marketing and Publishing for Low Profile and Debut Authors: Rethinking Book Publicity after the Digital Revolutions.* Acworth, GA: Wisdom Creek Press, 2011.

Schriever, Norm. *The Book Marketing Bible: 99 Essential Marketing Strategies for Self-Published and First-Time Authors, or any Writer Looking to Skyrocket Sales.* Seattle: Amazon Digital Services, n.d.

Scott, David Meerman. *The New Rules of Marketing & PR: How to Use Social Media, Online Video, Mobile Applications, Blogs, News Releases, and Viral Marketing to Reach Buyers Directly.* Seattle: Amazon Digital Services, 2013.

Scott, Steve. *61 Ways to Sell More Nonfiction Kindle Books.* US: Amazon Digital Services, n.d.

Weber, Steve. *Plug Your Book.* Falls Church, VA: Weber Books, 2007.

Index

Order Form

If you borrowed this copy from a library or would like to order a copy for a friend or family member, please send a check or money order to: Iron Gate Publishing, P.O. Box 999, Niwot, CO 80544. Our books are available online to institutions through Ingram, to individuals at Amazon.com and on our website:

www.irongate.com

Set Yourself Up to Self-Publish: A Genealogist's Guide
      ISBN 978-1-879579-99-6 $19.95 + $5.00 S&H

Publish Your Genealogy: A Step-by-Step Guide for Preserving Your Research for the Next Generation
      ISBN 978-1-879579-62-0 $24.95 + $5.00 S&H

Publish Your Family History: A Step-by-Step Guide to Writing the Stories of Your Ancestors
      ISBN 978-1-879579-63-7 $24.95 + $5.00 S&H

Publish a Local History: A Step-by-Step Guide from Finding the Right Project to Finished Book
      ISBN 978-1-879579-64-4 $24.95 + $5.00 S&H

Publish a Memoir: A Step-by-Step Guide to Saving Your Memories for Future Generations
      ISBN 978-1-879579-65-1 $24.95 + $5.00 S&H

Publish a Biography: A Step-by-Step Guide to Capturing the Life and Times of an Ancestor or a Generation
      ISBN 978-1-879579-66-8 $24.95 + $5.00 S&H

Publish a Photo Book: A Step-by-Step Guide for Transforming Your Genealogical Research into a Stunning Family Heirloom
      ISBN 978-1-879579-67-5 $24.95 + $5.00 S&H

Publish a Source Index: A Step-by-Step Guide to Creating a Genealogically Useful Index, Abstract or Transcription
      ISBN 978-1-879579-68-2 $24.95 + $5.00 S&H

Publish Your Specialty: A Step-by-Step Guide for Imparting Your Research Expertise to Others
      ISBN 978-1-879579-76-7 $24.95 + $5.00 S&H

www.ingramcontent.com/pod-product-compliance
Lightning Source LLC
Chambersburg PA
CBHW080325270326
41927CB00014B/3099